Positive Interactions with At-Risk Children

Find the tools and knowledge you need to build resilience in all children from an early age through appropriate interactions and conversations. Presenting a wide range of research in an accessible format, *Positive Interactions with At-Risk Children* explains how to understand and assess behaviors in the context of children's developmental stages.

This book introduces Bayat's original Resilience-based Interaction Model (RIM), which combines behavioral and emotion-based theories of development to provide practical steps for early childhood teachers and professionals. RIM features research-based practices, including relationship building, behavior guidance, body-mind exercises for both teachers and students, as well as strategies to promote strengths of character in children and aid future learning.

Ideal for new and veteran educators alike, *Positive Interactions with At-Risk Children* is an invaluable guide to early years behavior.

Mojdeh Bayat is Professor of Child Development and Education at DePaul University, USA and internationally recognized expert in early childhood development and education of children with developmental disorders and mental health issues.

Naseem Jamnia is a former scientist and a current MFA student at the University of Nevada, Reno. A freelance writer, editor, and activist, they have published in *The Washington Post*, *The Rumpus*, *Bitch Media*, and more.

Positive Interactions with At-Risk Children

Enhancing Students' Wellbeing, Resilience, and Success

Mojdeh Bayat and Naseem Jamnia

NEW YORK AND LONDON

First published 2019
by Routledge
52 Vanderbilt Avenue, New York, NY 10017

and by Routledge
2 Park Square, Milton Park, Abingdon, Oxon, OX14 4RN

Routledge is an imprint of the Taylor & Francis Group, an informa business

Library of Congress Cataloging-in-Publication Data
Names: Bayat, Mojdeh, author. | Jamnia, Naseem, author.
Title: Positive interactions with at-risk children : enhancing students' well-being, resilience, and success / Mojdeh Bayat and Naseem Jamnia.
Description: New York, NY : Routledge, 2019. | Includes bibliographical references.
Identifiers: LCCN 2018044818 (print) | LCCN 2018060089 (ebook) | ISBN 9781315110547 | ISBN 9781138087316 (hardback) | ISBN 9781138087323 (pbk.) | ISBN 9781315110547 (ebook)
Subjects: LCSH: Students—Mental health. | School children—Mental health. | Psychic trauma in children. | Resilience (Personality trait) in children.
Classification: LCC LB3430 (ebook) | LCC LB3430 .B39 2019 (print) | DDC 371.7/13—dc23
LC record available at https://lccn.loc.gov/2018044818

ISBN: 978-1-138-08731-6 (hbk)
ISBN: 978-1-138-08732-3 (pbk)
ISBN: 978-1-315-11054-7 (ebk)

Typeset in Palatino
by Apex CoVantage, LLC

Contents

Foreword

At a time when there are a record number of children receiving psychotropic medications and other therapies largely designed for and studied on adults and simply adapted or modified for children, this book is a critical addition to the literature. It takes various approaches to the central thesis that children's mental health requires specialized understanding of development as well as differences in the presentations of psychiatric disorders in children from those in adults.

This book is a joy to read. It is thorough, clearly written, and accessible—whether for students entering fields related to children's mental health or experienced clinicians and academics. It brings into focus for the reader the reality that toddler and young children's mental health is often overlooked—whether in the DSM-V, research-based pharmaceutical trials, or even in interventional options—by carefully describing the features of at-risk youth and approaching this population through a resilience-based diagnostic and therapeutic lens.

Several key points in this wonderful book warrant particular mention. First, Dr. Bayat develops a clear and persuasive argument that externalizing maladaptive behaviors often have underlying mental health etiologies. Understanding these behaviors is a critical factor in developing an appreciation of the key components of differences in the presentation of symptoms of mental illness in children as compared to the presentation in their adult counterparts. In order to fully grasp the significance of this point, one needs to situate assessments of children in the context of developmental stages. This point cannot be overstated.

Another strength of this book is its treatment of resilience. It goes beyond definitional considerations to thoughtful considerations of not just individual resilience, but also the central importance of resilience within family systems. Again, Dr. Bayat's inquisitive and knowledgeable insight into childhood development and thorough assessment and critique of existing research goes beyond the descriptive to the practical application of the study of childhood development to the compassionate and effective treatment of children and adolescents with mental illness.

A third notable contribution of this book is its incorporation of brain development and the impact of trauma into understanding the range of emotional responses children exhibit. This nuanced and developmentally sensitive approach lays a strong framework for exploring the behavioral and cognitive theories and interventions that have had therapeutic value and hold promise for children. It furthermore makes a compelling case for considering the potential of positive psychology for children in behavioral interventions and treatments that focus on areas of strength rather than deficit.

In sum, this is a book that anyone in the field of children's mental health would find an invaluable resource. Dr. Bayat has effectively woven together research, context, and practical relevance through a developmental lens to deliver an accessible volume that incorporates the complexity of and struggles faced by mentally ill children and their families while embracing approaches focused on resilience and strength rather than narrowly defined pathology.

Louis J. Kraus, MD
Woman's Board Professor
and Chief of Child & Adolescent Psychiatry
Rush University Medical Center
Chicago, Illinois
September 16, 2018

Preface

Mojdeh Bayat

This book is the result of a mother—daughter collaboration. I am delighted to have worked with my daughter, Naseem, in presenting this book. It has always been my wish to do away with the dry and somewhat "pompous" (my description) academic language, and to make my writings accessible to a larger audience. I have and continue to find it almost impossible to do without letting slip some hard-to-figure-out terminology or boring writing. This time around, I asked Naseem to help me modify my writing, particularly when it comes to explaining brain research, which is very technical and usually hard to understand for a reader unfamiliar with this literature. Naseem is a fabulous writer and writes popular science, creative young adult literature, and literary essays; their educational background is in neurobiology, and they are currently pursuing an MFA in creative writing. Naseem is of this generation and speaks the language of the millennials. So I hope that together, we have been able to hit the right notes with younger teachers and with readers who prefer a more conversational tone as opposed to an academic one. It has been a wonderful experience, and I am indebted to Naseem for their generous contributions to this book.

Finally, I would like to say some words about my motivation for writing this book. I entered the field of early childhood education in the 1990s with a passion for the education of children with developmental disabilities. This interest was ignited by my son, Seena, who is on the lower end of the autism spectrum (Level 3). Seena is now a 25-year-old adult. He has and continues to influence what I and my family do in our work and careers. Naseem's writings continue to show this influence, as they often write about autism and other disability related issues. My husband Ali has devoted a good bit of his engineering knowledge and martial arts talents in ways to help kids and adults with disabilities. I have, on the other hand, devoted much of my career to prepare educators in methods that reduce anxiety and promote socialization in children. I have equally learned from my own day-to-day interactions and work with Seena, as in my research and teaching. For example, the design of body-mind activities and effectiveness of meditation practices and physical activity in reducing anxiety, and increasing emotional and cognitive awareness, was inspired from my own nightly exercises and meditation routine with Seena before it was researched and studied.

If my passion for the education of children with developmental disorders began with my son, my interest in early childhood mental health and my subsequent studies and research in this area was motivated by Naseem. Since adolescence, Naseem has dealt with mental health issues: depression, anxiety, gender dysphoria, and an eating disorder. Like many parents with children who deal with mental health issues, my husband and I did not notice any signs until they were a young teenager. We took steps, and Naseem themself has done a marvelous job of being proactive, upfront, and open to ensure their own mental health and wellbeing. I believe, however, had I known what to look for in early years, I might have noticed some signs and better able to help them. More importantly, I might have been able to become aware of my own interactions with them as a parent and had taken steps to modify my reactions, responses, and language with them.

I strongly believe interactions with children, what we say to them, do with them, expect of them, and how we react to what they do and say, all build the foundations of their mental health and wellbeing. This book is all about this understanding. It presents the research that forms this belief, as well as the practices that are based on them.

Mojdeh Bayat,
August 2018

Naseem Jamnia

For much of my life, my brother Seena has been the driving motivator of everything I do. With only 19 months between us, every single memory I have is colored by my interactions with and love for him. It's what drove me to become a scientist. I started a PhD program at the University of Pennsylvania in the neurobiology department to further my work and understanding of the brain, but shortly left in order to pursue my true calling as a writer.

My ability to cope with and understand my own mental illness has been largely because I've watched my mother Mojdeh redefine herself in the wake of my brother's diagnosis. She went back to school when I was growing up not only to learn how to communicate and work with him but also to help other families and children with developmental disabilities. Her work has been one defined first and foremost by love, and it is with great pride that I watch her work to change the way people think about and work with all children, regardless of ability. For everything she does and more, she is my hero.

When my mom asked me to help her with this book, I jumped at the chance. Despite having left the sciences, I still care deeply about scientific literacy and working with children in a way that centers their mental and emotional health. I imagine how different my own childhood would have been if we had even a fraction of the understanding that we do today—and I grew up in the 1990s, not too long ago. I hope my small contribution in the form of working on this book will make even a small difference.

I hope reading this book gives you a new appreciation for and understanding of the science behind child mental health. I know it certainly has done so for me.

Naseem Jamnia,
August 2018

Acknowledgements

This work will not have been possible without the valuable work and contributions of a group of wonderful individuals. First and foremost, I am indebted to Heather Little who, at the time of inception of the Resilience-based Interaction Model (RIM), spent many hours and days with me over several months to help me develop components of RIM's conceptual framework. Heather began her work as a graduate student and my advisee, and is currently a part-time faculty at DePaul University in Chicago. She designed the graphic model of the conceptual framework of RIM. Without our numerous discussions, her probes, as well as ongoing encouragements, this model will not have developed.

Along with Heather, my other graduate advisees and doctoral candidates, Ai Hoang and Rafi Antar, assisted me in the first research project, testing the efficacy of RIM. I am grateful for their invaluable assistance. The three of them, with dogged determination, worked directly with and coached teachers in RIM training, spent time in the classroom with children, entered and analyzed data, and, more importantly, they generously did all of this work for many months on their own time. Laura Knotts and Julie Parson Nesbitt, other graduate advisees of mine, contributed to this book with their case studies. My good friend, Ms. Liliana Bilbao, let me use her beautiful photography for Chapter Five.

Last, but not least, many heartfelt thanks to my husband, Ali, for cooking, taking care of our home and family at the times when I had to lock myself in my office to write.

I am grateful to all!

Introduction

In the United States, early childhood education has been dominated by the long shadow of Piagetian ideas about cognition and learning. Despite the increasing evidence about the importance of behavioral and emotional wellbeing of children, early education of children is not about their social-emotional development (their mental and behavioral health), building positive relationships with peers and adults, socializing together, exploring together, and learning how to get along. Early childhood education is, for the most part, about early literacy and numeracy, social studies, science, and school-readiness skills: sitting at the desk for long periods, completing a worksheet, and following the teacher's instructions.

The mental health and wellbeing of children is far from being a focus in the US educational context—whether at an early childhood level or in elementary or high school. A focus on academic performance has dominated not only public education, but private schools as well. Buzzwords are STEM (Science, Technology, Engineering, Math), or its alternative, STEAM (Science, Technology, Engineering, Arts, and Math). "Microsoft kids" are the model for the school children of the future! There is no place for a child's wellbeing, happiness, and mental health in this picture.

This book is not about children's academic performance or success. It is not about technology or science in early childhood. This book is about promoting children's mental health and overall wellbeing. It lays the scientific research foundations to argue for a focus on emotional wellbeing and relationship-building with children in early school years. Positive relationships can buffer them from ongoing stress or trauma and build resilience. Drawing on bodies of empirical research on the neuroscience of trauma and stress, emotion research, child resilience studies, and positive psychology, we hope to have made a convincing argument for using positive approaches with children. This book also brings together theories that have historically competed and worked against one another. We borrow from different research areas to lay the groundwork for specific practices that will promote not only the mental health and wellbeing of children, but also set the stage for their future academic well-doing.

Finally, we introduce a model called the Resilience-based Interaction Model (RIM). This model consists of sets of practices that are grounded in scientific research and include relationship building with the child, behavior guidance, and body-mind exercises for the reduction of anxiety and stress in both teachers and students, as well as strategies to promote strengths of character (such as self-regulation, optimism, growth mindset, grit, kindness, friendship, and gratitude) in a community of children.

The Term "At-Risk Children"

"At-risk children" is a loaded term. It is used for different groups of kids: children who grow up in poverty; Black children and youth who live in dangerous and disadvantaged communities; children who are subject of trauma and traumatic events, including child neglect and abuse; infants and toddlers who might be vulnerable because of developmental and neurological disorders; children who are vulnerable for internalizing mental health conditions, like depression, anxiety, the development of suicidal ideations, etc.; and children who have diagnosed developmental disorders. Who does this term really refer to: one of the groups mentioned or all of them?

There are disadvantages to using the term "at-risk" because it often implies that this population of children, regardless of whichever group they belong to and what kind of vulnerabilities they are at-risk for, are "hard" to work with. It also sometimes implies that a certain expertise, training, and educational background, or at the very least some prior experience, is needed for work with this population. Some teacher candidates tell us that they "resent" the term "at-risk," because it demonizes the children who are labeled with it.

But there are also advantages to using this term, because it implies that whatever the danger, the damage is not inevitable, and that prevention and intervention could reverse or abort the danger. There is also a practical advantage to using the term "at-risk." It gets the attention of professionals, who are now faced with working in inclusive classrooms with children with diverse learning and social-emotional abilities. We think it necessary to use the term "at-risk" in the title because this book is written for teachers who have reservations about children whom they consider "hard" to work with.

Use of Plural Pronouns: "We," "They"

When I found out, to my delight, that my daughter would join me as the co-author in this writing project, I switched from "I" to the pronoun "we" to make sure the authorship belongs to both of us. However, the pronoun "we" is also used in context of "we, the educators." This meaning is usually clear within the context of topics under discussion within the book. The pronoun "you" is also used, albeit sparingly, to address the book readers directly. The pronoun "he/she" is avoided. Instead, you will notice, the pronoun "they" has been used when a "child" is discussed to observe gender neutrality. Finally, we intentionally use numbers for in-text citations and references, instead of the usual in-text APA format (i.e., author's last name and publication date) to maintain a conversational tone.

The Audience

This book is written for teachers and professionals who work with children in the early childhood age range (infants through age eight). However, the research and recommended practices in this book can be modified and are therefore also appropriate for parents to use with their young children at home. You'll note that we don't use the word "student" too often to refer to young children, unless the discussion is in a school context.

Book Chapters

Chapters of this book are arranged so that the research background can be appropriately laid out for the last two chapters that focus on practice. Thus, the first six chapters present research from the fields of developmental psychology, early childhood education, neuroscience, clinical psychology, special education, and positive psychology. The last two chapters introduce and discuss elements of our recommended model, the Resilience-based Interaction Model. The chapters are arranged in the following way:

- *Chapter 1* orients the readers to the issues surrounding the early education of children who face mental health issues that result from trauma or neurobiological vulnerabilities. It provides the grounds for the argument that the mental health of children should be at the forefront of early childhood education.
- *Chapter 2* presents general information about early signs of mental health issues which may manifest in young children. The chapter also advocates for acknowledging and addressing the emotional and mental health needs of children who are diagnosed with developmental disorders. The issues surrounding the restraint of children with challenging behaviors is also discussed in this chapter.
- *Chapter 3* is about trauma in children. Beginning with a discussion of modern attachment theories, current research in neurobiology, epigenetics, and neuro-epigenetics are presented to explain the brain

mechanisms of stress and early relational factors that may occur in infancy and beyond which can contribute to traumatizing children.

- *Chapter 4* explains the roots of the concept and science of resilience. It describes factors research has solidly established is promotive to resilience of children (e.g. positive relationships, optimism, executive functioning skills, grit and perseverance).
- *Chapter 5* begins a discussion around the theoretical foundations of the Resilience-based Interaction Model (RIM). In particular, this chapter argues for a unifying approach in which even theories known to be opposites can be brought together to address the needs and strengths of children.
- *Chapter 6* continues with the theoretical background of RIM. It focuses on positive psychology and lessons that can be learned from this new and popular science to help us form best positive practices with children.
- *Chapter 7* introduces the readers to our model (RIM) and its guiding principles. The chapter details an approach building positive relationships with children.
- *Chapter 8* continues with guiding principles and practices used in RIM. The chapter also presents examples for RIM practices.

Shaded Texts

There are a number of shaded texts in some of the chapters. These shaded areas usually tell of a personal anecdote or present a story. We have provided our initials (NJ or MB) at the end of the anecdotes to clarify the authorship. We have also presented a few anecdotes about a child or a situation. These are cases of real children and real situations in which either I (the first author, MB), or one of my graduate students have been involved. In the acknowledgement section, I have provided the names of these wonderful students and collaborators to whom I am grateful and indebted for their generosities.

1

Children's Mental Health in the United States

PHOTO 1.1

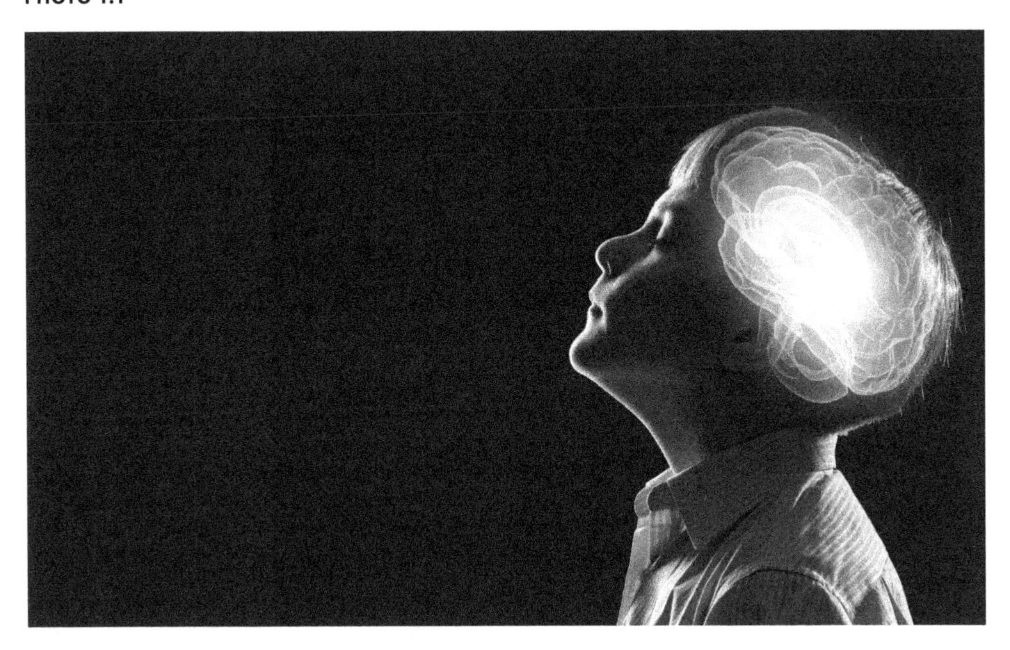

I grew up in the 1990s and early 2000s. Like most decades, it was a time of change, but millennials are unique for a reason: these were the years where the internet picked up traction, where computers were beginning to be found commonly in households. Now, nearly three decades later, it's practically inconceivable that someone wouldn't have a smartphone or laptop within easy reach. Every year, technological advancements grow to places we never would have conceived, showing us even more about human ingenuity.

This spread of technology is necessarily linked to a spread of information—and misinformation. Back in the '90s, my parents used to carry around WHAT IS AUTISM business cards to hand to people who'd stare at us in public; the "1 in 68" Autism Spectrum Disorder statistic wasn't plastered on billboards everywhere (we'll discuss more about autism in future chapters). Now, people are using #ActuallyAutistic to increase not necessarily awareness, but acceptance, of neurodevelopmental disorders like autism.

—NJ

Discussions about mental health and illness have shifted in the last few decades as the public becomes more aware of it. Thanks to the media coverage—propagated by the internet in this age of mass media—of political conflicts in the Middle East and other regions of the world, the term PTSD (post-traumatic stress disorder) and the condition it represents has permeated cultural consciousness in the United States. People are beginning to realize the serious and inevitable effects of war trauma in our returning combat veterans—and with it, a gradual understanding of the deleterious effects of any trauma on the brain and body of an individual. This is, of course, ignoring all the PTSD and other mental illness-related jokes people casually make, which adds to cultural stigma. But here's a question that not enough people are asking: If strong soldiers are adversely affected by trauma in such a severe way, how would developing children on the home front—those who face daily adversities and traumatic events in their lives—be able to weather it?

Trauma may seem like a far reality for children, but the truth is much bleaker than that. One op-ed in *The New York Times* stated for every soldier with PTSD, there are ten—ten!—children in the US who are traumatized for a variety of reasons like violence, abuse, assault, or neglect (1). What's worse, these children are suffering to a *comparable degree* as those adults who've been in literal war. And those children become adults; mental health scholars have frequently stated that individuals who have histories of childhood trauma—that is, neglect and abuse—make up almost the entire population of people who are incarcerated in the US criminal justice system (2, 3). (A brief note here: This is not to say experiencing trauma will result in incarceration. Problems with the criminal justice system aside, we'll come back to the issues of stigmatization of mental health and illness later in this chapter.)

These are staggering statistics. And yet, because children do not show signs of mental health issues the same way adults do, most adults think young children don't feel the effects of adversities and maltreatment, or that as they grow up, the effects will gradually disappear. There is also a perception that unless an event of a serious nature happens—a trauma with a capital T—daily adversities can't actually hurt children.

If it wasn't clear by now, this could not be further from the truth. Children do, in fact, experience trauma. But it's only been within the past decade or so that scholars have begun to understand that trauma in children doesn't have to result from a single or multiple serious events and that children may show the signs of trauma differently than adults. In this age of social media, there are already signs of this being true; as people step forward and share their own stories, we're able to see the ways both similar and different types of trauma have lifelong effects. In 2018, Pulitzer Prize-winning author Junot Diaz published an essay about how his childhood rape affected not just his relationships, but his entire life (4). His is not a unique story, and such trauma doesn't have to be from something as catastrophic as rape for the results to be the same.

As we will explore in Chapter 3, what might constitute a trauma for a child can be different from what is deemed as such in adults. The type of trauma children experience is almost always one of an interpersonal nature. Ongoing daily stressors, such as those that result from an unresponsive caregiver, or worse, from maltreatment, can have long-lasting traumatic effects on a child. Under certain conditions and based on the child's developmental capacities, sometimes even an event which one might deem ordinary can have a deleterious effect. This isn't to lessen what an actual "trauma" is—it's to broaden the definition.

Many children grow up in communities or in families dealing with an ongoing amount of daily interpersonal stress that may result from a family crisis, lack of financial and material resources, domestic and/or neighborhood violence, and parenting issues. These children are particularly at risk for becoming traumatized—for trauma to have lifelong effects that may become deleterious. Experiencing ongoing stress amounts to the same effects on the brain as stress from a single severe traumatic event. On that front, here's something else to consider—how often can we even find communities or families in which stress isn't ongoing for a child? The vast majority of children growing up in the world, including many children who grow up in the United

States, do, in fact, deal with ongoing stressors, which can present risks to their development.

We will explain later (Chapter 3) what "amount" of stress may be toxic and over time change the architecture of the developing brain. Research from the past three decades shows the brain cannot recalibrate after ongoing interpersonal stress and/or trauma without intervention. These effects are usually long lasting, often leading to more serious mental, behavioral, and physical health problems later on.

It's something we have to think about if we're serious about helping children, whether as healthcare practitioners, parents, or, yes, even teachers. Thanks to the work of child mental health scholars such as Cicchetti, Rutter, Masten, and van der Kolk, educators have recently become interested in understanding the nature of stress and its effects on a child's mental health. Terms such as "trauma-informed education," "trauma-informed schools," and "trauma-sensitive teaching" have found their ways into the US public education system and even in state- and federally funded early childhood programs. In fact, as of 2018, many states such as California and Washington have begun promoting conceptual maps for schools to implement trauma-informed teaching practices that support children who are experiencing mental health issues.

There's another thing to consider, too. Although stress and traumatic situations can change the brain, it's now understood that all mental health disorders have biological origins. Stress and trauma are some of the obvious environmental conditions that can interact with genetic factors to result in mental illness. Many children also display signs of mental and developmental disorders from birth due to inherited genetic and neurobiological factors—without having necessarily experienced any toxic levels of stress or any traumatic events. Children who are diagnosed with a developmental disorder, such as Autism Spectrum Disorders (ASD), Attention-Deficit Hyperactivity Disorder (ADHD), or global developmental delay (GDD), belong to this category. However—and this is vital to remember—these children are also, if not more so, vulnerable to trauma on top of experiencing interpersonal stress with adults, caregivers, and teachers around them.

Fortunately, in the last thirty years, because of the advocacy efforts of families of children with disabilities and the special education public law that followed, there has been a great deal of awareness about the nature and treatment of neurodevelopmental disorders, including ASD, intellectual disabilities, ADHD, and sensory processing disorders. (An important caveat: the last iteration of the Individuals with Disabilities Education Act was in 2004, and though it's been due for reexamination in Congress for several years, it hasn't been improved upon since its last amendment.) In fact, special education and most early childhood teacher preparation programs have integrated a good deal of scientific literature regarding developmental disorders into their curricula. Parents, siblings, and other family members have in particular taken an active role in understanding and advocating for the developmental and educational needs of children with various forms of neurodevelopmental disorders. And as we mentioned above, with the rise of the internet and social media, individuals with the disorders—especially in the autism community—have begun to advocate for themselves. (Some of this is even in direct contrast to what parents or educators think someone might need, telling us we still have a lot to learn even in these areas.)

While we, as educators and families, might have come a long way in understanding and advocating for the developmental needs of children with and without disabilities, we have grossly neglected one area of development of all children—their social-emotional, mental, and behavioral health needs. The US educational system, including its subsidiary special education, continues to be fragmented, taxed with lack of funding, budget cuts, and an inappropriately trained workforce. Furthermore, our educational system focuses on academic learning and performance—or "functional academic," in the case of special education—at the expense of the mental health needs of children. In publicly funded early education programs, such as Head Start, Early Head Start, and state pre-kindergartens, the primary emphasis continues to be on the implementation of early academic curricula, despite an abundant body of research supporting the importance of social-emotional development in young children *before* literacy and numeracy are taught. Of course, this is both ironic and frustrating, as these programs are designed for and serve children who are at risk for a host of developmental and mental health issues.

While having the best academic training will ensure a better future for a child, having an unhealthy mind will destroy any possibility to enjoy that future. Putting the mental health of children at the forefront of education is not only the best approach, but the right thing to do. And that means more than just doing our best to prevent any sort of trauma or illness—it also means actively encouraging the positive mental health and wellbeing of the child. We need to focus on not just the absence of illness, but the active encouragement of children's potential and abilities so they may lead whole, happy, and productive lives.

Mental Health Issues in Children

Mental health issues are far more widespread and prevalent in children and adolescents than people usually think. It is estimated 20 percent of teenagers and youth between the ages of 13–18 in the United States either

TABLE 1.1 Reported percentage range of US preschoolers with types of mental health issues, in research literature

Type of Mental Health Issues	*Reported Percentage Range*
◆ **Anxiety Disorders**	**2% to 20%**
➢ Phobias	➢ 0 to 12%
➢ Separation anxiety	➢ 1% to 5%
➢ Social anxiety	➢ 2% to 5%
➢ Generalized anxiety disorders	➢ 1% to 7%
➢ Selective mutism	➢ 1% to 2%
◆ **Attention Deficit Hyperactivity Disorder (ADHD)**	**2% to 17%**
◆ **Autism Spectrum Disorders (ASD)**	**1.5% to 2%**
◆ **Oppositional Defiant Disorder**	**2% to 13%**
◆ **Depressive Disorders**	**0.5 to 2%**
◆ **Conduct Disorder**	**1% to 3%**

currently live with or will live with serious mental illness (5, 6). The estimates for the number of young children with mental health issues ranges anywhere from 13 percent to 27 percent (7–9). (See Table 1.1 for statistics related to mental health issues in preschoolers.)

Because mental illnesses have neurobiological bases, it is possible many adolescents and adults who are identified with mental disorders might have displayed detectable behavioral signs in early childhood. This fact should make it obvious to parents/caregivers and educators that something can be and needs to be done both at homes and in schools to detect possible risks or conditions and to then take appropriate steps to intervene.

Some of the most harrowing events of our time, shooting tragedies such as Columbine in 1999, Virginia Tech in 2007, Northern Illinois University in 2008, Sandy Hook Elementary School, Denver in 2012, and, most recently, Parkland in 2018, which resulted in the death of tens of innocent children and adults, were perpetuated by teenagers and young adults with mental health issues. Could such tragedies have been prevented if teachers and other adults around these perpetrators recognized subtle signs of mental health issues earlier—perhaps as far back as in their early childhood years—and taken prompt steps to meet their needs?

Of course, we will never know the answer. However, if we understand the early signs and know what to do, we could make the case that we should and would be able to prevent most, if not all, such tragedies that have resulted from mental health issues. There is certainly enough evidence to support the efficacy of early intervention in the remediation—and in some cases, reversal—of various forms of developmental problems in children. Furthermore, both subtle and obvious signs of mental health issues do exist in young children. It therefore makes sense to educate early childhood teachers on possible early signs and prepare them to appropriately address these issues in children starting in preschool and beyond. It is, however, more important to help them cultivate practices that will promote children's wellbeing and well-doing.

Before going further, it's important to explain here that by making case examples of public shootings, we don't intend to imply that all individuals with mental health issues are or are likely to be violent (nor that all mass shootings are due to mental illness). On the contrary, the percentage of individuals with mental health issues who commit acts of violence toward others is indeed small. Many healthcare professionals will ask whether their patient has access to firearms not because they're worried for others, but because they think the individual will harm themselves. This is far more a prevalent issue; violence or aggression generally, but especially towards others, is *not* the most common characteristic of mental health problems, despite its frequent portrayal in the media and in works of fiction. Even hours after a tragedy, the media will announce that the perpetrator has some undefined mental illness. Regardless of whether that's true, the focus on the illness not only gives the perpetrator an "excuse" for their actions but simultaneously demonizes other individuals with mental illness. Indeed, viewing all children and individuals with mental health issues as being apt to commit violence or heinous acts is one stereotype we should avoid at all costs.

It is such perceptions that have often resulted in adults' inappropriate reactions toward emotional outbursts or challenging behaviors of children. The lack of empathy and understanding from adults often means adolescents who experience mental health issues understand the stigma attached to mental illness and learned early on to hide their struggles. Many develop strategies to hide the signs from their parents, peers, and teachers as young as five years of age.

This was certainly the case for many children who begin experiencing symptoms of depression before the end of the early childhood period. They repeatedly tell us that by middle childhood they have learned to hide what they are feeling from absolutely everyone around them. Many adolescents believe they would be a burden to their parents and friends, and carry these thoughts and feelings with them throughout college.

Our reactions to children's behaviors send these same messages despite our best intentions, and they have lifelong effects. It's even arguable that this attitude is why so many people still struggle to seek out help when they deal with a mental health issue. Common erroneous assumptions and stereotypes of individuals experiencing mental issues only reinforce the stigma attached to mental illness.

Regardless of some efforts in the direction of public awareness about the nature of mental disorders in children, educators and parents continue to have deeply embedded negative ideas. Such views are usually influenced by one's own cultural backgrounds and upbringing, which are difficult to change. But if we're going to make the difference in even one child's life, the changes must start with us.

Cultural Concept of Mental Illness and Stigma

In 1904, during a trip to Indonesia, the founder of comparative psychiatry Emil Kraepelin became interested in psychiatric illnesses in tropical regions. Some of the questions he asked himself then continue to be relevant for reflection today: Are there forms of mental illness unique to specific cultures? To what extent is the expression of mental illness shaped by social and cultural factors? (10–12). In this context, culture means "shared elements involved in 'perceiving, believing, evaluating, communicating, and acting' that are passed down from generation to generation with modifications" (11).

Concepts of mental health and illness are deeply rooted in one's culture. After all, the formal diagnosis of a mental illness or a mental disorder is usually given to someone whose behavior(s) deviate from the norm in that particular society.

For example, in some countries, conditions classified as psychiatric disorders based on the American Diagnostic Statistical Manual of Mental Disorders (DSM)—currently in its fifth edition (DSM-5)—are seldom recognized and hence identified as a disorder in a child (12). Such is the case of ADHD, which does not have a widespread prevalence—as identified through diagnosis—in most African and Middle Eastern countries compared to the US. This is because in these cultures, the behavioral symptoms of impulsivity and hyperactivity are acceptable for boys (in whose population ADHD happens to be most prevalent).

A brief but important aside: As mentioned above, diagnostic criteria are based on a culture's understanding of what is "normal." Sometimes, experts may not consistently agree upon what that means. In 2013, the National Institute of Mental Health (NIMH) withdrew its support of DSM-5 prior to its release. While it acknowledged the reliability of DSM as the "Bible" for the field, it criticized the DSM-5's lack of validity via an objective laboratory measure instead a cluster of symptoms. In the same year, the NIMH launched a Research Domain Criteria (RDoC) project to transform the diagnosis of mental health issues, incorporating genetics, imaging, cognitive science, and other information, in order to build a new classification system of diagnosis for mental disorders.

In my brief stint as a PhD student at the University of Pennsylvania, I considered doing a rotation with one researcher who was looking at child and adolescent brain scans to find some sort of commonality to use as a possible diagnostic marker. It's a project even he was frustrated with, because despite all we know about the brain, there is still so much we don't. Until we do find more clinical markers for mental illness, we're mostly required to diagnose based on symptoms and trial-and-error use of medications to alleviate those causing distress. That means, despite our best efforts, diagnosis remains based on list of deviations or symptoms.

—NJ

Unlike many other disorders, clinicians can't order a brain scan or blood test to detect whether someone has a mental illness. To add to the complexity, culture is also a fluid and ever-evolving phenomenon. For example, the criteria for what we consider atypical or a mental illness today in the US is not necessarily what they were three decades ago, nor will they be the same three decades from now. In general, culture plays an important role in determining whether one is mentally healthy or not.

We are not making a judgment call on this. In the absence of strong biological markers of illness, it's important to think about how we're deciding whether someone is mentally ill or not. Despite how we might individually feel about it, there are certain norms that, as a culture, we sanction, and anyone who behaves outside of that stands out. This is what can ultimately lead to social stigma—the negative effects a culture imposes on an individual for their unfitting or culturally defined unacceptable behaviors (13, 14).

A cultural stigma of being "crazy" or "bad" is understood in early childhood. Depending on what they see and hear others say about them, children can experience self-stigma and can form negative opinions about themselves as young as three years of age or even earlier (14, 15).

PHOTO 1.2 Stigmatizing a child socially results in the child's self-stigmatization

Xavier

A telling story is one that a doctoral student of mine recounted to me over an email in 2017. She was visiting an urban Head Start early childhood program and told me:

> Upon entering the Head Start classroom for a previously arranged observation visit, I was greeted by a young boy. The boy approached me and asked, "Who are you?" I smiled at this very typical directness of the child. I knelt down so that I could look him in the eyes and replied, "Hi. My name is Ms. Heather. What's your name?" He extended his hand out to me with the poise and grace of a child whom I thought had some leadership potentials and said, "Hi. I'm the bad kid."
>
> This child, whom I later learned was named Xavier, turned out to become a leader and exemplary student, after my student spent a few months coaching his teachers to appropriately address his emotional and behavioral needs.

—MB

The story of a "bad kid" is far too often repeated in the early schooling of young children, particularly in the education of at-risk children. This is the story of a child who resorts to aggressive behaviors and seems oblivious to the consequences of his actions, or is the one who has uncontrollable impulses, is easy to anger, and throws inconsolable tantrums. And to make explicitly clear, this happens much more commonly to children with disabilities, children whose families have low socioeconomic status, and children of color, particularly Black boys (16–21). Frequently, a story like this doesn't have a happy ending unless an appropriate intervention from some caring adult is provided.

In recent years, in order to prevent the stigma of mental illness and to encourage parents of children and adolescents with mental health issues to seek help, a number of advocacy efforts have begun to educate the public about the neurobiological sources of mental disorders. One such group is the Avielle Foundation, created by Jeremy Richman and Jennifer Hensel to honor their six-year-old daughter, who died in the Sandy Hook Elementary School shooting. In their advocacy efforts and publications, they use the term *brain health, brain illness,* and *brain disorder* to draw attention to the tangibility and physicality of mental health conditions and to create awareness about their causes. Their goal is to eliminate the stigma attached to mental illness so help can be sought early on for children and adolescents. Ultimately, their aim is to encourage timely intervention to prevent any violence, self-inflected or otherwise.

The Concept of Early Childhood Mental Health

In the United States, the relatively new field of *infant mental health* defines mental health as children's capacity to regulate and express emotions, form secure relationships, and explore their family and community environment (22). Infant mental health is a multidisciplinary field which was developed in the 1970s and currently integrates knowledge gained from research in neuroscience, behavioral epigenetics, developmental psychology, psychiatry, social work, and counseling. Interesting, this definition of mental health necessarily incorporates positive mental health—which, as we described above, means defining health as not just the absence of illness but the ability to thrive.

Infant mental health is revolutionary in its own way. Traditionally, early childhood mental health focuses on children from birth through five years (23). It is not clear why the field does not include children older than five (as the early childhood period is defined as birth to age eight), who, despite being functionally on target, may display signs of mental health distress.

The field also covers those who are "functionally younger," which harkens back to the issue of "lower/higher function" with which children with cognitive impairments and autism are often designated. (It's important to note this terminology is ladled with misconceptions and stigma and focuses on what the child cannot do, instead of what the child can and is capable of doing).

Intervention in early childhood mental health has primarily focused on relational approaches that promote healthy, positive relationships between young children and their immediate caregivers in their family system. There is some difficulty in doing this, however. Although in the US children as young as infants often spend more time in center or home-based daycares and early childhood education programs than with their families, the infant mental health field has not begun efforts to implement early childhood care and education outside the home—for example, at early childhood education programs—through policy change.

The concepts of challenging behaviors—"behavioral problems" in early school years or the label "emotional and behavioral disorders" in elementary

PHOTO 1.3 The field of infant/child mental health focuses on interventions which improve the quality of attachment between the child and their caregivers

or high school—are different iterations of mental health issues applied to children who show maladaptive behaviors. Behavioral interventions in early childhood education either rely on special education methodologies that use *Positive Behavior Support* or *function-based* behavioral approaches or disciplinary approaches grounded in a specific school district's policies and philosophies. In general, in most public education settings from state prekindergarten through high school, many maladaptive behaviors are addressed using approaches that are severely punitive, often ineffective, and mostly counterproductive.

In most public schools in the United States, displaying any behavior that deviates from the class norm—in particular those that, from the perspective of the teacher, are problematic—happens to result in the strongest and often uncalled for types of disciplinary actions. Some disciplinary practices in our public schools have led to a widespread and ongoing discrimination against children who display any kind of perceived challenging behaviors. In no place is this stronger than in public preschools.

In state preschool programs, the rate of expulsion of three to five-year-olds who display challenging behaviors is 3.4 times higher than in kindergarten through high school (16–18). Boys as compared to girls, Black children as compared to Whites, and children with a diagnosed condition as compared to those without a diagnosis are three to four times more likely to be expelled from preschools (18). In fact, a 2016 report from Yale Child Study Center identified implicit racial and gender biases in preschool professionals that often results in expulsion and suspension. It's ironic that the child who is suspended from preschool is usually the very same child who needs to remain in the preschool environment, because most likely, the school environment is the most appropriate—and for some children, the safest—to thrive in (19).

While we are specifically discussing public preschools here, we don't mean to imply that private early childhood programs fare better in this regard. A 2017 analysis of national data on children's health shows in private preschools, 250 children are suspended every day (20). However, private schools in general are not regulated by states and hence are not required to comply with the principles of the Individuals with Disabilities Education Act (IDEA) regarding behavioral support. Therefore, unless a private school receives funding from the state or federal government, or unless parents bring lawsuits against such schools, expulsion or other discriminatory actions against children with challenging behaviors in these settings do not attract enough attention.

Regardless of whether in private or public school, the early childhood environment is likely the one place that can give a child with challenging behaviors the support needed. It is also the place in which the most effective intervention can take place, since, typically, children spend most of their waking hours in school environments. It therefore makes sense that teachers should be just as equipped as parents and caregivers to promote a child's mental health. Exclusion of a child from a place in which they have a right to be is not only discriminatory but extremely punitive. Furthermore, such actions not only lead to failure in future school experiences but could be the very factor that creates undue stress and further mental health issues (21). Unfortunately, exclusionary and restrictive policies regarding challenging behaviors, inappropriate and counterproductive behavioral interventions, and a lack of teacher knowledge and skills about child mental health and intervention are among the most persisting problems in early childhood education programs in the United States today.

The mainstream *Developmental Appropriate Practices* (DAP), advocated by early childhood professional organizations such as the National Association for the Education of Young Children (NAEYC), do not necessarily include informed approaches for children who display behaviors that are signs of mental health issues. This shortcoming might be due to an erroneous belief that children who have mental health issues are usually "extreme cases" and should have a specific intervention plan in place. Thus, the term *mental health* continues to evade early childhood teacher preparation programs and, therefore, teaching practices. As such, it's important for educators and caregivers alike to learn early signs of risks for mental health issues in children. In the rest of the chapter, we'll discuss some of those signs and risk factors. Our hope is this is only a starting point for people to educate themselves on mental health in children.

Classification of Mental Health Issues in Children

The history of classification of mental health issues in children goes back to at least half a century. Thomas Achenbach, a renowned scholar of children's maladaptive behaviors, began his long-standing research on children and youth with mental health issues in the 1960s. At the time, the DSM, which was in its first and second editions, did not have a differentiated diagnosis category for children, except for two disorders: *Adjustment Reaction of Childhood* and *Schizophrenia Reaction in Childhood*. But Achenbach understood children showed behavioral symptoms of mental health problems differently than adults; in the 1970s, his studies resulted in the development of what is currently the most widely used assessment instrument of a child's behavior, the *Child Behavior Checklist*, currently known as the *Achenbach System of Empirically Based Assessment* (ASEBA; 24).

Achenbach classified children's symptomatic maladaptive behaviors into two categories: *externalizing* (maladaptive behaviors that are visible) and *internalizing* (maladaptive behaviors that are internal and not openly visible) (25). Since then, much has been written about the association of both behaviors in early childhood with later forms of mental illness in adolescence or adulthood. Although ASEBA has become more detailed and sophisticated—for example, specifying symptoms that can then be aligned with DSM-5 classifications for easier diagnoses—its general classification of symptoms remains mostly the same.

Achenbach's classification relies on the identification of maladaptive behaviors which indicate risks for mental health issues. This creates an overlap between mental and behavioral health. Interestingly, in adults, *behavioral health* is usually distinguished from *mental health*. Behavioral health problems in adults usually refers to maladaptive behaviors formed as a result of unhealthy habits, like excessive smoking or drinking. Although the link between the behavioral health and physical health seems to be clear—as described in the related literature—its connection with psychological and mental health is less defined. No matter the age, there is usually a link between most maladaptive behaviors—which are sometimes used for coping—and one's state of mental health (26).

In children, a distinction between behaviors from their emotional state and mental health issues is not as clearcut. Thanks to the work of infant mental health scholars such as Tronick, Brazelton, and Zeanah, it is understood children's behaviors and their social-emotional state, and hence their state of mental health, cannot be separated. Furthermore, it's shortsighted to rely only on symptoms that are laid out in diagnostic manuals (like the one in the DSM-5; ICD-10 *International Classification of Mental and Behavioral Disorders;* or DC:0–5 *Diagnostic Classification of Mental Health and Developmental Disorders of Infancy and Early Childhood).* We should always look at a child's behaviors within the context of their relationships with their primary caregivers. This is even putting aside the consideration of culture discussed earlier in this chapter. Therefore, Achenbach's classification, although pinpointing the presence of a risk or a condition, is not sufficient on its own. As a part of diagnosis and intervention, a child's relationships should also be examined carefully.

As a starting point, Achenbach's descriptions of *internalizing* and *externalizing* behaviors are useful tools. By grouping together similar behaviors, we can make connections between those and diagnosable mental illnesses. While such behaviors are not a sufficient cause for concern, they certainly can help pinpoint the type of social-emotional support a child might need.

Children's Externalizing Behaviors: Problems of Undercontrol

Externalizing behaviors are maladaptive behaviors directed toward outside environments, such as peers and adults, as well as materials, objects, or animals. Externalizing behaviors are also called problems of undercontrol (27), in that the child fails to self-regulate or inhibit outbursts of strong emotions or to calm down in a reasonable length of time when faced with a distressing, stressful, or stimulating situation.

Externalizers usually have a hard time understanding others' perspectives, thoughts, feelings, and intentions—what is known as a *theory of mind*. Development of theory of mind begins around eighteen months. By age three, children should have developed a basic theory of, that others might feel and think differently from them. By age five or six, children have developed a more sophisticated theory of mind, that others might have different intentions or beliefs from them. However, externalizers are usually not aware that their aggressive acts directed toward others can result in hurting others.

Achenbach classifies externalizing behaviors into two categories: *attention problems* and *aggressive behaviors*. As such, externalizing behaviors are easily noticed and detectable; by their very nature, they immediately gain the attention of peers and adults and are often alarming and threatening. Children with externalizing behaviors often also consume the energy of caregivers, teachers, and adults around them. (See Figure 1.1 for the cluster of externalizing behavioral symptoms in young children based on ASEBA.)

FIGURE 1.1 Achenbach's classification of externalizing behaviors in preschool children who are risks for further mental health issues

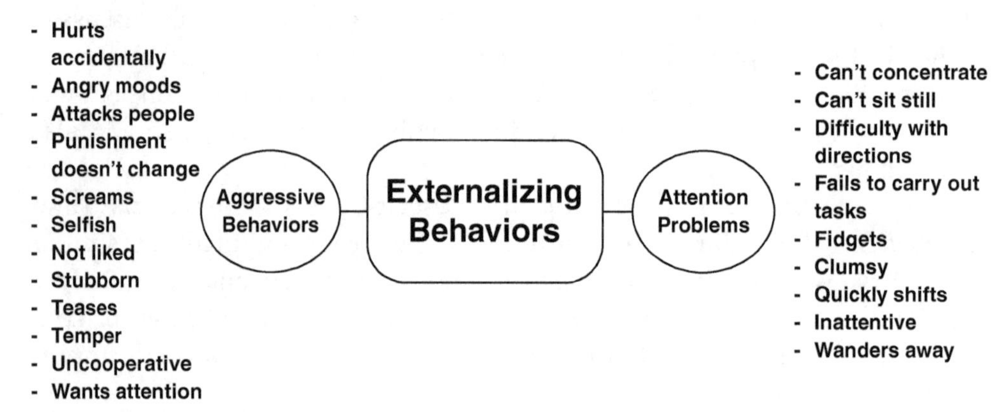

Children's Internalizing Behaviors: Problems of Overcontrol

Internalizing behaviors are maladaptive behaviors are directed toward oneself and are not necessarily disruptive. Internalizing behaviors are also called problems of overcontrol (26), in that the child inserts too much restraint or inhibition on themselves and prevents themselves from expressing emotions and feelings openly when faced with a distressing or an overstimulating situation. Achenbach clusters internalizing behaviors into two categories: *emotionally reactive* and *anxious/depressed* (26). (See Figure 1.2 for the clusters of internalizing behavioral symptoms in young children based on ASEBA.)

Prior to Achenbach's studies, psychologists did not think young children could experience depression. The prevalent psychoanalytical tradition of the time dictated children did not develop depression until adolescence,

FIGURE 1.2 Achenbach's classification of internalizing behaviors in preschool children who are risks for further mental health issues

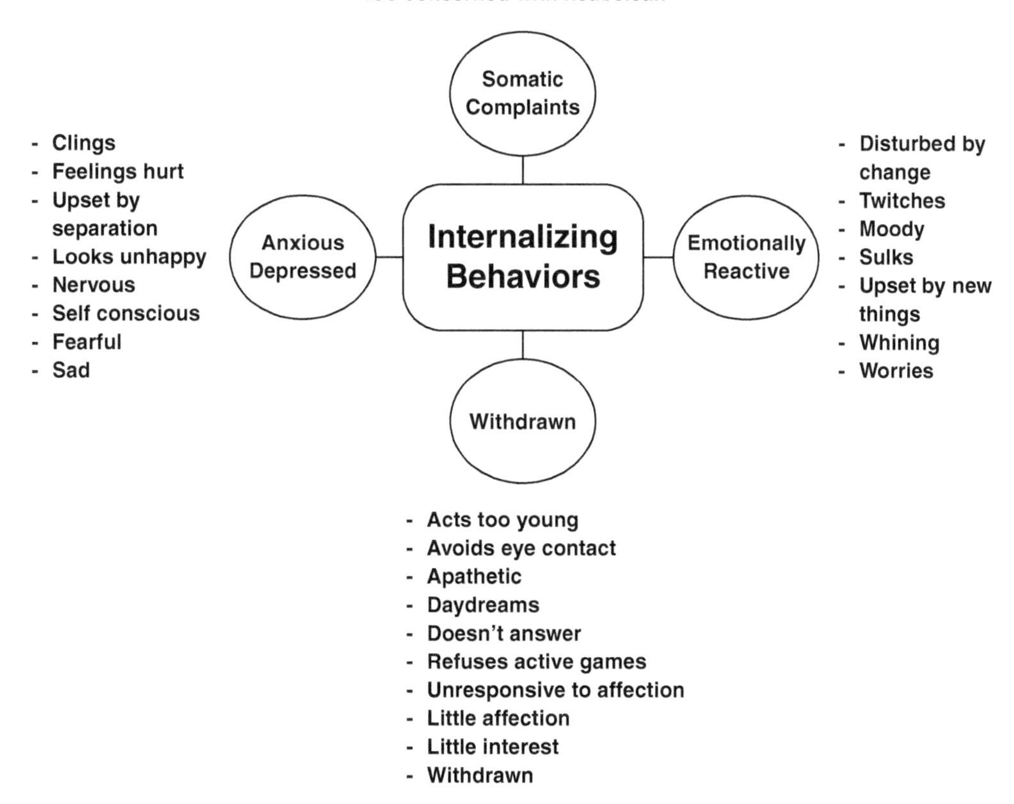

when the superego is developed. This is no longer believed to be a valid argument. Young children can and do experience depression and anxiety. Unfortunately, these issues are most often invisible to families and teachers as internalizers do not typically engender negative feelings in their caregivers or peers, because they don't usually act out. In addition, major symptoms of anxiety and depression are quietness and withdrawal from social activities, which could be virtues in typically noisy classrooms and homes.

Early Externalizing and Internalizing Behaviors and Mental Health Issues

Since the 1990s, a lot of research articles have been written about the association of externalizing and internalizing behaviors with existing or future mental health issues. In general, research consistently shows in the absence of intervention, externalizing and internalizing behaviors present in childhood will continue, often becoming more complex, or sometimes leading to more serious mental disorder diagnoses (28–33). The range and nature of cited mental health diagnoses that might exist or appear in later years are daunting and alarming.

Studies (26–31) show that preschoolers with undercontrolled (externalizing) behaviors are likely to be diagnosed with conditions like conduct disorder (CD), ADHD, anxiety disorders, bipolar disorder, and clinical depression in later years. Similarly, preschoolers with overcontrolled (internalizing) behaviors may receive diagnoses of anxiety disorders, depressive disorders, and bipolar disorder as they get older. The number of girls with internalizing issues seem to be higher compared with boys, although maladaptive behavior in girls are not usually identified early (33). The reason may be due to social gender roles; for example, girls are expected to be quieter and calmer compared to boys. This may seem almost trivial, but it is, perhaps, the disparity between the socialization of genders that has indirectly contributed to the underdiagnosis of some disorders, such as ADHD in girls.

In terms of social functioning, children with maladaptive behaviors usually have relationship problems which start in preschool and continue well throughout their adult lives. In particular, preschool externalizers tend to have much more difficulties forming and/or maintaining positive relationships with peers and adults, including members of their family (34). Because these children instigate strong negative thoughts, feelings, and behaviors in those around them, others are not often enthusiastic to initiate or maintain friendships with them. Having conflicts with teachers and peers is particularly detrimental to the future of children with externalizing behaviors. Studies show externalizers often experience school failure and learning problems that are more related to negative interactions and relationship experiences than to a learning or cognitive issue (32, 33).

Perhaps the most alarming is the research that has reported children with symptoms of both internalizing and externalizing behaviors are likely to develop suicidal ideations, thoughts of death, and/or actually attempt suicide when they are older (35–37). This should immediately concern everyone—that no matter what the behavioral symptoms early on, there is a connection to suicide. As suicide is the third leading cause of death in youth aged 10–24 (5), early childhood could be a critical time to saving the lives of these children.

Final Thoughts

We began this chapter by considering the way that trauma and mental health have come into public attention. The truth is, as long as these topics are treated with stigma, they'll be rife with misinformation. Furthermore, we'll never move forward socially or scientifically without listening to those who have been affected by childhood trauma and mental illness.

It seems easy to dismiss these concerns as being "outside of the norm" or "overcautious." At this point, they're neither. Between the beginning of 2018 and April 22, there were 69 mass shootings in the US (38). Not all of these are at the hands of someone the media has called mentally ill, but that refrain is still common. That means the discussions around mental health issues still center tragedies and stigmatize those who deal with it.

In order to educate and prevent future tragedies of any kind—not just mass shootings, but suicides, for example—we must take mental health at all ages seriously, but especially in children. By providing children with the adequate social-emotional support they need, we can help them thrive and grow. In order to do that, we must educate ourselves, our teachers, and the public at large. In a society in which everyone is on their smartphones, getting the right information out there is possible—it's just a matter of others stepping up.

References

1. van der Kolk, B. A. (2011, May 11). Post-traumatic childhood. *New York Times* (p. A25).
2. van der Kolk, B. A. (2005). Developmental trauma disorder: Toward a rational diagnosis for children with complex trauma disorder. *Psychiatric Annals, (35)*5, 401–408. http://psycnet.apa.org/doi/10.1111/j.1939-0025.2012.01154.x

3. Teplin, L. A., Abram, K. M., McClelland, G. M., Dulcan, M. K., & Mericle, A. A. (2002). Psychiatric disorders in youth in juvenile detention. *Archives of General Psychiatry, 59*(12), 1133–1143. https://doi.org/ 10.1001/archpsyc.59.12.1133
4. Diaz, J. (2018, April). The silence: The legacy of childhood trauma. *New Yorker*. Retrieved from www.newyorker.com/magazine/2018/04/16/the-silence-the-legacy-of-childhood-trauma
5. National Alliance on Mental Illness. (2017). *Mental health facts: Children and teens*. Retrieved from www.nami.org/getattachment/Learn-More/Mental-Health-by-the-Numbers/childrenmhfacts.pdf
6. Centers for Disease Control. (2017). *Treatment of children with mental illness*. Retrieved from www.nimh.nih.gov/health/publications/treatment-of-children-with-mental-illness-fact-sheet/index.shtml
7. Bufferd, S. J., Dougherty, L. R., Carlson, G. A., & Klein, D. N. (2011). Parent reported mental health is preschoolers: Findings using a diagnostic interview. *Comprehensive Psychiatry, 52*, 359–369. https://doi.org/10.1080/15374416.2012.759225
8. Wichstrom, L., Berg-Neilsen, T. S., Angold, A., Eggert, H. L., Solheim, E., & Sveen, T. H. (2012). Prevalence of psychiatric disorders in preschoolers. *Journal of Child Psychiatry, 53*, 695–705. https://doi.org/10.111/j.1469-7610.2011.02514.x
9. Egger, H. L., & Angold, A. (2006). Common behavioral and emotional disorders in preschool children: Presentation, nosology, and epidemiology. *Journal of Child Psychology and Psychiatry, 47*, 313–337. https://doi.org/10.111/j.1469-7610.2006.01618.x
10. Hans, P. (2011). Emil Kraepelin on culture and ethic factors in mental illness. *Psychiatric Times*. Retrieved from www.psychiatrictimes.com/articles/emil-kraepelin-cultural-and-ethnic-factors-mental-illness
11. Triandis, H. C. (1996). The psychological measurement of cultural syndrome. *American Psychologist, 51*, 407–415. http://psycnet.apa.org/doi/10.1037/0003-066X.51.4.407
12. American Psychiatric Association. (2013). *Diagnostic and statistical manual of mental disorders* (5th ed.). Arlington, VA: American Psychiatric Publishing.
13. Anagnostopoulos, D. (2017). Bridging culture and psychopathology. *European Child and Adolescence Psychiatry, 26*, 263–266. https://doi.org/10.1007/s00787-016-0922-6
14. Crowe, A., Averett, P., Glass, J. S., Dotson-Blake, K. P.l., Grissom, S. E., Ficken, D. K., . . . & Holmes, J. A. (2016). Mental health stigma: Personal and cultural impacts on attitudes. *Journal of Counselor Practice, 7*(2), 97–119. https://doi.org/10.22229/spc801925
15. Lopez Ibor, J. J. (2002). The power of stigma. *World Psychiatry, 1*(1), 23–24.

16. Gilliam, W. S. (2005). Prekindergarteners left behind: Expulsion rates in state prekindergarten programs. *Foundation for Child Development: FCD policy brief series No. 3*. Retrieved from www.challengingbehavior.org/explore/policy_docs/prek_expulsion.pdf
17. Perry, D., Holland, C., Darling-Kuria, N., & Nadiv, S. (2011, Nov.). Challenging behavior and expulsion from child care. *ZERO TO THREE*, 4–11.
18. Office of the State Superintendent of Education. (2014). *Reducing out-of-school suspensions and expulsions in District of Columbia public and public charter schools*. Retrieved from https://osse.dc.gov/sites/default/files/dc/sites/osse/publication/attachments/OSSE_REPORT_DISCIPLINARY_G_PAGES.pdf
19. Gilliam, W., Maupin, A. N., Reys, C. R., Accavitti, M., & Shick, F. (2016). Do early educators' implicit biases regarding sex and race relate to behavior expectations and recommendations of preschool expulsions and suspensions? *Yale Child Study Center*. Retrieved from https://medicine.yale.edu/childstudy/zigler/publications/Preschool%20Implicit%20Bias%20Policy%20Brief_final_9_26_276766_5379_v1.pdf
20. Data Resource Center for Child and Adolescent Health (2017). *The national survey of children's health*. Retrieved from http://childhealthdata.org/learn/NSCH
21. Koivunen, J., Van Alst, D., Ocasio, K., & Allegra, C. (2017). Understanding engagement in mental health services for preschool children: An analysis of teacher, clinician, and parent perspectives. *Early Childhood Education Journal*, *45*, 313–320. https://doi.org/10.1007/s10643-016-0799-5
22. Zeanah, C. H., & Zeanah, P. D. (2009). The scope of infant mental health. In C. H. Zeanah (Ed.). *Handbook of infant mental health* (3rd ed.) (pp. 5–21). New York: Guilford Press.
23. Brandt, K. (2014). Core concepts in infant family and early childhood mental health. In K. Brandt, B. D. Perry, S. Seligman, & E. Tronick (Eds.). *Infant and early childhood mental health: Core concepts and clinical practice* (pp. 1–20). Washington, DC: American Psychiatric Publishing.
24. Achenbach, T. M., & Rescorla, L. A. (2000). *Manual for the ASEBA Preschool Forms & Profiles*. Burlington, VT: University of Vermont, Research Center for Children, Youth, & Families.
25. Achenbach, T. M., & Edlebrock, C. S. (1978). The classification of childhood psychopathology: A review and analysis of empirical efforts. *Psychological Bulletin*, *85*(6), 127–1301. http://psycnet.apa.org/doi/10.1037/0033-2909.85.6.1275
26. Barley, E., & Lawson, V. (2016). Using health psychology to help patients: Common mental health disorders and psychological distress. *British*

Journal of Nursing, *25*(17), 966–974. https://doi.org/10.12968/bjon.2016.25.17.966

27. Rubin, K. H., & Coplan, R. J. (2004). Paying attention to and not neglecting social withdrawal and social isolation. *Merrill-Palmer Quarterly*, *50*(4), 506–535.
28. Bufferd, S. J., Dougherty, L. R., Carlson, C. A., Rose, S., & Klein, D. N. (2012). Psychiatric disorders in preschoolers: Continuity from ages 3 to 6. *American Journal of Psychiatry*, *169*, 1157–1164. https://doi:101176/appi.ajp.2012.12020268
29. Lavign, J. V., Arend, R., Rosenbaum, D., Binn, H. J., Christoffel, K. K., & Gibbons, R. D. (1998). Psychiatric disorders with onset in preschool years: I. stability of diagnosis. *Journal of the American Academy of Child and Adolescent Psychiatry*, *37*, 1246–1254. https://doi:10.1097/00004583-199812000-00007
30. Luby, J. L., Si, X., Belden, A. C., Tendon, M., & Spitznagel, E. (2009). Preschool depression: Homotypic continuity and course over 24 months. *Archives of General Psychiatry*, *66*, 897–905. https://doi:10.1001/archgenpsyhiatry.2009.97
31. Tendon, M., Si, X., Beldon, A., & Luby, J. (2009). Attention-deficit hyperactivity disorder in preschool children: An investigation of validation based on visual attention performance. *Journal of Child and Adolescent Psychopharmacology*, *19*, 137–146. https://doi:10.1089/cap.2008.048
32. Woodward, L. J., Lu, Z., Morris, A. R., & Healey, D. M. (2017). Preschool self-regulation predicts later mental health and educational achievement in very preterm and typically developing children. *Clinical Neuropsychologist*, *31*(2), 404–422. https://doi: 10.1080/13854046.2016.1251614
33. Dougherty, L. R., Leppert, K. A., Merwin, S. M., Smith, V., Bufferd, S., & Kushner, M. R. (2015). Advances and directions in preschool mental health research. *Child Development Perspectives*, *9*(1), 14–19. https://doi:10.1111/cdcp.12099
34. Sheftall, A., Asti, L., Horowitz, L. M., Felts, A., Fontanella, C. A., Campo, J. V., & Bridge, J. A. (2016). Suicide in elementary school aged children and early adolescents. *Pediatrics*, 138(4), 1–10. https://doi:10.1542/peds.2016-0436
35. Kovess-Masfety, V., Pilowsky, D. J., Goelitz, Dietmar, ... & Carta, M. G. (2015). Suicidal ideation and mental health disorders in young school age children across Europe. *Journal of Affective Disorders*, *177*, 28–35. https://doi:10.1016/j.jad.2015.02.008

36. Venables, N. C., Sellbom, M., Sourander, A., . . . & Patrick, C. J. (2015). Separate and Interactive contribution of weak inhibitory control and threat sensitivity to prediction of suicide risk. *Psychiatry Research, 226*(2/3), 461–466. https://doi:10.1016/j.psychres.2015.01.018
37. Serra, G., Koukopoulos, A., De Chiara, L., . . . & Baldessarini, R. (2017). Child and adolescent clinical features preceding adult suicide attempts. *Archives of Suicide Research*, 21(3), 502–518. https://doi.org/10.1080/13811118.2016.1227004
38. Gun Violence Archive (2018).*2018 Mass Shootings*. Retrieved from www.gunviolencearchive.org/reports/mass-shooting

2

Early Signs of Possible Mental and Behavioral Health Issues in Young Children

PHOTO 2.1

Most parents and teachers do not notice signs of internalizing mental health conditions like anxiety or depression in early childhood. It's common for many parents to expect for their children to grow out of their maladaptive behaviors as they get older. On the other hand, adults usually do not recognize early signs of internalizing issues because many children who deal with sadness or anxieties do not demand much attention from grownups; they are usually quiet and complaisant. Furthermore, young children who begin experiencing conflicting and often confusing emotions are simply not able to fully understand the range and complexity of their own feelings and thoughts, and so are not necessarily able to articulate how they feel. These reasons make professionals reluctant to make a definitive diagnosis of a child who may be experiencing mental health issues.

I was first aware of my depression when I was twelve. It wasn't that I hadn't experienced symptoms of depression before; I just didn't have the words or understanding to express how I felt when I was younger. But when I was in seventh grade—at a new school, getting grades for the first time, deep in the throes of puberty—I could finally label the complex feelings of anger, self-hatred, self-doubt, and sadness that pulsed through me since early childhood. Yes, part of it was entering preteen years, but part of it was also the beginnings of my mental health issues and their manifestations. It took me years to realize that I'd been dealing with anxiety and depression simultaneously for several years.

Undoubtedly, if you ask my parents, they may be able to reflect back and recognize some signs of anxiety that were there from an early age—what likely they didn't realize were signs of childhood depression. As a preteen, I was convinced I was able to hide away how I felt so no one would worry about me. But I hadn't developed those kinds of defense mechanisms until I was about nine or ten. The years before then are an open and blank book—one that might have much to tell, if it could have been read.

—NJ

Michael Rutter, a pioneer in the field of developmental psychiatry, has written extensively about risk and resilience mechanisms and factors that can amplify or mitigate mental health issues in children. He talks about the underlying biomarkers (biological markers)—objective and quantifiable characteristics of biological processes indicative of a condition, disorder, or disease—or genetic mechanisms that are common or connected in many existing psychiatric disorders. Unfortunately, most biomarkers are unknown, because there is usually a mix of multiple genetic and multiple environmental factors that work together to manifest a disorder—which vary from individual to individual (1). We'll talk a bit more about the biomarkers and biology related to trauma specifically in the next chapter. In addition, what happens during someone's life usually influences the developmental course and expression of a mental and/or physical condition through time; in other words, mental health issues in children can change with age and over time. A child may display one or more maladaptive behaviors together or at different periods during their childhood, further complicating the matter.

Many of the behaviors we will describe in the upcoming sections may overlap or coexist with one another in some children. We'll go through the most common of them. Keep in mind, there may not be anything wrong with some of these behaviors on their own; what makes them harmful or maladaptive is when they disrupt a child's life, taking up more of their mental space than is typical. It is also concerning when a child exhibits multiple maladaptive behaviors, another indicator that they need social-emotional support for building their mental health.

Anxiety and Depression

Anxiety is an excessive fear of a perceived danger or threat. It drives most maladaptive behaviors of both internal and external natures in children. Clinical anxiety disorders in children, according to the *Diagnostic Classification of Mental and Developmental Disorders of Infancy and Early Childhood* (DC:0–5), have been classified into six categories: *generalized anxiety disorder*, *separation anxiety disorder*, *social anxiety disorder* (*social phobia*), *selective mutism*, *inhibition to novelty*, and *other anxiety disorder* (2).

Classification of anxiety disorders in the DSM-5 includes an addition of specific conditions like *panic disorder/attack* and *agoraphobia*, the fear of being in specific places, like being outside of one's home or in closed spaces. As the names imply, classification of anxiety in children is often related to the child's early interpersonal relationships and attachment.

Regardless of type or whether diagnosed or undiagnosed, anxiety drives children to find a way to make themselves feel safe, whether or not their behaviors actually accomplish that. These behaviors range from clinginess to a caregiver to withdrawal from a perceived threatening situation, place, or a person. Other behaviors include aggression (to defend against a perceived threatening situation or person), perfectionism, somatic complaints, or hyperactivity. Research on anxiety in children has grown drastically in the last twenty years, resulting in the recognition of this condition as a much more common phenomenon in childhood than previously thought or reported (3–5).

> I know my depression had definitely settled in by the time I was twelve. However, lack of self-worth, perfectionism, and perpetual sadness were all common feelings for me far before then. When I was diagnosed with clinical depression at nineteen, it was really to no one's surprise. It's easy to look back and see the "warning signs."
>
> —NJ

Depression, on the other hand isn't traditionally thought of as a common phenomenon in early childhood. However, in the past decade, an emerging body of literature along with anecdotal reports from early childhood educators have shown that depressive moods, such as sadness and irritability, do occur in preschool-aged and older children, with patterns similar to adults (2). In some children, depressive moods may be accompanied by anger or aggression; in others, it might be lack of appetite or sleep, sluggishness,

PHOTO 2.2 In young children, disinterest in play activities and frequent sadness could be signs of childhood depression.

disinterest in activities, and a lack of focus. While sadness and irritability are typical in all children, depressive moods that persist across time and for many activities are a cause for concern. It's a serious risk factor for lifelong depression, future maladjustment issues, or a mental health condition like bipolar disorder.

Perfectionism

Perfectionism when adaptive is not a negative trait. Individuals who persist on a task to get it "right" are highly valued in Western societies—like Steve Jobs, the Apple® technology wizard, whose insistence and perseverance in perfection is legendary. However, there is also *maladaptive perfectionism*, which can be noticed even in early childhood. Maladaptive perfectionism occurs when the person, in completing a task or achieving a goal, aims for a set of self-imposed and personally demanding standards, despite the fact that doing so may have negative consequences for themselves or for others (6).

Sue Klebold, the parent of Dylan Klebold, one of the two teenagers involved in the Columbine shooting, has been outspoken about her son and the years leading to the tragedy. She describes Dylan in childhood as being task-oriented and persistent to the point of perfection:

> As a child, Dylan made parenting easy. From the time he was a toddler, he had a remarkable attention span and sense of order. He spent hours focused on puzzles and interlocking toys (7, p. 2) . . . As a toddler, he was fascinated by snap-together construction toys; as he grew older, he spent countless hours building with Legos. Precise and methodical, he loved to follow the printed instruction exactly, meticulously building ships, castles, and space stations, only to dismantle and build them again (8, p. 63).

This level of meticulousness does not have to fall under obsessions and compulsions (discussed next). It can also be different from the type of focus some individuals on the autism spectrum exhibit. Maladaptive perfectionism leads to undue stress and anxiety, even if some adults think otherwise.

Unfortunately, adults can sometimes confuse behaviors commendable for adults with what is developmentally appropriate for a child. They appreciate it when young children are orderly, quiet, focused, and task-oriented. When a preschooler is able to keep themselves occupied for a long period, teachers and family members usually tell each other, "He's

PHOTO 2.3 Perfectionism and insistence for organization and order may be a sign of anxiety or obsession.

so good!" or "He can play on his own for hours." However, focusing and persisting on a task to make it perfect isn't necessarily a sound developmental characteristic for toddler or a preschooler. Young children are apt to make errors and are usually fine with imperfections (unless adults are highly critical of them, which we'll discuss in the last chapter)—for example, wearing their clothes inside out or putting the wrong shoe on each foot. Perfectionist children, on the other hand, are constantly critical of themselves and often deal with self-doubt (9). When they do not meet their own high standards, perfectionists tend to view themselves as "failures." Although early childhood perfectionism is not well researched or understood, there is enough evidence to suggest its early appearance could indicate a risk for later depression, anxiety, obsessive-compulsive disorder, eating disorder, and other mental health issues (9).

For me, it took until I developed and underwent treatment for an eating disorder in college to let go of my perfectionism. Until then, I was focused on doing everything right. In high school, I always took on the brunt of group projects.

In middle school, I didn't have grades as a marker of my success, so I had to do whatever I was doing to completion, to the best of my abilities—whether that was catching all the Pokemon in my game or knowing a book forwards and backwards. It took me my first-ever C+, a severe eating disorder, and a suicide attempt to let go of my ideal of perfect, and sometimes, I wonder whether I could have stopped it when the tendency started popping up—that is, when I was little.

—NJ

Obsessions and Compulsions

Obsessions and compulsions are two common features of obsessive-compulsive disorder (OCD) and is sometimes present in children with anxiety, or with neurological disorders such as in ASD. Some common behaviors in these children are: insisting they eat or do the same things in a specific way, having certain organizations and order, or thinking and performing actions in a specific ritualistic or repetitive way (10–13). Obsessions are unwanted, obtrusive thoughts, and compulsions are the uncontrollable actions that placate or quiet those thoughts—until the cycle begins again. Like most maladaptive behaviors, obsessions and compulsions are usually indicative that an underlying issue, like anxiety, exists (13). In some children, obsessive behaviors—for example, sexual behaviors which are not appropriate for their developmental level—may signal a child's experience with abuse (14).

A brief aside regarding child sexual behavior: Most young children between the ages of two and five show developmentally appropriate sexual behaviors, such as liking to be naked; looking at other children's genitals or showing their own during play; or imitating certain adult sexual behaviors, such as kissing. In some children, both boys and girls, occasionally masturbating is also developmentally appropriate. These behaviors gradually disappear around and after age six, as children begin to learn about privacy and private behaviors. However, when these behaviors become excessive, or when they appear in a much later or much earlier age, they might signal a child's experience with sexual abuse.

Obsessive behaviors may be observed in young children who do not have histories of abuse or a diagnosed condition like ASD and OCD. Furthermore, Certain levels of ritualistic behaviors are expected in young children. For example, playing with the same toy or game, eating the same food, or wearing their favorite clothes over and over again are typical within the developmental context of a young child. It's when such behaviors become severe to the extent that interfering with them, and causes excessive distress that they should be of concern. Early obsessive behaviors can be a risk for further problems.

In her memoir *The Center Cannot Hold*, Elyn Saks, a legal scholar who was diagnosed with schizophrenia when she was a young adult, recalls herself as a child who was obsessed with having everything organized, neat, and in order. Saks would become inordinately upset when things got disorganized and messy in her room (15). Children are usually messy and explorative, so being too obsessed and preoccupied with cleanliness or organization of toys and objects is not usually a positive sign. It's more typical for a young child to get dirty, leave their toys scattered around the room, or not care about appearances than to insist everything has to be in a particular order.

Aches and Pains

It is not unusual for children to complain about certain aches and pains in early childhood. Stomach aches, for example, are a common malady in three- to five-year-olds (16). Pains and aches that do not have physical causes are commonly referred to as *somatic* complaints. Repeated somatic pains in young children are usually related to an underlying anxiety or emotional issue, which could be situational, related to maltreatment, stress related, or be ongoing (17, 18). Research has shown children who have aches are not only generally anxious, but often deal with sleep problems as well (16).

As a note, it is not uncommon that children who have experienced abuse and trauma have similar sort of complains (19). Chronic stomach pains and headaches are two such examples. (More common indications of abuse and trauma are nightmares and bedwetting.) Though not all physical symptoms are a sign of something so traumatic, it is important to note such patterns exist.

Social Isolation

Kenneth Rubin and Robert Coplan have studied different forms of social withdrawal in children since the 1980s. They distinguish between different types of *social isolation* based on the motivation that underlies a child's act of isolation. For example, a *socially withdrawn* child may opt not to interact with other children as a result of anxiety. Socially withdrawn children may be anxious because they have negative self-regard, or they perceive some difficulties for themselves in a given social situation.

Shy children, on the other hand, usually get reticent when faced with a novel social situation or if they feel self-conscious if they think they're being socially evaluated (20, 21). Shyness in boys seems to be a more maladaptive behavior as compared to girls because it is much more socially acceptable for girls to be shy (22). Negative and inappropriate reactions toward shy boys can result in some issues for them as they enter teenage years. For example, in middle childhood, shy boys seem to be less adjusted as compared with girls of the same age (22). Shy adolescent boys seem to have poorer social skills, lower self-esteem, more negative coping strategies, and experience more frequent depressive moods (23). However, in the context of the US and other developed countries, shy children do not typically tend to be at any imminent risk for further mental health problems as they grow up; in Western societies, many children are content to play alone for long periods of time, such as on the computer or with video games (22, 23). Remember, again, the cultural context of these discussions is key.

A third group of children who may not participate in groups or play with others are those who prefer to play alone simply because other children don't want to play with them. These children are called *actively isolated* or *withdrawn* (20–22). Active isolation occurs when a child is aggressive, socially immature, or belongs to a minority group and hence is discriminated against. In this situation, the child has no option but to withdraw (22). Active

PHOTO 2.4 Over clinginess and seeking isolation are maladaptive behaviors usually caused by anxiety.

isolation in preschoolers can result in anger and aggression in their middle childhood and adolescence (24).

The fourth group of socially withdrawn children are those who avoid the company of others or refuse to participate in social and group situations, not because of anxiety or exclusion, but because they are not interested in being with a group. Not much is known about the developmental course of these *socially disinterested* children. There is some evidence to suggest that excluding shy children, those who are socially disinterested tend to have depressive moods and are likely to develop depression and anxiety in middle childhood and beyond (24).

Anger Outbursts, Aggression, Defiance, and Opposition

Emotional reactivity is a term used to describe a child's emotional "instability," or a tendency to experience frequent intense and strong emotions and expressions when faced with various situations. Although extreme reactivity is a characteristic of several conditions, such as ASD, intellectual disability, and ADHD, some children who do not have these disorders may also be emotionally reactive (25).

There is no doubt emotional regulation and emotional reactivity belong to a joint process involved in the development of social-emotional competence and social behavior of children (26, 27). Although there isn't an agreed-upon definition of emotional regulation, experts do agree it requires a child to be able to manage, change, and control emotions in response to an experience and then behave accordingly (28). Children who are not able to modulate and exert control over their emotions often have extreme reactions, such as anger outbursts/temper tantrums and aggression toward themselves and others, in response to situations that do not typically provoke such reactions in others.

The inability to regulate anger is particularly problematic in the early socialization and development. Frequent temper tantrums and bouts of aggressive behaviors are among the most cited reasons for the exclusion of a child from social play and expulsion in preschools and kindergartens. Children who have frequent anger outbursts usually fail to calm down quickly; are easily irritated by others; and tend to be noncompliant, argumentative, defiant, and oppositional. Anger dysregulation in children can result in *reactive aggression* toward peers and authority figures, such as hitting, kicking, biting, throwing, or could lead to *proactive aggression*, such as the child being coercive, controlling, or saying and doing things that seem purposeful in hurting others (2).

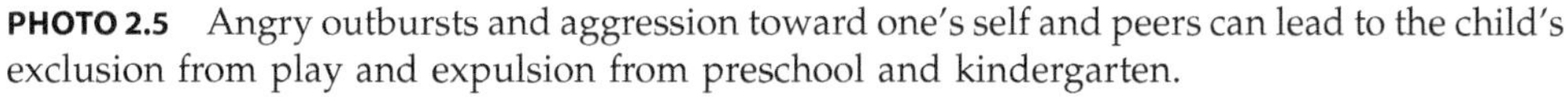

PHOTO 2.5 Angry outbursts and aggression toward one's self and peers can lead to the child's exclusion from play and expulsion from preschool and kindergarten.

Opposition and defiance that fall under the diagnostic criteria for oppositional defiant disorder (ODD) in the DSM-5 are associated with anger and purposeful hostility and aggression toward authority figures. ODD is a diagnosis typically given to a young child who is aggressive and tends to irritate and bother others purposefully. Without intervention, ODD often leads to serious conduct disorder (CD) in later years. The DSM-5 system emphasizes the coexistence (or *cormorbidity*) of aggressive and oppositional behaviors in children with ODD, along with symptoms of anxiety, depression, and other emotional distress.

However, in child mental health literature and certain diagnostic systems (DC:0–5), there is a clear distinction between the processes involved in the dysregulation of emotions and reactivity that might lead to a temper tantrum or aggression, and the processes related to opposition and defiance that might lead to ODD/CD. However, there is an overlap between both processes, as with many mental health disorders. In general, children who show symptoms of uncontrollable anger, aggression, defiance, and opposition are at risk for both a host of mental health disorders and academic and work-related issues in later years (2, 10).

Hyperactivity and Attentional Problems

Hyperactivity often, but not always, coexists with an inability to sustain attention. Signs of hyperactivity and attentional problems in young children are a lack of concentration, an inability to sit still, being clumsy, quickly shifting from one action to the next, and wandering away. Children with hyperactivity usually have a difficult time following directions, controlling their impulses, being organized, and/or doing things in an appropriate sequence.

Hyperactivity and a lack of sustained focus are features of Attention-Deficit Hyperactivity Disorder (ADHD). Children who have challenging behaviors are frequently diagnosed with ADHD, and many of them also experience anxiety and depression (29). While anxiety may be present in early childhood, depressive moods in children with ADHD seem to appear in later years (29, 30). The body of research on ADHD and its treatment has grown in the last thirty years, with a variety of educational and medical—or a combination of both—intervention options. Russell Barkley, one of the foremost experts in the field of ADHD research and treatment, recommends a combination of medical and behavioral/educational approach for children with ADHD.

Common Diagnosed Conditions in Childhood

Nowadays, the public is well aware of different diagnosed conditions in early childhood. The ongoing flow of information and misinformation makes new parents watch their infants closely and get anxious that all might

TABLE 2.1 Childhood neurodevelopmental disorders with common ages for diagnosis

Common Childhood Neurodevelopmental Disorders	*Common Age for Diagnosis*
Autism Spectrum Disorder (ASD)	➢ Clearly recognizable as early as 12 to 18 months; diagnosed around and after age 2.
Sensory Processing Disorder (SPD)*	➢ Diagnosed around and after age 2
Speech Language Disorders	➢ Diagnosed around and after age 2.
Attention Deficit Hyperactivity Disorder (ADHD)	➢ Diagnosed around age 3.
Oppositional Defiance Disorder (ODD)	➢ Diagnosed around and after age 3.
Obsessive Compulsive Disorder (OCD)	➢ Recognizable early; diagnosed in middle childhood and later.
Learning Disorders (LD)	➢ Diagnosed in primary grade, when performance in reading, writing and math are formally assessed.

*SPD is not an approved diagnosis in the DSM

not be right. There are a group of developmental disorders usually diagnosed in childhood, and most early childhood and primary grade teachers are knowledgeable about behavioral signs and characteristics of these disorders and are able to alert families or refer the child for diagnostic services and intervention. Table 2.1 gives a list of common neurodevelopmental disorders. This table excludes genetic disorders that are identifiable during neonatal development or right after birth (e.g.; fetal alcohol disorders, Down syndrome, Fragile X syndrome, etc.).

Emotional Needs of Children Aside from Their Diagnosed Conditions

Most professionals who work with children with neurocognitive and developmental disorders do not think of these children in terms of their mental health needs above and beyond their behavioral symptoms and learning difficulties. In special education, skill learning is within either behavioral or developmental methods and is isolated from the child's emotional context. Similar to previous beliefs about young children not being affected by trauma, there is either a disregard for the emotional wellbeing of children with developmental and intellectual disorders, or a perception that because of their cognitive limitations, they do not feel stress and trauma the same way neurotypical children would. We can even come up with reasons to back these beliefs: Because children with cognitive impairments often have limited verbal abilities to express their thoughts and emotions, it is particularly difficult to gauge their feelings about things and their interpretations of events—especially stressful events. Furthermore, because we believe them to be incapable of sound judgment due to their cognitive limitations, we fall into the trap of thinking they cannot feel and emote as typical children do.

There are several additional considerations to keep in mind. First, neurocognitive disorders and intellectual disability are already classified under *mental disorders* as far as psychiatric diagnostic systems (e.g., DSM, ICD-10, or DC:0–5) are concerned. Therefore, there has been little discussion or research about the way stressors in the caregiving environments of these children can adversely influence their already vulnerable neurobehavioral systems and cause further developmental and mental health issues.

Second, the same three areas of brain implicated in severe stress (e.g. the hippocampus, amygdala, and prefrontal cortex; more in Chapter 3) are already implicated in most developmental disorders, such as ADHD, ASD, and some forms of intellectual disability (ID). In fact, some behavioral characteristics in these disorders (usually due to impairments in executive functioning, regulation of emotions, memory, theory of mind, social relatedness, and sensory processing) overlap and, in many cases, are identical to behaviors of children who have experienced trauma. For example, the fight-or-flight behaviors in response to being held in a child who has been maltreated or traumatized, and in a child with ASD in reaction to various sensory stimuli and/or being held, are identical, although the underlying causes of those behaviors for each condition is very different. Furthermore, as mentioned, limitations in language and cognitive development make the task of identifying traumatic stress in children with developmental disorders difficult.

Third, professionals primarily use behavioral approaches both in special education and in clinical intervention for children with developmental disorders and intellectual disability. Because behavioral methods have over fifty years of evidence to back their efficacy in treatment, their use dominates special education teacher training and practice in early childhood and elementary grades (after the child exits the early intervention system). Early intervention, which is the system of prevention and intervention for children with disabilities from birth to age three, uses a family-centered approach, in which the needs and strengths of the family are assessed and considered. Developmental therapists and other service providers use play-based developmental approaches in their therapy with the child and work within the context of and in collaboration with family members to achieve positive outcomes for both the child and the family. Unfortunately, this focus is usually lost as the child ages out of the system.

Behavioral techniques are also the means by which special education professionals teach lessons and help the child achieve their annual IEP (individual education plan) goals—which often include behavioral and social-emotional goals. While there is not necessarily a problem with using direct instructional strategies and behavioral techniques, using only behavioral techniques as a means of teaching social-emotional skills and addressing challenging behaviors, emotional needs, and mental health issues is ineffective in the long run.

Fourth, variations in the training and skill level of special education professionals and school administrators who work with children with disabilities contribute to some serious problems, particularly when it comes to addressing challenging behaviors. Some highly unethical behavioral treatment, such as the use of electrical shock to control aggressive behaviors, remain in practice at least in one school (Judge Rotenberg Education Center) in the United States. In July 2018 response to a 2013 lawsuit against the Judge Rotenberg Education Center in Massachusetts, a judge ruled the use of electric shock in that school was allowed, stating no evidence had been presented that showed the use of electric shock did not conform to the accepted standard of care for treating individuals with intellectual and developmental disabilities.[1]

Restraint is another procedure some public schools use in a number of states for children with developmental and intellectual disabilities, usually in conjunction with seclusion. It's defined as any action or procedure that prevents a child's free body movement to a position of choice and/or prevents normal access to their body by any method attached or close to the child's body, which the child cannot control or remove easily (31). These are procedures that have also been in use in residential treatment centers for children and youth with mental disorder.

Issues with Restraining Children

The issue of restraining children is one that provokes arguments and strong emotions on all sides. While it may be obvious to some why restraint is questionable and unethical, there are a good number of professionals and parents who believe restraining children with intellectual and developmental disorder is an effective procedure and is done for their own benefit, to prevent

PHOTO 2.6 Schools and professionals differ in their beliefs and approaches to address and prevent challenging behaviors of children.

self-harm and aggression toward others. This argument is rooted in institutional practices in behavioral psychology that are half a century old. Science has come far and long in showing us what damage can be done to children when we restrain them (or give them electric shocks) for any reason. Despite a growing body of scientific evidence to the contrary, many school principals and teachers continue to believe restraining children is the only way to "keep the child themselves and other children safe."

In a series of training conferences I presented for a state in which restraint was allowed, I cautioned participant professionals about its deleterious effects, briefly discussing some neuroscience research about the effects of restraint on the child's brain and likening the effects to those that occur as a result of child maltreatment (emotional and physical abuse). After the series of trainings had ended, one participant wrote to me:

> "I would just share that while not at my current job, a portion of my career was spent where restraint and seclusion were used. Maybe not needed to share, but I struggled at both October and April training calling that [practice] emotional and physical abuse. In [the name of state], while not everywhere, it is legal if a behavioral plan is in place and signed off on. Children with highly psychotic presentation, when attempting to attack other children and staff, could not have been ignored. I am defensive, and I know this. I am thinking of my coworkers who were harmed and are still harmed today. I very much see your point through the trauma lens; however I do believe there is a valid place for restraint and/or seclusion. I would just like this to be noted as a true struggling point for me throughout training."

Several years ago, I would have emphatically agreed with this genuine and honest professional, and furthermore, I would, myself, have recommended restraint for those children whom this participant describes. Like this professional, I used to perceive many children with severe intellectual and developmental disorders to be unavoidably "dangerous" and "harmful." Today, however, I know my beliefs were misguided, my perceptions wrong, and my knowledge of child brain development completely lacking! Science has come too long a way for us to keep ourselves in the dark any longer. We did not have a good understanding of the human brain and behaviors fifty years ago, when electric shock and physical restraint were recommended to stop children's aggressive behaviors. We do now. We understand under what circumstances children (whether with or without an intellectual and/or behavioral disorder) might become aggressive. We cannot use the excuse "It is for their own good" to treat children with cruelty. We have no cause to refuse them the right to be treated with the same dignity and regard as any other human would expect—no matter what a child's behaviors or diagnosis. Think about this: If anyone treated an incarcerated individual in a US prison this way, under the US Constitution, that individual would have the right to object to it as *cruel and unusual punishment*. Why can't we give our children these same rights?

—MB

There is a slowly growing yet limited body of research studies that shows the physical restraint of children, even those in psychiatric residential treatment centers, can either traumatize or re-traumatize them (see 32–36). Most psychiatric residential centers and institutions in Europe, Canada, and Australia have taken steps to reduce or completely do away with seclusion and restraint procedures (31, 35, 36). In the US, however, as of 2015, 82 percent of residential treatment centers continued to use seclusion and restraint for children and adolescents with developmental and intellectual disorders, or those with other psychiatric condition. This procedure is used in response to agitation, anxiety and panic, and aggression (37), and to our knowledge the procedure has not changed to date. In terms of the education system, although restraint (with and without seclusion) has always been recommended as a last resort, schools currently use it as a ready response to the smallest behavioral outbursts of children of all ages in special education.

From a neurological perspective, the brain's command to the body to fight (e.g. aggression or attack) is in response to repeated stress and situations in which the person feels threatened. (We will discuss this in detail in Chapter 3.) Children with developmental and intellectual disorders almost always resort to acts of aggression out of frustration and anger, anxiety and fear, and agitation. Even in situations of frustration and anger, it is the anxiety that works in their disfavor and drives them to act in a fight-or-flight mode.

No child resorts to aggression without a cause. To children who deal with anxiety, many situations are perceived as threatening. Their automatic reaction to these situations is agitation, temper tantrums, and aggression as a way to defend themselves. In all children who resort to aggression, anxiety plays a prominent role. When we restrain them in this high state of emotional arousal, we make them feel the threat even more severely. Their brain's stress response system (the HPA axis, which we'll discuss in the next chapter), which is already activated, goes into an overdrive. Repeated or prolonged activation of the brain's stress response system amounts to the same effects as repeatedly maltreating (abusing) a child; that is, it can result in PTSD symptoms. Needless to say, during the restraint procedure, the child does not take in any information we might want to communicate to them, such as "You need to calm down," "You can hurt your classmates," "This is the consequence of your aggression," etc. Their brain is, for all practical purposes, shut down, and the only thing they can think of is to be safe from danger. There is not any educational value in this procedure.

There is another neurological reason for not restraining children. In Chapter 4, we will discuss the concept of helplessness and its neurological underpinnings. Briefly, helplessness is a default condition which the brain resorts to when a person is in a situation of repeated failures or repeated pain (e.g.: electric shock or restraint hold). Reflecting back on our discussion of electric shock on children, it's ironic that in the series of studies on helplessness in the 1960s and 1970s, electric shocks were given to dogs, which is now banned—no researcher resorts to shocking dogs any longer, due to its inhumane implications. In those situations, the dogs had no way to escape the shock, the same way in which children have no way to escape from being held/restrained/given an electric shock. In 2016, neuroscientists found in situations where the brain has no way of escaping, a brain structure called the dorsal raphe nucleus (DRN) is activated. The DRN releases serotonin, a neurotransmitter implicated in psychiatric conditions, onto the amygdala, the area of the brain that controls our fear response. This DRN activation produces helplessness, a belief that one cannot do anything to change the situation. Therefore, the child learns to become passive when faced with restraint. This is why there are professionals who believe that restraint works—because it makes the child helpless—but at what cost? Helplessness is an important precursor for depression, suicidal ideations, and other psychiatric conditions in children (38) (see Chapter 4 for details).

In our experience, in states in which restraint is allowed in public schools, the practice is actually not used as the last resort. Rather, it is used as an immediate solution to any aggressive outburst of children, particularly those who are known to have a difficult time with self-regulation. In some schools, there are designated personnel who receive "safe restraint" training and are called upon by the teacher as soon as an aggressive outburst takes place in the classroom.

Finally, this approach has no teaching value, since children who are subject to this treatment don't actually learn self-control. If there is a decrease in the amount of aggressive behaviors, as some single-subject behavioral studies suggest, it is not because they have learned a new behavior of self-control. Rather, as new scientific studies tell us, it is because their brain has resorted to a helpless state (38). In other words, over time, they have learned they have no control over the situation.

The opposite can also happen in children, particularly in those with higher cognitive abilities to interpret the situation. In these children, restraint creates anger, animosity, and resentment toward the authority figure and teaches them further aggression in addition to other traumatic effects. We cannot be more clear: In all circumstances, restraint traumatizes the child. It teaches the child more aggression and anger. In the best-case scenario—when there is a decrease in aggression—it creates helplessness, which can result in later mental health issues.

Aggression can be prevented when we are attuned to a child's mental state, teach them strategies to calm their anxieties and panic, and help them appropriately manage their frustrations and anger. Because many instances of behavioral outbursts are related to a child's frustration and anger with their environment, they can also be prevented when we keep children engaged on interesting and meaningful tasks, no matter what their cognitive ability is. In our model, if and when aggressive behaviors occur, which is very seldom, we have a specific and effective procedure that is not traumatizing to the child. This procedure has been previously explained in detail elsewhere (39). We will briefly describe it in our last chapter.

Toward A New Understanding of Children

The current early educational approaches, dominated by the mainstream model *Developmentally Appropriate Practices*, are behind the scientific discoveries in the emerging field of developmental neuroscience—such as behavioral epigenetics and the effects of toxic stress and trauma on the brain—that must inform the practice of anyone who works with children on a daily basis. These discoveries help us develop a new understanding of not only causes but also symptoms of mental health issues in young children. Such understanding can and must inform our work far more effectively than is currently the norm. This will hopefully help us be open to finding better ways of parenting, caring for, teaching, working with, and interacting with children; ways that will acknowledge, value, and respect children's shared personhood with us; ways that will prevent their stigmatization, social isolation, and worse, maltreatment.

Note

1. The Judge Rotenberg School uses GED, an electric shock device, to control unwanted behaviors in enrolled children and adolescents. Parents agree to the use of GED via signed consent. There have been several lawsuits against the school, but thus far, the school has managed to fight them off. Information on the last court ruling in July of 2018 was retrieved from *The Guardian*, available at www.theguardian.com/education/2018/jul/12/judge-rotenberg-educational-center-electric-shocks.

References

1. Rutter, M., & Pickles, A. (2016). Annual research review: Threats to the validity of child psychiatry and psychology. *Journal of Child Psychology and Psychiatry*, 57(3), 398–416. https://doi:10.111/jcpp.12461
2. ZERO TO THREE (2016). *Diagnostic classification of mental health and developmental disorders of infancy and early childhood: Revised edition (DC:0-5)*. Washington, DC: ZERO TO THREE.
3. Ellin, S., & Verboon, P. (2016). Psychological inflexibility and child anxiety. *Journal of Child and Family Studies*, *25*(12), 3565–3573. https://doi:10.1007/s10826-016-0522-6
4. Morales, S., Taber-Thomas, B. C., & Perez-Edgar, K. E. (2017). Patterns of attention to threat across tasks in behaviorally inhibited children at risk for anxiety. *Developmental Science*, *20*(2), e12391, 1–9. https://dx.doi.org/10.1111%2Fdesc.12391
5. Poirier, C. S., Brendgen, M., Girard, A., Vitaro, F., Dionne, G., & Boivin, M. (2016). Friendship experiences and anxiety among children: A genetically informed study. *Journal of Clinical Child & Adolescent Psychology*, *45*(2), 655–667. https://doi:10.108/15374416.2014.987382
6. Shafran, R., Cooper, A., & Fairburn, C. G. (2002). Clinical perfectionism: A cognitive-behavioural analysis. *Behaviour Research and Therapy*, *40*, 773–791. https://doi:10.1016/S0005-7967(01)00059
7. Klebold, S. (November, 2009). I will never know why. *O, The Oprah Magazine*. Retrieved from www.oprah.com/omagazine/susan-klebolds-o-magazine-essay-i-will-never-know-why
8. Klebold, S. (2016). *A mother's reckoning: Living in the aftermath of the Columbine tragedy*. London: WH Allen.
9. Morris, L., & Lomax, C. (2014). Review: Assessment, development, and treatment of childhood perfectionism: A systematic review. *Child and Adolescent Mental Health*, *19*(4), 225–234. https://doi:10.1111/camh.12067

10. American Psychiatric Association. (2013). *Diagnostic and statistical manual of mental disorders* (5th ed.). Arlington, VA: American Psychiatric Publishing.
11. Sheftall, A., Asti, L., Horowitz, L. M., Felts, A., Fontanella, C. A., Campo, J. V., & Bridge, J. A. (2016). Suicide in elementary school aged children and early adolescents. *Pediatrics*, 138(4), 1–10. https://doi:10.1542/peds.2016-0436
12. Mack, H., Fullana, M. A., Russell, A. J., Mataix-Cols, D., Nakatani, E., & Heyman, I. (2010). Obsessions and compulsions in children with Asperger's syndrome or high functioning autism: A case-control study. *Australian & New Zealand Journal of Psychiatry*, *44*(12), 1082–1088. https://doi:10.3109/00048674.2010.515561
13. Obsessions and compulsion in children. (2012, January). *Harvard mental health letter*, *19*(1), 4. Retrieved from www.health.harvard.edu/newsletters/harvard_mental_health_letter/2012/january
14. Akpinar, A., Bakim, B., Alpak, G., Cevik, M. Yavuz, B. G., & Karamustafalioglu, O. (2013). Childhood trauma, sexual functions, psychiatric comorbidity and socio-demographic data in obsessive compulsive disorders with sexual obsessions. *Dicle Medical Journal*, *40*(2), 183–191. https://doi:10.5798/diclemedj.092.2013.02.0252.
15. Saks, E. R. (2007). *The center cannot hold: My journey through madness*. New York: Hyperion.
16. Palmer, C., & Alfano, C. A. (2017). Sleep architecture relates to daytime affect and somatic complaints in clinically anxious but not healthy children. *Journal of Clinical Child and Adolescent Psychology*, *46*(2), 175–187. https://doi:10.1080/15374416.2016.1188704
17. Beyears-Carlson, E., Stevenso, M. M., Gonzalez, R., Oh, W., Volling, B. L., & Yu, T. (2017). Developmental trajectories of children's somatic complaints after the birth of a sibling. *Monographs of the Society for Research in Child Development*, *82*(3), 118–129. https://doi:10.1111/mono.12315
18. Villanueva, B. L., Prado-Gaseo, V., Gonzalez Barron, R. (2016). Emotion awareness, mood and personality as predictors of somatic complaints in children and adults. *Psicothema*, *28*(4), 383–388. https://doi:10.7334/psicothema2015.265
19. Darkness to Light. (n.d.). *Identifying child sexual abuse*. Retrieved from www.d2l.org/get-help/identifying-abuse/
20. Asendorpf, J.B. (1991). Development of inhibited children's coping with unfamiliarity. *Child Development*, *62*, 1460–1474. https://doi.org/10.1111/j.1467-8624.1991.tb01618.x
21. Doey, L., Coplan, R. J., & Kingsbury, M. (2014). Bashful boys and coy girls: A review of gender differences in childhood shyness. *Sex Roles*, *70*, 255–266. https://doi:10.1007/s11199-013-0317-9

22. Rubin, K. H., Coplan, R. J., & Bowker, J. C. (2009). Social withdrawal in childhood. *Annual Review of Psychology, 60*, 141–171. https://doi:10.114/annurev.psych.60.110707.163642
23. Coplan, R. J., & Armer, M. (2007). A "multitude" of solitude: A closer look at social withdrawal and nonsocial play in early childhood. *Society for Research in Child Development, 1*(1), 26–32. https://doi.org/10.1111/j.1750-8606.2007.00006.x
24. Kopala-Sibley, D. C., & Klein, D. N. (2017). Distinguishing types of social withdrawal in children: Internalizing outcomes of conflicted shyness versus social disinterest across childhood. *Journal of Research in Personality, 67*, 37–35. https://doi:10.1016/j.jrp.2016.01.003
25. Lugo-Candelas, C., Flegenheimer, C., McDermott, J. M., & Harvey, E. (2017). Emotional understanding, reactivity, and regulation in young children with ADHD symptoms. *Journal of Abnormal Child Psychology, 45*, 1297–1310. https://doi.10.1007/s1802-016-0244-7
26. Eisenberg, N., & Fabes, R. A. (1995). The relation of young children's vicarious emotional responding to social competence, regulation, and emotionality. *Cognition and Emotion, 9*, 203–228. https://doi:10.1.080/02699939508409009
27. Bengtsson, H., & Arvidsson, Å. (2011). The impact of developing social perspective-taking skills on emotionality in middle and late childhood. *Social Development, 20*, 353–375. https://doi:10.1111/j.1467-9507.2010.00587.x
28. Compas, B. E., Jaser, S. S., Bettis, A. H., Watson, K. Hl, Gruhn, J. P., Dunbar, E. W., & Thigpen, J. C. (2017). Coping, emotion regulation and psychopathology in childhood and adolescence: A metal analysis and narrative review. *Psychological Bulletin, 143*(9), 939–991. https://doi:10.1037/bul0000110
29. Segenreich, D., Paez, M. Regalla, M., Fortes, D., Faraone, S., Sergeant, J., & Mattos, P. (2015). Multilevel analysis of ADHD, anxiety and depression symptoms aggregation in families. *European Child & Adolescent Psychiatry, 24*(5), 525–536. https://doi.org/10.1007/s00787-014-0604-1
30. Hammerness, P., Geller, D., Petty, C., Lamb, A., Bristol, E., & Biederman, J. (2010). Does ADHD moderate manifestation of anxiety disorders in children? *European Child & Adolescent Psychiatry, 19*(2), 107–112. https://doi:10.1007/s00787-009-0041-8
31. Cusack, P., Cusack, F. P., McAndrew, S., McKeown, S., & Duxbury, J. (2018). An integrative review exploring the physical and psychological harm inherent in using restraint in mental health inpatient settings. *International Journal of Mental Health Nursing, 27*(3), 1162–1176. https://doi.org/10.1111.12432

32. Timbo, W., Sriram, A., Reynolds, E. K., DeBoard-Lucas, R., Spect, M., Howell, C., McSweeney, C., & Grados, M. A. (2016). Risk factors for seclusion and restraint in a pediatric psychiatry day hospital. *Child Psychiatry and Human Development*, *47*, 771–779. https://doi.org/10.1007/s10578-015-0608-1
33. Hammer, J. H., Springer, J., Beck, N. C., Menditto, A., & Coleman, J. (2011). Relationship between seclusion and restraint use and childhood abuse among psychiatric inpatients. *Journal of Interpersonal Violence*, *26*(3), 567–579. https://doi.org/10.1177/0886260510363419
34. Boel-Studt, S. M. (2017). A quasi-experimental study of trauma-informed psychiatric residential treatment for children and adolescents. *Research on Social Work Practice*, *27*(3), 273–282. https://doi.org/10.1177/1049731515614401
35. Gaskin, C. J., McVilly, K. R., & McGillivary, J. A. (2013). Initiative to reduce the use of seclusion and restraint on people with developmental disabilities: A systematic review and quantitative synthesis. Research in Developmental Disabilities, 34(11), 3946–3961. https://doi.org/10.1016/j.ridd.2013.08.010
36. Scanlan, J. N. (2010). Interventions to reduce the use of seclusion and restraint in inpatient psychiatric settings: What we know so far, a review of literature. *International Journal of Social Psychiatry*, *56*(4), 412–423. https://doi.org/10.1177%2F0020764009106630
37. Green-Hennesy, S., & Hennessy, K. D. (2015). Predictors of seclusion or restraint use within residential treatment center for children and adolescents. *Psychiatric Quarterly*, *86*(4), 545–554. https://doi.org/10.1007/s11126-015-9325-8
38. Maire, S. F., & Seligman, M. E. P. (2016). Learned helplessness at fifty: Insights from neuroscience. *Psychological Review*, *123*(4), 349–367. http://dx.doi.org/10.1037/rev0000033
39. Bayat, M. (2015). *Addressing challenging behaviors and mental health issues in early childhood*. New York: Routledge.

3

Child Stress, Trauma, and the Brain: What Does Science Tell Us?

PHOTO 3.1

Up until quite recently, children younger than six years old were excluded from trauma studies because everyone assumed young children were not affected by trauma as older children and adults are (1).

> Every time I talk to people about childhood and trauma, they immediately relate a story either from their past or someone they know. One person told me that her husband's childhood trauma—the death of his brother—still haunts him in ways he doesn't admit to, or want to admit to. Knowing this, and knowing my own history of trauma, it is bizarre to me that it wasn't until the last three decades that researchers found support for something we already know: infants and young children do experience trauma.
>
> —NJ

In 2007, William Copeland and his colleagues conducted an epidemiological study of trauma in over 1400 children (2). They found two-thirds of their subjects had had at least one traumatic experience in their lives before they reached age sixteen. Copeland and his team also found in the general population of children, being subjected to a traumatizing event is fairly common. Was it novel that there were final numbers behind a phenomenon people were already aware of, or that it was found to be as common as it is? When we remember that what can be traumatic for a child might not be for an adult, or even for a different child (as we discussed in Chapter 1), then this number shouldn't be surprising.

Most children face adverse conditions that may persist over time. In the majority of world countries, children grow up experiencing ongoing psychological adversities and material depravity. A great number of children live in dangerous regions, in states of war and armed conflict, where their own lives and those of their loved ones are threatened on a daily basis. Many experience displacement and separation from their parents, as well as homelessness. In countries ravished by colonialism, the long-term cultural effects that trickle down into everyday life are another layer, a type of collective trauma experienced both socially and even genetically.

Children who grow up in more affluent countries similarly face adversities. Many children growing up in the United States face ongoing community violence and/or experience discrimination in their schools and communities by peers and adults. In the US, one of the richest countries of the world, 22 percent of children live in poverty and are deprived of needed material and cognitive resources for healthy development.

Research shows early-life adversities results in ongoing emotional distress which, over time, can change a child's brain structure. Admittedly, prevention of all adverse events is not possible. In the best-case scenario, in the aftermath of a highly stressful event or under conditions of persisting adversities, adults are present to provide appropriate support for the child. In reality, however, many children end up experiencing trauma without receiving adequate support.

What is Trauma in Children?

The exact definition of *psychological trauma* is not clear due to its subjectivity. Psychological trauma is usually defined as an event or experience which would have an enduring negative effect that could, in turn, compromise or overwhelm the person's (or child's) ability to cope with the experience appropriately. There are ongoing disputes in the field about what conditions or events may result in a trauma and what kind of emotional and cognitive experiences are severe enough to be considered experiences of trauma.

The American Psychiatric Association (APA) has looked at these issues since a formal diagnosis of PTSD entered the DSM-III in 1980. To this day, the APA workgroup continues to regularly revise and refine criteria for a diagnosis of PTSD. Part of the problem of having a clear definition might be due to the association of the word *trauma* with *PTSD* (3). However, many children and adults in the world who experience trauma and whose lives are affected by it may never receive this diagnosis. That could be due both to the lack of a solid definition and to a healthcare provider dismissing someone's concerns, finding that their symptoms don't match the textbook definition of PTSD or that their trauma either isn't severe enough or isn't rooted in a single, concrete event. Terms like *complex PTSD*, or C-PTSD, have recently cropped up in reference to trauma that happens over time; as of now, however, C-PTSD is not considered a formal diagnosis in the DSM-V or ICD-10 (3). (It is, however, proposed for addition in the ICD-11.) But healthcare judgment and skepticism is not uncommon.

It's no wonder professionals are wary to designate something as traumatic. After all, the media uses the term to refer to a variety of distressful events, from a soldier's witnessing his friend's body being torn in combat to a celebrity's loss of jewelry (4). People use the term "triggered" (often in relation to political differences) without recognizing that psychological triggers do, in fact, exist. When such topics are thrown around lightly, it explains people's wariness to designate something as traumatic.

Most of us consider an experience traumatic when it has left a lifelong emotional scar on us. While some people use the concept to refer to an event, others use it to describe an emotional experience. Without a doubt, trauma is subjective. There are, of course, events most experts agree would cause severe emotional distress in almost anyone, such as natural disasters, wars, accidents, or any situation that is life threatening. However, not all events, regardless of their level of severity or threat, have the same effect or the same meanings for the people who experience them.

When it comes to understanding trauma in infants and children, the issue is even more complicated. Early childhood is a sensitive period, and children have different neurobiological and developmental capacities, as well as different family systems and support, which together determine how an infant or child could react to a stressful event. More importantly, because young children cannot articulate their own emotions or reactions to what they perceive as threats, understanding how trauma affects infants and children is specifically hard.

As a result, childhood trauma research is a relatively new venture. In 2005, Bessel van der Kolk, an expert and respected scholar in the study and treatment of trauma, proposed a new diagnosis for the DSM-5. He called it *Developmental Trauma Disorder*, for children who experience and show symptoms of trauma. He contended there were clear differences between children and adults in the presentation of symptoms of trauma, and that the common types and trauma for children—often being interpersonal in nature—should be taken into account, therefore needing a separate diagnostic category than the existing PTSD (5). However, despite the calls and support from numerous scholars and practitioners in the field, a separate category for the diagnosis of trauma in children was not approved in the final iteration of DSM-5. And so, to this date, no consensus has been reached regarding a separate diagnosis for children.

Wrapping Our Heads Around Trauma

Typically, when an event is highly stressful, our brain primes our body to deal with and oust the stressor so we can feel calm and secure. In many of my (NJ) biology classes, whether in college or grad school, my professors would often use the example of bear in the woods to explain this situation. It goes like this: You're walking in the woods and see a bear coming toward you. Your brain kicks into action, increasing your heart rate, dilating your pupils, switching the focus from functions like digestion to a focus on either "fighting" or "fleeing"—this is called the fight-or-flight response. So, when we perceive a threatening condition, our brain warns our body to get away from the source of threat through some physiological changes (e.g.: raised heart rate and hormonal production). Our *stress response system* is what alerts us and prompts our bodies to move away from the stressor. When the stressor is gone—either because we removed ourselves from the situation, or it otherwise resolved itself—our brain signals our body to go back to its usual equilibrium.

The biological systems that underlie this response are the hypothalamus (in the brain), pituitary gland (right under the hypothalamus), and the adrenal glands (above the kidneys). Thus, the stress response is governed by the hypothalamus-pituitary-adrenal axis, or the *HPA axis*. An activation of the HPA axis means an activation in the stress response and vice versa; when something stressful occurs, the HPA axis is activated.

Trauma usually occurs when the system cannot resolve a highly stressful condition—for example, when one is prevented from fleeing a situation the individual perceives as life-threatening. Children who are maltreated—abused or neglected, those who witness violence to a loved one, and those who live in unsafe homes and neighborhoods—are in these types of situations, where escape is not possible, and their stress response systems are frequently activated. In such a situation, the HPA axis is activated without a resolution. Frequent HPA axis activation means stress hormones keep producing long after the actual danger has passed, which has long-term effects we'll discuss further in this chapter. In other words, trauma causes continual HPA axis activation.

An *interpersonal trauma* occurs in the context of the child and adult's relationship. It is perhaps the most common form of trauma for children. Interpersonal trauma includes not only *child abuse* and *neglect*, but also less severe yet ongoing problematic relationships that can begin early on, during the time that the child begins forming an attachment with one or more primary caregivers. Thus, trauma can occur over time as a result of continual and repeated exposure to high stressors. *Complex trauma* is a common diagnosis given to children who are subjected to a lifetime of traumatic experiences, such as abuse or neglect. (Recall our discussion of C-PTSD above; while similar, C-PTSD is still not a formal diagnosis.) Children who experience complex and/or interpersonal trauma are at risk for developing not only a host of lifelong psychiatric disorders, like anxiety, depression, poor impulse control, and psychosis, but also for serious physical health issues such as obesity, cardiovascular diseases, and lung disease (5–7). To understand interpersonal trauma in children, it is important to look at the history of child development in this regard.

Modern Attachment Theory and Interpersonal Trauma

More than 65 years ago, in his report to the World Health Organization (WHO), John Bowlby brought to attention the importance of a healthy relationship between the primary caregiver and a child (8). Bowlby explained an impaired parent-child relationship can result not only in developmental and mental health problems in the child, but might well be the instigator of further long-term issues, such as antisocial or criminal behaviors, when the child is older (9). Bowlby went on to develop his well-known *attachment theory*. He grounded this theory in Freudian psychoanalysis and Darwinian evolutionary biology to explain a human development model that remains valid to this day.

Bowlby argued attachment is an inherent biological rather than emotional mechanism, and that attachment has an evolutionary purpose, therefore making it a common and necessary survival mechanism in all animals (10). Human infants, he explained, like those of other animals, stay in close proximity to their parents so they can be protected from predators. For this reason, an infant's primary task in development is to form attachments.

From Bowlby's perspective, a responsive attachment figure would be a primary caregiver who responds to a baby's bids for attention at times of need so the baby can be kept safe and secure to grow and develop. Early on, infants demand their primary caregiver's attention by crying. Later, they learn to bring their caregivers to their side by smiling. As they grow older, they add other *attachment behaviors*, like crawling, shuffling, raising their hands to be picked up, and walking toward their attachment figure. Depending on the consistency of the caregiver's responses, an infant learns to consider that caregiver a *secure base*. Children may form attachments to more than one figure and in a hierarchical manner from the most attached to least.

Bowlby's theory and the resulting work of his collaborator, Mary Ainsworth, in the *classification of attachment* types in children continues to be respected in the fields of child development and developmental psychology (9–13). Their valuable contributions have made us aware that the quality of adult-child attachment can result in a baby's *secure* or healthy attachment, or end in an *insecure* type of attachment, which can lead to further issues in the social-emotional development of the child.

Over the next sixty years, an increasing body of contemporary theorists have advanced Bowlby's work by drawing on recent neuroscience discoveries to explain the intricate biobehavioral mechanisms in the development of attachment and interpersonal relationships between the caregiver and infant. Among modern attachment theorists, Alan Schore, Alan Sroufe, and Edward Tronick have presented separate but similar models of attachment using both neurobiological and adult-child relationship studies. Modern attachment theories are theories of *social-emotional regulation*. They use the mechanisms of interpersonal development as the catalyst for the child's development of emotional regulation and development of a sense of self, others, and the world.

Schore, a modern attachment theorist, believes an infant begins to initiate nonverbal and affective communications with their caregivers immediately after birth, because the brain begins the process of lateralization. *Brain lateralization*, or brain hemispheric specialization, enables the right half of the brain to develop and mature faster. The right brain allows babies to communicate with their caregivers through visual, tactile, gestural, and auditory means without a need for language. The caregiver similarly synchronizes their responses with the baby's affective communicative overtures, for example, through their own verbalization and facial and tonal gestures. Based on the quality of the caregivers' responses and synchronization, over time, the infant learns to self-regulate and gradually develop an implicit, subjective, integrated, and coherent sense of self (14).

PHOTO 3.2 An infant develops a healthy sense of self and others through forming a secure attachment with a caring and responsive caregiver.

In the *Minnesota Longitudinal Study of Parents and Children*, which began in 1975 and has continued to date, Sroufe demonstrated that caregivers not only help to keep the arousal level of infants low and regulated, but they also help the infants learn how to regulate and modulate their own levels of physiological arousal. Sroufe found erratic caregiving behaviors usually result in emotional and physiological dysregulation in children—in that these children tend to remain physiologically aroused and are not able to handle stress or control their behaviors when facing stressors or conflicts. Following up such children in his studies, he found these were children who often ended up with metal health issues in their adulthood.

Recall that the purpose of this chapter is to discuss the manifestation of trauma in children and infants. It's important, therefore, to understand what the source may be. Because infants are unable to move or care for themselves, it makes sense that any psychological trauma they experience is interpersonal in nature, especially with a caregiver. That's not to say every time an infant cries and a caregiver doesn't respond, they'll have a lifelong psychological scar—only that we must be cognizant of the ages and communicative abilities of children as we interact with them.

It's All About Relationships

Ed Tronick's *Mutual Regulation Model (MRM)* further articulates what exactly happens between the infant and the caregiver in early relationship formation and how the mechanism of adult-child relationship can become the catalyst for self-regulation and further development in a child. We'll explore his theory in relation to Bowlby's in order to think about ways in which trauma might happen to an infant or child.

Tronick conducted extensive experiments in which he video-recorded face-to-face *dyadic* interactions between mothers with their infants in a laboratory procedure called the *still-face paradigm*. Briefly, the paradigm involves the interactions between a primary caregiver (like a parent) and a twelve-to fourteen-month-old infant. At some point, a caregiver is directed to freeze and become unresponsive to the child to record the child's reaction. The experiment was designed to discover how a caregiver's interactions and emotional state may influence the infant's emotional state and overall social-emotional development. Through completing a frame-by-frame analysis of each recording, Tronick discovered both caregivers and infants mutually regulate each other's social-emotional states and co-create not only their interactions, but unique features of their own relationships (15, 16).

From this perspective, two distinguishing characteristics of a relationship between a caregiver (parent) and a child are *mutuality* and an ongoing *co-creation* of meaning. Because the child and primary caregiver spend many hours and do many activities together, such as eating, sleeping, and playing, they have numerous contexts and opportunities in which they co-regulate and co-create meaning together, and thus implicitly know one another.

Tronick believes each adult and child mutually co-create a unique relationship together. Therefore, a relationship between one parent and the child differs from the other parent with that child. It is also the equal role in co-creation of meaning and understanding of one another that makes a relationship different from mere interactions. For example, in every dyadic interaction, both child and adult quickly evaluate and communicate with each other their own relational affects and intensions—that is, for example, how they each feel in that moment, if they are in sync and connected with one another, and whether they should stop interacting or go on. Each side then makes a communicative move via facial and vocal expressions and body language. Then, based on one's emotions and the affective overture, the other individual adjusts their behavior to match.

In a dyadic interaction, when one party's reaction does not match the other—for example, when the parent's affect is flat or sad as the baby is laughing, or when the baby is crying and the parent isn't responding—a *mismatch* of emotions will occur between the two. In this situation, the corresponding party attempts to *repair* this mismatch. For example, the baby may smile, laugh, make noises, or move to get the parent to respond in a similar positive fashion, or the parent may begin to sooth the crying baby. In the best-case scenario, each party responds to the other's attempts in a positive way, for example, by smiling back and co-regulation resumes.

Tronick's explanation makes sense in light of the great discovery of the *mirror neuron system* in the 1990s (17). Mirror neurons are specialized cells in the motor cortex that are key in the development of action understanding and imitation. Mirror neuron activity, therefore, is related to both action execution and action observation; furthermore, later research has found that motor neurons—following the definition of a neuron that is active during both action execution and observation—while discovered in the premotor cortex, have been found elsewhere as well (18). Keep in mind that despite over 900 papers published on the subject, the existence of mirror neurons and their roles are still somewhat controversial, with some scientists refuting their existence and others questioning both their development and function (19).

Regardless, over the past ten years, there has been research supporting the link between empathy, synchrony, and *tuning into others' feelings* through mirror neurons. Though the evidence regarding the presence and function of mirror neurons in infants is mixed (20), many scholars do believe there is evidence that imitation in infants, along with mirror neuron activation, is strongly linked to later social, cognitive, and motor development (21). Thus, though the neurobiology may still be debated, we can at least say it is worth further investigation.

On a behavioral level, infants do learn how to tune-in, respond, and gradually make meaning through their early relationships. Tronick calls this coordination of meaning a *dyadic state of consciousness*, which says every individual creates their own state of consciousness, or state of brain organization, which can be changed by interacting with another independent state of consciousness (15). In other words, a child's internal state, though functioning independently, can become more complex and larger through caregiver interactions. It makes sense, then, that a dyadic state of consciousness is critical in the social-emotional development and functioning of the child. In fact, an infant's experience of the world and the state of consciousness depends on this coordination of meaning making between the adult and the child (16).

PHOTO 3.3 In every typical adult-infant dyadic relationship, there are many *mismatches* and *repairs*. A mismatch occurs when one person is not emotionally in sync with the other. A repair takes place when the reciprocating person adjusts their behavior to regulate the other's emotional state.

One of the tenants of classical attachment theory is the formation of one's *self-image* and that of others. Bowlby explains that in the first two years of life, as a result of repeated interactions with the primary caregiver, the baby begins to construct an *internal working model* of the primary attachment figure (10). He describes an internal working model as a formed image of the primary caregiver that develops based on that caregiver's repeated interactions and responses toward the child, as well as a complementary image of the child's self. When the attachment figure is consistently responsive, warm, and positive, the child forms a positive and trusting image of not only the attachment figure, but of themselves as someone who is worthy of love and trust. On the other hand, when a caregiver has inconsistent responses, is neglectful or indifferent, and, worse, is negative and punitive (showing anger toward the infant), the child sees the adult as unreliable and threatening, and develops an image of themselves that is similarly negative—for example, of someone who is unworthy of love and trust. Many scholars believe once a negative self-image is created within a child early on, it is resistant to change (22).

Though Tronick does not dispute the classic explanation of self-image development, he believes the process of co-regulation and co-creation is one that dynamically changes over time and with each experience. A relationship therefore gradually evolves and expands into new possibilities, with additional meaning making in different contexts, and as progress is made in the child's cognition, language, and social-emotional development. Therefore, a caregiver-child relationship over time becomes detailed, specific, concrete, personified, and more unique to each individual (23). And so, both the child and adult develop narratives of self, each other, and the context and events around them.

From Tronick's view, there is no "perfect" form of parent-child relationship, and all relationships are *messy*. This is because in every adult-child relationship, there are, and there should be, many mismatches and discords that happen in each episodic interaction. These "misses" are typical and quite necessary to help each side learn new ways of repairing a discord and co-create new meanings about each other and their world (15, 16). In fact, it is through these mismatches that the child learns self-regulation and the foundation of executive functioning skills, such as the planning, waiting, focus, and execution of an action. Thus, in this way, both the child and caregiver not only discover different ways of being together, but the child learns the foundational skills in social-emotional development and self-regulation. The important point is for the child and adult to make reparations that will result in newly discovered and positive knowledge about each other and togetherness.

PHOTO 3.4 Each adult-child relationship is unique. It evolves over time to expand and include circumstances in which both the adult and child make new meanings about each other and their relationships.

This modern take on adult-child relationships is somewhat different from Bowlby's theory that a parent-child relationship is the prototype for the future relationships of that child, whether with the same parent or with others. In Tronick's model, what happens in a relationship between two persons is strict, and the relationship of the child with one adult is not transferable to a different adult. However, relationships do influence one another, and there is no doubt that a parent-child relationship does have an influence on how the child learns to connect and form relationships with other adults and with peers.

We find Tronick's theoretical contributions helpful to understand why early positive relationships with adults are essential for children. It helps them to not only develop healthy social-emotional functioning and a sense of self and others, but to learn how to establish, build, and maintain a healthy relationship with another. It also illustrates the reciprocal dynamics of a relationship that help a child understand their own emotions and those of others, and to gradually make either positive or negative meanings about their surroundings.

This model is also useful to explain how an interpersonal trauma can occur when things go wrong. Repeated negative patterns of caregiving behaviors that persist over time—for example, caregivers who are emotionally flat, indifferent, neglectful, punitive, angry, or shaming—can make the infant fearful and dysregulated. When negative caregiving behaviors persist and become a pattern, over time the child might become confused, hypervigilant or hyperactive, fearful or anxious, disengaged or withdrawn, angry or mistrustful, sad or depressed, and, in harsher scenarios, helpless and/or hopeless (23).

Toxic Stress and the Child's Brain

In the last ten years, much has been written about toxic stress and its effects on the brain in children. The question is, what is toxic stress? One might reason it is best to shield a child from experiencing *any* kind of stress. Research, however, suggests otherwise. Resilience studies of children (discussed in detail in Chapter 4) have shown it's necessary that children are exposed to a small but reasonable amount of day-to-day stress so they can learn how to cope, problem solve, and effectively deal with difficulties as they arise. Research also shows parents who hover over their child's head and protect them against any conflicts or displeasures actually do more harm than good. For example, studies of *helicopter parents* show that their children tend to be less resilient, more anxious and depressed, and have fewer life skills to deal with difficulties (24–26). So the question remains, what kind of stress is harmful to children?

An increasing body of research shows early persisting negative and/or neglectful caregiving behaviors are the kinds that result in toxic levels of stress in the brain of a child (27–32). When a caregiver is consistently unresponsive and neglectful, or when the adult responds harshly and negatively to the baby, the infant begins to display certain *biobehavioral* distress signs. Two important signs are increased heart rate and elevated levels of endocrine production, such as an increase in the stress hormone cortisol. These biobehavioral signs are the brain's alarm system, alerting the body to stress and helping it prepare for fight or flight. Studies show all infants—even those who are securely attached to their caregivers—show a marked increase in their heart rates, as well as elevated cortisol production, when their caregivers are not responsive or react negatively to their bids for attention (27, 28).

When the biological stress and defense system is activated frequently, or when it's in fluctuation, the stress level reaches a toxic level. *Toxic stress* overwhelms the body's capacity to strike a balance for functioning or maintain a homeostatic state. This creates what's called an *allostatic load* (29). An allostatic load occurs when the system is not able to achieve stability in times of change and thus becomes the body's "wear and tear" when a person is repeatedly or chronically exposed to toxic stress (30).

The interpersonal life of an infant predominantly consists of repeated interactions with their primary caregivers. It's therefore natural that when these interactions are chronically negative, stress levels elevate frequently and therefore remain at a toxic level. It's important to keep in mind here that the effects of toxic stress are compounded by other environmental conditions and adversities as well, such as not having enough material resources or cognitive stimulations (31). When toxic stress is present, the child's susceptibility to stressors, the nature and architecture of brain, and overall development are affected in such a way that they last a lifetime and are *epigenetically* inheritable (28–32).

Lessons on Childhood Stress from Neuroepigenetics

Since the 1990s, the evolving field of epigenetics has revolutionized the field of human development. Epigenetics has compelled us to look at development not in terms of genetics versus environment, which has been the focus of developmental learning theories, but rather as a dynamic and complex biochemical interplay of genes and environment together (33, 34).

Almost every cell in the body has a package of genetic information within the nucleus, and this genetic information is the exact same for every cell. How is this possible? Common knowledge dictates humans are born from the unity of two cells, a sperm and egg. That means every cell in the body came from just two initial cells, one package of genetic material.

So, then, how can we have the same genetic material in our skin as we do in our brain? The answer lies in gene expression. Our genes act as functional "codes" that eventually build up a cell's function, therefore making one cell different from another. The central dogma of molecular biology states genetic information is carried in the form of DNA, which is *transcribed* as messenger RNA (mRNA), and then *translated* into proteins, which carry out the work of the cell.

But if every cell has the same genetic material, how does one cell decide what genes to transcribe? This is where epigenetics comes into play. By placing specific molecular "tags" onto certain genes, the cell knows what genes to transcribe and what genes to ignore. As a field, epigenetics examines what those tags are, how those tags are placed, and whether those tags can be heritable both from parent cell to daughter cell and from human parent to human child. And research shows us that they are.

The term *epigenetics*—with the prefix *epi* meaning *above*—was coined by the developmental biologist Conrad Waddington in 1942. Waddington explained a mechanism through which all cells, even though carrying the same genetic information, can also carry an additional layer of information over and above their genetic code to allow for the cell to become specialized and remain that way in subsequent cell divisions (35). Today, we commonly refer to the additional information that genes can carry as *DNA/gene tags*.

In the 1990s, several important research findings established the field of epigenetics as a growing and complex science. One of the important contributions of this field is the research explaining that through experience and learned behavior, human chromosomes can become modified to the extent that the expression of certain genes (phenotype) can change and become heritable, without any change having taken place in the genes' DNA sequence (genotype). The field has therefore extended to include *behavioral epigenetics* and *neuroepigentics*. Behavioral epigenetics focuses on how one's lifestyle and learned behaviors (both maladaptive and adaptive)—such as habits, diet, exercise, nutrition, and social experience—can modify gene expression and therefore be inherited. *Neuroepigenetics*, on the other hand, helps us understand how a variety of physical, mental, and behavioral health conditions can be inherited epigenetically.

One of the contributions of neuroepigenetics is research studies that demonstrate how an impaired early adult-child relationship could lead to lifelong and heritable mental and physical health issues. Since early 2000, Michael Meaney of McGill University in Canada and his team have conducted a series of groundbreaking studies on the epigenetics of early adult-child relationships. Their work illustrates how the quality of early caregiving changes the patterns of gene expression in the infant's brain and can lead to mental health disorders in the child (34, 36–44).

Meaney and his team examined the molecular mechanisms by which maternal care alters gene expression and further alters neuronal growth, function, and health. These studies not only demonstrated how early care and experiences in life alters the endocrine responses to stress—which in turn changes the physical health, mental health, and behaviors of a person—but also how these changes can persist over the lifespan and be passed on to the next generation.

Like most epigenetics studies, Meaney and his colleagues used a rat model to understand human epigenetics processes. In one of their earlier studies, they found that naturally occurring differences in the maternal behaviors of rats toward their pups trigger different patterns of gene expression in the brains of pups (36). For example, pups who were licked and groomed more often by their mothers showed a different pattern of gene expression in various brain regions (specifically their hippocampus, prefrontal cortex, and amygdala) than pups whose mothers did not lick and groom them often. They found the well-cared-for pups were more social, faster to approach, less fearful, and explored things frequently. The pups who were less cared for and less frequently licked and groomed were fearful, unsociable, and did not explore things readily.

Meaney's team discovered the stress response system of the pups who were well cared for was much less reactive as compared to the pups who were less cared for (35). This was due to an epigenetic change to the glucocorticoid receptor (GR), which is responsible for a variety of metabolic and growth processes. GR is the receptor to which cortisol, the human stress hormone, and other glucocorticoids bind. Glucocorticoids belong to a group of corticosteroids, like hydrocortisone, that are involved in the metabolism of carbohydrates, proteins, and fats and have anti-inflammatory functions. They're not just involved in the body's stress response, which is why toxic stress affects so many aspects of health.

Meaney's group found the epigenetic change to GR in the cared-for rats caused an increase in GR expression. Increased GR expression in the hippocampus and prefrontal cortex, two key brain areas involved in memory and executive function, causes an overall decrease in the activation of the stress response. In other words, pups who were cared for had decreased levels of stress overall (35).

The question is: Can animal studies actually give us a glimpse into the human condition. The answer is yes, they can. The purpose of an animal model is to create something that can predict the human condition. Because there are rodent analogs to many human proteins and biomarkers—ones that use the same or very similar cellular processes—we can draw conclusions from these rodent models. Even modeling psychiatric disorders isn't impossible in an animal; the point isn't to model, say, depression as a disorder, but rather, aspects of depression—depressive-like behaviors.

PHOTO 3.5 In epigenetic studies, scientists found pups who were licked and groomed more by their mothers were less stressed, more social, ready to approach others and explore their environments, and less fearful.

However, any good researcher will either independently check that there are similar changes in humans after examining a rodent model or else turn to the literature. Meaney's team was one such that ran human studies to check. In addition to their mother/pups studies, they also compared patterns of gene expression in postmortem brain tissues obtained from young victims of suicide, who had been abused in their childhood, against those obtained from young individuals without a history of child abuse. They discovered the same results they had found in their animal studies—that is, the brain of individuals who had been abused showed an increased epigenetic change in GR promoter methylation and decreased levels of GR mRNA. (The GR promoter is what causes the GR gene to be transcribed into mRNA, which eventually becomes the GR itself.) This increase epigenetic change of the GR promoter directly causes the decreased levels of GR mRNA, which implies that there were fewer GR receptors in these patients' hippocampi. Fewer GRs within the hippocampus means an increase in the stress response (42). To summarize: In young suicide victims with a history of abuse, Meaney found evidence that there were likely fewer GRs in their hippocampi, thereby meaning these patients' brains were more reactive to stress and had higher activations of the stress response. Just as the pups study found neglected pups had increased stress, this study found abused suicide victims likely did as well.

The implication of Meaney's studies are far-reaching. The stress response system and related mechanisms are natural ways by which the brain defends a person from a threat. When a child is emotionally and physically well cared for, the environment is safe for the brain to develop, and therefore responds to threatening events in the most productive way possible. On the other hand, when there is adversity, such as not receiving the minimal emotional and physical care necessary for healthy development, or worse, receiving harsh treatment, the brain responds to the perceived threats with hypervigilance. The effects can therefore be lifelong—even if that life is cut short.

Stress-Related Changes in the Brain

In times of high stress, when the HPA axis is activated, three areas of brain functioning are adversely affected. These brain defensive areas are the hippocampus, prefrontal cortex, and amygdala (30). The three areas work together to process information that the child perceives, like *what* and *where*, and connect them to contextual information like *when* and *whom* (42). Hence, the child can make sense of this contextual information, using memory, awareness, and emotion, and respond accordingly. In other words, these areas are responsible for memory, general awareness, regulation of emotion, and executive functioning of the brain.

In threatening situations, the hippocampus, amygdala, hypothalamus, and the rest of the limbic system work together to ensure our defense and survival. For example, the hypothalamus (while also involved in the stress response) and the limbic system help adjust and control our actions, while the three other areas help us make sense of the dangerous situation quickly, such as whether we should defend ourselves, or to run, hide, or stay put—in short, *fight* or *flight* (42–45). When a child/person is blocked from reacting appropriately to a threatening event in the way that the brain compels one to do—for example, when the child is held down—the brain's stress and defense system remains activated long after the threat is passed (45). Freezing instead of fighting or fleeing a dangerous situation, for example, is thought to be related to repeated activation of HPA axis while a person is unable to get away.

In an easily reactive system, the brain can interpret even non-threatening situations as physically and emotionally threatening, and therefore react accordingly for survival. It is thus typical for a child who experiences chronic

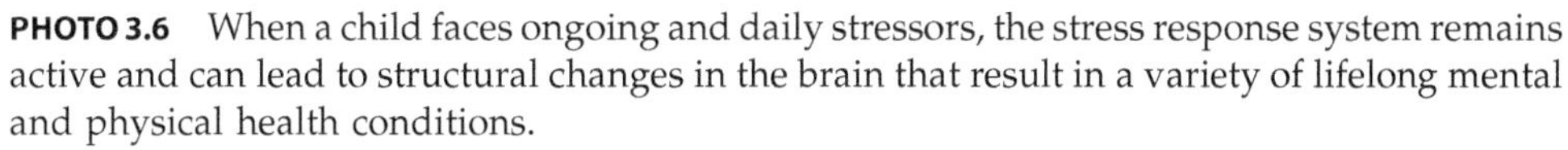
PHOTO 3.6 When a child faces ongoing and daily stressors, the stress response system remains active and can lead to structural changes in the brain that result in a variety of lifelong mental and physical health conditions.

and toxic levels of stress to respond with extreme reactions to situations others may find benign. In addition, a series of studies have also shown children who are subject to abuse and neglect tend to misread emotions in the faces of others, often seeing anger where, in fact, none exists (46–48).

Furthermore, repeated activation of the stress and defense mechanisms of the brain in a child causes the connected functions of the hippocampus, prefrontal cortex, and amygdala to become impaired, so that not only the perception of a stressful event, but the context and other related information about the event becomes distorted (44, 45, 49). This distortion of memory is a phenomenon common in both children and adults who have experienced trauma. Recollection of a stressful event in these individuals is often patchy, remembering a single image, an action, a sensation, or even a scent the individual experienced along with the stressful condition during that episode, as opposed to the whole episode (49). For a child, recollection and memory of the event may not be manageable, and as a result, they respond with fear (44).

Teachers often find children who deal with ongoing stressors, particularly those who have witnessed or been the subject of violence, frequently misinterpret facial expression and behaviors of others negatively—usually as anger. They misread children's and adults' actions as threatening or offensive and react with extreme negative emotions or actions. These children similarly have a distorted recollection of conflictual events in which they have been involved; when teachers engage them in conversations about specific conflictual episodes at a later time, their recollection of the event is not aligned with what others witnessed. As it is, memories in non-traumatized individuals are reconstructed and can be different from another's recollection of the same event. Trauma adds a further haze.

Sources of Trauma in the Family

Child abuse and neglect are well-known causes of trauma in children. Child maltreatment is usually perpetrated by a member of the family or someone whom the child knows well and trusts. In Chapter 3 of *Addressing Challenging Behaviors and Mental Health Issues in Early Childhood* (written by the first author, MB),[1] there is a detailed discussion of types of child abuse (sexual, physical, and emotional) and child neglect (emotional, supervisory, medical, and physical), along with issues that surround the maltreatment of children. To avoid redundancy, we won't go into definitions and types of child maltreatment. Suffice it to say, from the discussions we have presented in this chapter, it should become obvious that any form of mistreatment of children, whether physical or emotional, is likely to have a lifelong physical and mental effects on them.

Unfortunately, not enough attention has been paid to the issue of child abuse and neglect in the US. It is only recently that the field has started to acknowledge child maltreatment is more widespread than is typically thought. In 2011, in an essay published by BBC News (50), Michael Petit, the president of the US child advocacy organization Every Child Matters Education Fund, wrote,

> Over the past 10 years, more than 20,000 American children are believed to have been killed in their own homes by family members. That is nearly four times the number of US soldiers killed in Iraq and Afghanistan. The child maltreatment death rate in the US is triple Canada's and 11 times that of Italy. Millions of children are reported as abused and neglected every year.

In 2015, US Child Protection Services (CPS) received reports of 7.2 million cases of child maltreatment, with 75.3 percent of them being victims of neglect, 17.2 percent being physically abused, 8.4 percent being sexually abused, and 6.9 percent being emotionally abused (51, 52). In the same year, CPS referred over 3.4 million children for further investigation and 2.3 million children for prevention services. Keeping in mind a great number of child maltreatment cases are not reported or detected, these are indeed sobering statistics.

There are other traumatic events that can occur in both the family system and environment. Most of them are associated with or co-occur with interpersonal trauma in children. For example, intimate partner violence, a parent's mental health issues, and parental addictive behaviors are conditions that, whether alone or in conjunction with other factors, can cause trauma in children.

Roughly 15.5 million children are annually exposed to intimate partner violence in their homes (53, 54). Intimate partner violence is a threatened, attempted, or completed abuse (of any kind: sexual, physical, emotional) between partners. The majority of children who witness violence being committed toward their parents are children under age of six (54). Additionally, studies show parents who are subject to or are engaged in violence are likely to have harsh discipline strategies or negative parenting, which in turn puts children in their households at risk for further emotional distress (53, 54). Further research is emerging that young children who witness intimate partner violence are at risk for either becoming victims of bullying or perpetrate bullying or violence on peers themselves (55).

Parental mental health issues as well as substance addiction are also thought to be risk factors for interpersonal trauma in children. Depression, for example, is consistently associated with a parent's lack of facial affect, which can influence the dynamics of early interactions and relationship building with their child. Anxiety and other mental health issues can similarly influence caregiving behaviors and daily interactions, which can lead to toxic stress for the child.

A multitude of other events and crises can occur in the family system that can have negative social-emotional and mental health consequences for the child. Severe, chronic, or life-threatening illness of a family member; a disability in a sibling or other family members; separation from the primary caregivers, such as in military deployment, immigration detention and deportation; or parental incarceration are among the contemporary issues that are traumatic for children.

School Risk Factors and Trauma

With the exception of bullying, not a whole lot is written about the type of seriously stressful and traumatizing events that could occur in schools. A school is and should be a community that offers any child a safe haven, a place where the child can learn, grow, make friends and socialize, and find out more about the world. For a child who faces multiple risks in their families and neighborhoods, school is likely the only safe place to be. So, it's not typical to think of schools as environments which can present stressors or risks.

In the past two decades, the phenomenon of bullying and its detrimental effects on school-age children and adolescents have come to increasing attention in both research and practice around the world. Bullying is generally thought of as aggression toward one or more peers with seemingly an intention to harm. The phenomenon of *cyberbullying*, which typically starts in late elementary school, has received a lot of coverage in the media, especially due to a number of teen suicides that resulted from cyberbullying in recent years. However, the bullying phenomenon in early childhood is not well understood nor well researched.

In early childhood, being either a bully or the bullied can indicate underlying developmental, relational, and social-emotional issues in that child. There is, however, only a very small body of literature available that links bullying in early childhood to developmental issues in the child, like a delay in language and cognition, problems with theory of mind development, and issues in social-emotional development (56).

Similarly, there are few studies that have looked at the relationship between childhood interpersonal trauma and the phenomenon of bullying. Research is just beginning to emerge that links both bullying behaviors and being the victim of bullying to domestic violence at home and to child maltreatment (54, 55). Whether related to developmental impairments or having experienced an interpersonal trauma, bullying itself presents a traumatic event for its victim, with the same consequence for the child as any other traumatic event would have.

Racism and Discrimination

Another stressor at school is child discrimination. Discrimination is often inherent and systematic and exists in societal and cultural structures that are institutionalized. Research is emerging that adverse social circumstances and experiences of discrimination that occur in childhood can shape and reshape brain and development, with resulting effects on educational and occupational success as well as physical and mental health (31). One groundbreaking and notable study in this area is a large-scale public health study done by Arlene Geronimus and her colleagues at the University of Michigan and Yale University in 2006 (57). Using National Health and Nutrition Examination Survey data, Geronimus and her team proposed and found support for the "*weathering effects*" hypothesis. They found Black people experience early health deterioration as a consequence of the cumulative impact of repeated experiences with economic and social adversities, discrimination, and marginalization. They also found chronic stress due to racism and societal discrimination leads to an ongoing high allostatic load in Black people that gradually results in a host of physical and mental health issues. They showed Black people had high allostatic load regardless of their socioeconomic status, whereas this phenomenon did not occur in their White counterparts.

In 2017, Craig and Bruce McEwan confirmed this finding for children and presented a *toxic stress model* (31) (discussed earlier) within a framework of discrimination and early social adversities that children can face. They argued both biological and epigenetic mechanisms interact with social inequities, discrimination, and culture, resulting in altered patterns of cortisol production, and hence in toxic stress and an allostatic load. This, they argued, would lead to embedded mental and physical health issues in children who face inequities that begin in early childhood. They reasoned the presence of toxic stress directly implicates the functioning of amygdala, prefrontal cortex, and hippocampus in these children, which is apparent in their difficulties with emotional regulation and logical problem solving; issues with executive functioning, like organization, planning, and impulse control; being hyperactive or hypervigilant; and resorting to aggressive behaviors. All of these, they predicted, will put these children in jeopardy for lifelong physical, mental, and behavioral health problems.

In the first chapter, we discussed the high number of expulsions of Black children and children with disabilities in state preschools in the United States as a common discipline strategy. It's logical to assume the high number of expulsions of minority children used in most public schools would exacerbate existing other discriminatory practices in outside communities, and hence create more stress for children and their families. Thus, preschools and kindergartens likely are the first social institutions in which minority children and children with disabilities experience the stressors of discrimination, ableism, and racism. Black children who display any infractions are particularly at risk to be the target of ongoing mistreatment by their teachers and peers.

In addition to expulsions, there are other common disciplinary procedures in some public schools that result in children experiencing undue stress. For example, a young kindergarten teacher who taught in an inner city public elementary school once discussed with me (MB) some of the disciplinary strategies used with children in her school. Teachers in her school enforced a military-like set of behaviors and had designated particular consequences to address any "misbehaviors" or infractions. The way consequences were set and implemented were generally based on an incorrect understanding of positive behavioral support (PBS), a school-wide approach based on principles of applied behavior analysis. For example, teachers used a point reward system, and students constantly lost points they had already earned whenever they "misbehaved." Other strategies consisted of shaming, belittling, humiliating, name calling, threatening to call parents, and isolating children for breaking rules or displaying "inappropriate behaviors." Rule breaking and inappropriate behaviors varied from not bringing school utensils out of their bag fast enough—while the teacher counted from one to ten—speaking without raising hands or out of turn, asking to go to the bathroom outside of a sanctioned time, being out of a seat, or talking to a peer during a lesson. It is perhaps needless to mention here that repeated shaming, belittling, threatening, and humiliating are highlights of emotional abusive behaviors no one should be subjected to anywhere. On the other hand, loss of earned points is similar to loss of income for any person who has already earned a salary for a work completed. These practices are discriminatory and unfair.

Aside from emotionally abusive behaviors, some schools use practices that have a potential to be traumatic, such as corporal punishment or physical restraint. Currently, nineteen states have corporal punishment status, which allow their public schools to use physical punishment as a discipline strategy, like paddling the behind of a child. This has created a controversy; since parents freely give their consent for this treatment, it is therefore the decision of the school leaders, and the civil rights of parents, to allow using the type of strategy they see fit with their children. While this is true and there is no disputing the rights of parents, research is clear on this account: Any harsh treatment of children, whether physical or emotional, is highly stressful, and either is or has the potential of becoming abusive (58–60). Harsh psychological or physical punishment cause emotional distress in the child, and in the long run are likely to result in the very behavior—if not worse—the punishment is being used to stop (55). Furthermore, corporal punishment is often unfairly and overly used in marginalized children, like children of color or children with disabilities, who, as we've discussed, are already at risk for toxic stress.

Further Thoughts: Interconnection of Mental, Behavioral, and Physical Health

The topic of trauma and stress and its effects on children is complex and multifaceted and deserves a complete book. We hope the discussions presented in this chapter make a convincing case for the deleterious effects of toxic stress on the child. In this discussion, we did not include the lifelong physical effects that toxic stress (including trauma and maltreatment) has on children. There are chronic and serious illnesses, like obesity, high blood pressure and heart disease, ongoing joint and body pain, autoimmune diseases, cancer, and dental problems, that have been linked to toxic stress. We intentionally stayed away from discussing these topics to keep the focus of the book on the social-emotional development and mental health of young children. This, of course, does not detract from the importance of paying attention to all deleterious effects that toxic stress can have.

Note

1. Bayat, M. (2015). *Addressing challenging behavior and mental health issues in early childhood*. New York, NY: Routledge.

References

1. Scheeringa, M. S., Wright, M. J., Hunt, J. P., & Zeanah, C. H. (2006). Factors affecting the diagnosis and prediction of PTSD symptomatology in children and adolescents. *American Journal of Psychiatry*, *163*, 644–651. https://doi.org/10.1176/ajp.2006.163.4.64
2. Copeland, W.E., Keeler, G., Anglod, A., & Castello, E. J. (2007). Traumatic events and posttraumatic stress in childhood. *Archives of General Psychiatry*, *64*, 577–584. https://doi.org/10.1001/archpsyc.64.5.577
3. ZERO TO THREE (2016). *Diagnostic classification of mental health and developmental disorders of infancy and early childhood: Revised edition (DC: 0-5)*. Washington, DC: ZERO TO THREE.
4. Dalenberg, C. J., Straus, E., & Carlson, E. B. (2017). Defining trauma. In S. N. Gold (Ed.), *APA handbook of trauma psychology: Foundation in knowledge, vol. 1* (pp. 15–33). Washington, DC: American Psychological Association.
5. van der Kolk, B. A. (2005). Developmental trauma disorder: Toward a rational diagnosis for children with complex trauma disorder. *Psychiatric Annals*, (*35*)5, 401–408. https://doi.org/10.1111/j.1939-0025.2012.01154.x

6. Mullen, P.E., Martin, J. L., Anderson, J. C., Romans, S. E., & Herbison, G. P. (1996). The long-term impact of the physical, emotional, and sexual abuse of children: a community study. *Child Abuse and Neglect, 20,* 7–21. https://doi.org/10.1016/0145-2134(95)00112-3
7. Felitti, V. J., Anda, R. F., Nordenberg, D., Williamson, D. F., Spitz, A. M., Edwards, V., . . . Marks, J. S. (1998). Relationship of childhood abuse and household dysfunction to many of the leading causes of death in adults. The Adverse Childhood Experiences (ACE) study. *American Journal of Preventive Medicine, 14*(4), 245–258. https://doi.org/10.1016/S0749-3797(98)00017-18
8. Bowlby, J. (1952). *Maternal care and mental health: A report prepared on behalf of the World Health Organization as a contribution to the United Nations Programme for the welfare of homeless children.* Geneva: World Health Organization. Retrieved from https://apps.who.int/iris/bitstream/10665/40724/1/WHO_MONO_2_%28part1%29.pdf
9. Bowlby, J. (1944). Forty-four juvenile thieves: their characters and home lives. *International Journal of Psychoanalysis, 25,* 19–52.
10. Bowlby, J. (1958). The nature of the child's tie to his mother. *International Journal of Psychoanalysis, 39,* 350–373.
11. Ainsworth, M. D. S. (1964). Patterns of attachment behavior shown by the infant in interaction with his mother. *Merrill-Palmer Quarterly, 10,* 51–58.
12. Ainsworth, M. D. S. (1967). *Infancy in Uganda: Infant care and growth of love.* Baltimore, MD: John Hopkins University Press.
13. Ainsworth, M.D.S. (1979). Infant mother attachment. *American Psychology, 34,* 932–937.
14. Schore, A. N. (2017). Modern attachment theory. In S. N. Gold (Ed.), *Handbook of trauma psychology: Foundation in knowledge vol. 1* (pp. 389–406). Washington, DC: American Psychological Association.
15. Tronick, E. (2003). "Of course all relationships are unique": How co-creative processes generate unique mother-infant and patient-therapist relationships and change other relationships. *Psychoanalytic Inquiry, 23*(3), 473–491. https://doi.org/10.1080/07351692309349044
    Tronick, E. (2007). *The neurobehavioral and social emotional development of infants and children.* New York, NY: W.W. Norton.
17. Rizzolatti, G., & Craighero, L. (2004). The mirror-neuron system. *Annual Review of Neuroscience, 27,* 169–192. https://doi.org/10.1146/annurev.neuro.27.070203.144230
18. Kliner, J. M., & Lemon, R. N. What we know currently about mirror neurons. *Current Biology,* 23(23): R1057—R1062. https://doi.org/10.1016/j.cub.2013.10.051

19. Heyes, C. (2010). Where do mirror neurons come from? *Neuroscience & Biobehavioral Review*, *34*(4), 575–583. https://doi.org/10.1016/j.neubiorev.2009.11.007
20. Southgate, V. (2013). Do infants provide evidence that the mirror system is involved in action understanding? *Conscious Cognition*, *22*(3), 1114–1121. https://doi.org/10.1016/j.concog.2013.04.008
21. Simpson, E. A., Murray, L., Paukner, A., & Ferrarie, P.F. (2014). The mirror neuron system as revealed through neuronal imitation: Presence from birth, predictive power and evidence of plasticity. *Philosophical Transactions of the Royal Society London Biological Science*, *369*(1644), 20130289. https://doi.org/10.1098/rstb.2013.0289
22. Cicchetti, D., & Doyle, C. (2016). Child maltreatment, attachment, and psychopathology: mediating relations. *World Psychiatry*, *15*(2), 89–90. https://doi.org/10.1002/wps.20337
23. Troncik, E., & Beeghly, M. (2011). Infant's meaning-making and development of mental health problems. *American Psychologist*, *66*(2), 107–119. https://doi.org/10.1037/a0021631.
24. Odenweller, K. G., Booth-Butterfield, M., & Weber, K. (2014). Investigating helicopter parenting, family environments, and relational outcomes for Millennials. *Communication Studies*, *65*(4), 407–425. Retrieved from www.tandfonline.com/author/Booth-Butterfield%2C+Melanie
25. Nelson, M. K. (2010). *Parenting out of control: Anxious parents in uncertain times*. New York, NY: University Press.
26. Locke, J. Y., Campbell, M. A., & Kavanagh, D. (2012). Can a parent do too much for their child? An examination by parenting professionals of the concept of overparenting. *Australian Journal of Guidance and Counseling*, *22*(2), 249–269. https://doi.org/10.1017/jgc.2012.29
27. Spangler, G. & Grossman, K. E. (1993). Biobehavioral organization in securely and insecurely attached infants. *Child Development*, *64*, 1439–1450. https://doi.org/10.2307/1131544
28. Klein, B., Gorter, J. W., & Rosenbaum, P. (2012). Diagnostic shortfalls in early childhood chronic stress: A review of the issues. *Child: Care, Health, and Development*, *39*(6), 765–771. https://doi.org/10.1111/cch.12009
29. Silberman, D. M., Acosta, G. B., & Zorrilla Zubilete, M. A. (2016). Long-term effects of early life stress exposure: Role of epigenetic mechanisms. *Pharmacological Research*, *109*, 64–73. https://doi.org/10.1016/jphrs.2015.12033
30. Cerqueira, J. J., Mailliet, F., Almeida, O. F., Jay, T. M., & Sousa, N. (2007). The prefrontal cortex as a key target of the maladaptive response to stress. *Journal of Neuroscience*, *27*, 2781–2787. https://doi.org/10.1523/JNEUROSCI.4372-06.2007

31. McEwen C.A., & McEwen, B. S. (2017). Social structure, adversity, toxic tress, and intergenerational poverty: An early childhood model. *Annual Review of Sociology, 43,* 445–472. https://doi.org/10.1146/annurev-soc-060116-053252
32. McEwen, B.S. (1998). Protective and damaging effects of stress mediators. *New England Journal of Medicine, 338,* 171–179. https://doi.org//10.1056/NEJM199801153380307
33. Sweatt, D. J. (2013). The emerging field of neuroepigenetics. *Neuron, 80*(30), 624–632. https://doi.org/10.1016/j.neuron.2013.10.023
34. Meany, M. J. (2010). Epigenetics and the biological definition of gene x environment interactions. *Child Development, 81*(1), 41–79. https://doi.org/10.1111/j.1467-8624.2009.01381.x.
35. Isles, A. R. (2015). Neural and behavioral epigenetics; what it is, and what is hype. *Genes, Brain, and Behavior. 14,* 64–72. https://doi.org/10.1111/gbb.12184
36. Caldji, C. Diorio, J. Meaney, M. J. (2000). Variations in maternal care in infancy regulate the development of stress reactivity. *Biological Psychiatry, 48*(12), 1164–1174. https://doi.org/10.1016/S0006-3223(00)01084-2
37. Champagne, F., Diorio, J., Sharma, S., & Meaney, M. J. (2001). Naturally occurring variations in maternal behavior in the rat are associated with differences in estrogen-inducible central oxytocin receptors. *Proceedings of the National Academy of Sciences of the United States of America, 12*(12), 1145–1148. https://doi.org/10.1073/pnas.221224598
38. Champagne, F. A., Francis, D.D., Mar, A., & Meaney M. J. (2003). Variations in maternal care in the rat as a mediating influence for the effects of environment on development. *Physiology and Behavior, 79*(3), 359–371. https://doi.org/10.1016/S0031-9384(03)00149-5
39. Weaver, I. C. G., Cervoni, N., Champagne, F. A., D'Alessio, A. C., Sharma, S., Seckl, J . . . . & Meaney, M. J. (2004). Epigenetic programming by maternal behavior. *Nature Neuroscience, 7,* 847–854. https://doi.org/10.1038/nn1276
40. Kaffman, A., & Meaney, M. J. (2007). Neurodevelopmental sequelae of postnatal maternal care in rodents: clinical and research implications of molecular insights. *The Journal of Child Psychology and Psychiatry, 48*(3–4), 224–244. https://doi.org/10.1111/j.1469-7610.2007.01730.x
41. McGowan, P.O., Saski, A., D'Alessio, A. C., Dymov, S., Labonte, B., Szyf, M . . . . & Meaney, M. J. (2009). Epigenetic regulation of the glucocorticoid receptor in human brain associates with childhood abuse. *Nature Neuroscience, 12*(3), 342–348. https://doi.org/10.1038/nn2270
42. Conradt, E. (2017). Using principles of behavioral epigenetics to advance research on early-life stress. *Child Development Perspectives, 11*(2), 107–112. https://doi.org/10.1111/cdep.12219

43. Heim, C., Meinlschmidt, S. M., & Nemeroff, C. B. (2003). Neurobiology of early life stress. *Psychiatric Annals, 33*(1), 18–26. https://doi.org/10.3928/0048-5713-20030101-05
44. Cross, D., Fani, N., Powers, A., & Bradley, B. (2017). Neurobiological development in the context of childhood trauma. *Clinical Psychology: Science and Practice, 24*(2), 111–124. https://doi.org/10.1111/cpsp.12198
45. van der Kolk, B. A. (2015). *The body keeps the score: Brain, mind, and body in the healing of trauma*. New York, NY: Penguin Books.
46. Pllak, S., Cicchetti, D., Hornung, K., & Reed, A. (2000). Recognizing emotion in faces: Developmental effects of child abuse and neglect. *Developmental Psychology, 36*(5), 679–688. https://doi.org/10.1037//0012-1649.36.5.679
47. Pollack, S. D., & Tolley-Schell, S. A. (2003). Selective attention to facial emotion in physically abused children. *Journal of Abnormal Psychology, 112*(3), 323–338. https://doi.org/10.1037/0021-843X.112.3.323
48. Ardizzi, M., Martini, F., Umilta, M. A., Evangelista, V., Ravera, R., & Gallese, V. (2015). Impact of childhood maltreatment on the recognition of facial expressions of emotions. *PLoS ONE, 10*(10), e0141732. https://doi.org/10.1371/journal.pone.0141732
49. van der Kolk, B. A. (2002). Trauma and memory. *Psychiatry and Clinical Neuroscience, 52*(Suppl.), S97—S109. https://doi.org/10.1046/j.1440-1819.1998.0520s5S97.x
50. Petit, M. (2011, October). *Why child abuse is so acute in the US*? Retrieved from www.bbc.com/news/magazine-15193530
51. American Society for the Positive Care of Children. (n.d.). *Child abuse statistics in the US*. Retrieved from https://americanspcc.org/child-abuse-statistics/
52. National Children's Alliance. (n.d.). *National statistics on child abuse*. Retrieved from http://nationalchildrensalliance.org/media-room/nca-digital-media-kit/national-statistics-on-child-abuse/
53. Modrowski, C. A., Miller, L. E. Howell, K. H., & Graham-Bermann, S. A. (2013). Consistency of trauma symptoms at home and in therapy for preschool children exposed to intimate partner violence. *Psychological Trauma: Theory, Research, Practice, and Policy, 5*(3), 251–258. https://doi.org/10.1037/a0027167
54. Graham-Bermann, S. A., Castor, L. E., Miller, L. E., & Howell, K. H. (2012). The impact of intimate partner violence and additional traumatic events on trauma symptoms and PTSD in preschool-aged children. *Journal of Traumatic Stress, 25*, 393–400. https://doi.org/10.1002/jst.21724
55. Lucas, S., Jernbro, C., Tindberg, Y., & Janson, S. (2016). Bully, bullied, and abused: Association between violence at home and bullying in childhood.

Scandinavian Journal of Public Health, 44, 27–35. https://doi.org/10.1177/1403494815610238

56. Jenkins, L. N., Mulvey, N., & Flores, M. T. (2017). Social and language skills as predictor of bullying roles in early childhood: A narrative summary of the literature. *Education and Treatment of Children, 40*(3), 401–418. https://doi.org/10.1353/etc.2017.0017
57. Geronimus, A., Hicken, M., & Keene, D., & Bound, J. (2006). "Weathering" and age patterns of allostatic load scores among Blacks and Whites in the United States. *American Journal of Public Health, 96*(5), 826–833. https://doi.rog/10.2105/AJPH.2004.060749
58. Knox, M. (2010). On hitting children: A review of corporal punishment in the United States. *Journal of Pediatric Health Care, 24*(2), 103–107. https://doi.org/10.1016/j.pedhc.2009.03.001
59. Losen, D. (2013). Discipline policies, successful schools, racial justice, and the law. *Family Court Review, 51*(3), 388–400. https://doi.org/10.1111/fcre.12035
60. Mortorano, N. (2013). Protecting children's rights inside of the schoolhouse gates: Ending corporal punishment in schools. *Georgetown Law Journal, 102*. 481–518.

4

Teaching Our Students to Be Resilient

PHOTO 4.1

My understanding of child development changed dramatically when I was in graduate school and came across the concept of *resilience*. One evening, in one of my doctoral seminars, the professor asked, "Why is it that some individuals respond to life's challenges differently from others? "What makes them better able to not only withstand crises, adversities, and trauma, but to come out of these experiences stronger, as compared to others going through identical problems who fall apart or deal with the emotional and physical after effects for years to come?"

My professor's questions resonated with me. I was, at the time, raising a young child with a severe developmental disorder. In meeting other parents and family members who had children with disabilities, I had met some parents who seemed completely devastated, extremely stressed, sometimes angry, but more often defeated and depressed. On the other hand, I had met other parents, who, despite the daily challenges and stressors that raising a child with a disability presented, had well-functioning and balanced lives. Many of these parents and their children became advocates and mentors for other family members or took on new personal and professional roles and goals, often in a disability-associated field. Members of these families seemed to laugh more, and their families seemed to have a better quality of life as compared with others who dealt with the same challenges. What was different about this second group from the first one? It was natural that after my professor raised those questions, I became interested in resilience as a topic of my doctoral dissertation, for which I interviewed 175 parents and family members of children with Autism Spectrum Disorder to find some answers.

I found about 30 percent of families I interviewed met the established criteria for being considered *resilient families*. These families not only ended up becoming closer and growing stronger after their child's diagnosis, they also were able to face small and large difficulties with more ease instead of "sweating the small stuff." I had hypothesized that the way family members perceived and conceptualized a highly stressful situation, a crisis, or a trauma, had something to do with the way the family as a unit functioned and faced difficulties and stressors on a daily basis. I found out that in general, whether parents viewed their child's disability in a pessimistic way ("My child's autism has broken our family apart") or made positive meaning out of it ("Autism has made us realize how precious and great to make each day and to love life") played a key role in the way they, as a family, handled the challenges of a disability and met their daily routines successfully (1). Family members' spiritual belief system and overall worldview also played an important role. Positive meaning making of a challenging situation together with the family's overall faith and positive outlook in life galvanized the members to come together and pool their resources, affirm each other's strengths, and meet their daily tasks and challenges. As it turns out, *perception*, *meaning making*, and *spirituality* are all central elements in post-traumatic growth and resilience research.

—MB

Resilient Children Come to Light

The Latin root of the word resilience is *resilire,* meaning to bounce or rebound. Since the introduction of the concept into psychology in early 1970s, resilience has grown into its own unique science, with over hundreds of research studies conducted by psychologists, social workers, educators, and neurobiologists. Resilience means different thing to different people. Some researchers talk about it in relationship to *at-risk children,*—children who grow up in poverty and other risk conditions. Others define it as the human ability to bounce back from adversities. Some have described it as a process—instead of a phenomenon—of adaptation and growth in response to stressors and crises in one's life (2). No matter what definition people use, stories of resilient individuals are about those who succeed "against the odds."

It's interesting that the trailblazers in resilience research can fit the definition of resilient individuals themselves. Early pioneers of resilience science withstood the perils and trauma of World War II. Norman Garmezy, the "grandfather of resilience research," was a young American soldier serving in the infantry in Europe. He fought in the Battle of the Bulge and experienced the devastation of the war firsthand. Michael Rutter, another resilience pioneer who collaborated with Garmezy on many projects, was one of thousands of British children who were evacuated and sent to North America, along with his sister, during the London Blitz of 1940. Emmy Werner, who published the first book on resilient children, was an adolescent at the time of World War II; she spent five years mostly living in a cellar during saturation bombings in Germany (3).

Garmezy was a clinical psychologist, and his interest in resilience began during the time he worked with patients with schizophrenia in Worcester State Hospital in Massachusetts. In an interview (4), Garmezy said during his work in the hospital, he noticed there were two distinct groups of schizophrenic patients. One group was called "process" patients, the other "reactive" patients. Garmezy saw that the "process" patients spent more than thirteen years in a mental hospital, whereas the "reactive" patients were more functional; most of them were competent, had jobs, and were married with families. If they had breakdowns, they usually recovered quickly and went back to their families and communities. Garmezy and his colleague looked into the family history and backgrounds of these patients and found there were clearly some areas of competence in the history of the "reactive" schizophrenic patients—meaning "reactive" patients had experienced and overcome traumatic incidents before. Garmezy began to think how he might study the background of children in order to understand the way they develop competency and skills, which in turn could enable them to adapt to and overcome obstacles, such as symptoms of a mental disorder. (Of course, let's not ignore that schizophrenia and other psychiatric diseases have a biological basis that isn't exactly possible to "overcome," but having these tools would lead them to cope with their symptoms in healthier, more productive ways.)

Garmezy and other scientists came together in the first conference on resilience in 1972 in Bled in Slovania (former Yugoslavia). There, Gormezy met Michael Rutter (we mentioned above that he was evacuated from England during World War II), which resulted in their collaboration at London's Institute of Psychiatry. They organized a year-long seminar on stress and coping in 1979 in Palo Alto, California (5). Emmy Werner, who had just finished writing a book on a longitudinal study of a large group of children on the Hawaiian island of Kauai, participated in this seminar. She presented the results of her study, which was later published in *Vulnerable but Invincible: A Study of Resilient Children* (6). The seminar was a groundbreaking beginning for the science of resilience.

For forty years, Garmezy undertook a study of thousands of children in schools in order to understand why one child would be more resilient than another. Project Competence began with interviewing school principals, asking them, "Can you identify stressed children who are making it here in your school?" Garmezy said,

> to be asked about children who were adaptive and good citizens in the school and making it even though they came out of very disturbed backgrounds, that was a new sort of inquiry. But that's the way we began. It was always interesting. The principal would turn to the social worker and say, "What about what's-his-name?" and they would tell the child's story. The story that I found most moving was the description of a boy, a young boy about 9 years old whose mother was an alcoholic. There was no father in the family, and the boy was basically on his own. He would bring a sandwich to school but there wasn't much food available to him and so he took two pieces of bread with nothing in between and he became known to us as the boy with the bread sandwich. The reason that he took a "bread sandwich" to school was so no one would feel pity for him and no one would know of the ineptitude of his mother. You know, if you get hit with a case like that and you begin to think, "Let's look beyond this case. Let's take a look at other children who are resilient in other kinds of stresses and circumstances" (4, p. 7).

Garmezy and other researchers began to think about and study resilience in two different fashions. On one hand, there were instances of acute stress

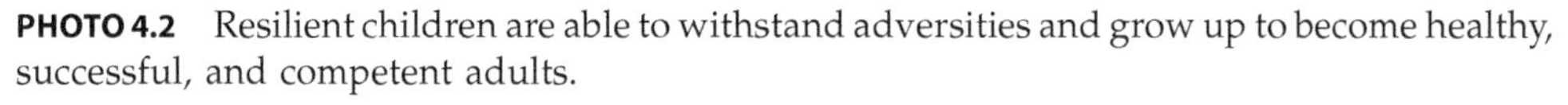

PHOTO 4.2 Resilient children are able to withstand adversities and grow up to become healthy, successful, and competent adults.

and trauma, for example, of the kind that Garmezy had witnessed himself during World War II, or similar cases of high emotional intensity. On the other hand, there were cases of cumulative stress, resulting from repeated and ongoing adversities that persisted over months or years, like children growing up in low-resource communities or those who had been subjected to maltreatment. This led to two different research focuses: Some began to conduct resilience research in the context of war, or an acute stress or trauma, while others like Garmezy turned their attentions to children growing up in the midst of adversity.

Like Garmezy, Emmy Werner also wanted to study children who faced adversity, specifically focusing a large group of children in Kaui, one of the islands of Hawaii. She began in 1955 by looking at 698 children, who were mostly descendants of sugar and pineapple plantation workers. Werner and her team, which included nurses and mental health professionals, monitored these children at ages one, two, ten, eighteen, thirty-two, and forty. About 30 percent of children were born and raised in poverty, had parents with mental illness, were raised by parents with less than eighth grade education, and/or faced other chronic family discord and issues. In other words, these children were at-risk. What Werner found was that about two-thirds of this at-risk group ended up with various problems, such as learning and mental health issues or delinquency, by the time they were eighteen. However, one out of every three of them grew into healthy, successful, and competent adults. By the time they were forty years old, all were employed, and none were receiving social services or had any problem with the law (2, 6, 7). Werner and her colleagues articulated the capability of these children to overcome odds and adversities as *resilience* and pointed to several common qualities or elements in these children's lives.

Resilience: A Balancing Act Between Risk and Protection

These early studies opened the door for looking at specific processes and factors that might contribute to the phenomenon of resilience. Rutter and Garmezy articulated several *protective factors*, or mechanisms which would counteract the effects of trauma or stressful conditions, ultimately resulting in resilience. (As you might imagine, *risk factors* are those qualities and/or conditions which enhance the effects of trauma or other stressors.) In other words, there are always both negative and positive events or conditions present in one's lifetime. Certain positive conditions, when present in a person's life, have the capability of not only withstanding but counteracting the effects of negative events and therefore result in resilience in that individual.

Scientists have faced some basic challenges regarding the overall framework for resilience. For example, at what point can an individual be considered resilient? Whether you are deemed resilient or not very much depends on the way your life's events unfold. If you don't face any significant and stressful event or an accumulation of stressors over time, it is hard to know if you are resilient. If you, on the other hand, do face one or more traumatic events, or live with an ongoing pile of stressors, at what point are you considered resilient? Do you need to show you do not succumb during, right after, or after a certain period of time has passed? What if you "regress," experiencing the negative aspects of some events but not others?

I think about resilience a lot. When I was in college, I took a months-long workshop called the Resilience Project with Dr. Alex Lickerman, author of *The Undefeated Mind: On the Science of Constructing an Indestructible Self.* At the time, I was in an abusive relationship masquerading as a best friendship, dealing with severe clinical depression, and in a recovery program for an eating disorder. I often wondered why and how I could get "better," whether my whole life would be defined by these issues.

Dr. Lickerman taught those of us in the workshop that formulating a *personal mission statement* would help guide us to find a path that would increase not just our happiness, but our resilience as well. The point was to find something we ourselves were already passionate about and use that to drive us forward in a meaningful way. Dr. Lickerman emphasized that a mission statement wasn't an immutable object; it would likely change over the course of our lives.

Though I've long since forgotten the specifics of the workshop, this idea of finding something meaningful to drive my life has been a question over which I've been preoccupied since I was a child. Although handing children a guide to creating a life worth living may not make a lot of sense, learning the things that drive us at a young age and how to cultivate that will, eventually, be useful. Even young children can understand that there are things in their lives they're passionate about, and holding onto that may help them be more resilient against the thing that most often stops them from indulging or pursuing it: themselves.

—NJ

PHOTO 4.3 Every resilient child has a positive relationship with a capable and caring adult.

Photo credit: Liliana Bilbao

Of course, resilience does not come about overnight. This might take an entire childhood, or it might happen much later in life. Ann Masten, a resilience scientist at University of Minnesota who worked with Garmezy, calls children who begin showing signs of resilience early on *early bloomers*, and those who demonstrate resilience later in life *late bloomers* (8).

Child resilience scientists have identified several important protective factors in the lives of children they study. Some of these factors have to do with the child, some with the environment, and others with the caregivers and adults around. For example, resilient children usually have *strong* and *affectionate relationships* with at least one capable person, like a supportive caregiver or parent, a teacher, or a mentor.

As a child, I didn't have these kinds of strong relationships with adults. Like many depressed children, I believed my struggles would burden others and that my parents were the last people I could turn to—not because they didn't love me, but because I needed to protect them from myself. I sometimes wonder if my childhood wouldn't have been different if I hadn't believed this so strongly, if I'd told my parents when I was struggling and sought to build that strong and affectionate relationship with them. As an adult, it certainly has contributed to the way I handle difficult or even traumatic situations now.

—NJ

Despite the conventional wisdom that resilient children have high IQ, the current research finds resilient children have some unique skills which are not necessarily related to their IQ. (We are both proponents of multiple intelligence over a singular intelligence score, but as multiple intelligences necessarily do *not* have a measurement, IQ is used as a quantitative variable.) Instead, they have a set of skills that are non-cognitive or indirectly related to cognition. For example, resilient children are resourceful, *socially competent* and *emotionally expressive*, *autonomous* and *easygoing*, have *self-control* and quite a good bit of *grit* (9–12).

As researchers continue to work to answer more questions about resilience, some things are becoming more obvious than others. For example, there is usually a *turning point* in the lives of resilient children and adults. This turning point usually happens after there is a break for the person with the disadvantaged past or a traumatic event, which opens the door to a different option for the future (11). Also, children and adults show different patterns of behavior in resilience. In fact, resilience can develop and change over time. For example, some resilient individuals can become overwhelmed and lose their ability to withstand difficulties, while others who seem fragile or show little competence in key areas can learn skills of resilience and overcome adversities later in their lives.

This is important for several reasons. First, it implies resilience can indeed be taught and learned. Second, teaching resilience skills makes most sense if they are taught early and continually reinforced throughout school and later in adulthood. Third, at-risk children who learn resilience skills early on are more likely to overcome advertises related to their upbringing as they grow up. So what are some key resilience skills we can teach children?

The answer may lie in *positive psychology*. Martin Seligman is the director of the Positive Psychology Center at the University of Pennsylvania and has devoted over thirty years to identifying, nurturing, and understanding human wellbeing and the ways in which positive factors can be used to withstand and overcome the negative. He and his cadre of several renowned colleagues and researchers have conducted a multitude of longitudinal controlled studies, examining positive factors contributing to wellbeing. Seligman and his team have identified common positive emotional, cognitive, and behavioral factors that can be cultivated to promote wellbeing. (We will describe these factors more fully in Chapter 6.) Interestingly, yet unsurprisingly, several of these factors happen to be those also identified by resilience scholars as promotive factors of resilience. These are: grit, key abilities of executive function (self-control and emotional regulation), optimism, and positive relationships.

Grit and Mastery

In 1964, Seligman was working on his doctoral studies in experimental psychology in the laboratory of Richard Soloman at the University of Pennsylvania. Soloman's graduate students experimented with Pavlovian conditioning in dogs to understand how fear motivated adaptive behaviors. They repeatedly gave dogs electric shocks paired with tone or light signals so the dogs could associate the electric shock with the signal and react accordingly. In other words, the dogs learned when the tone played or the light went off, there would be a shock that followed. The second part of the experiment involved putting the dogs in a chamber where only one side was electrified. Jumping over a low fence to the other side of the chamber would take them to the safe portion of the chamber. Seligman noticed the dogs who had been conditioned to the electrical shock did not try to escape. They just sat there passively and did not make any attempts to figure out how to avoid the shock. Seligman called this phenomenon *helplessness* (13).

Seligman was so intrigued by this phenomenon that he teamed up with two of his colleagues, Steven Maier and Bruce Overmier, and repeated the experiment with dogs who both had and had not been conditioned to the electric shock. He and his colleagues spent the next several years conducting experiments to understand the causes, preventions, and cure of helplessness. They discovered the dogs who had not been conditioned quickly jumped over the fence and went to the other side of the chamber to escape the shock. Seligman and his team explained what led to the dog's passivity was not the electric shock itself but having learned they could do nothing to escape it. In other words, the dogs who had experienced the shock had *learned* to be helpless. These dogs had learned they could not change their condition, so they didn't bother trying. Seligman explained *learned helplessness* happens when the past has taught you nothing you can do can change your situation (14).

So, how could these learned helpless dogs be cured? Through a number of sophisticated experiments, Seligman and his colleagues found helplessness could be reversed by teaching the dogs to keep trying. In one experiment, they physically picked up the dogs and moved their legs, until they gradually started to willfully escape the shock. This means, then, learning to master skills is key to preventing helplessness. Not only that, but as one of his students found out later, mastery and grit is a key resilience skill that prompts a person to overcome obstacles and be successful.

Fast forward to 2004. Angela Duckworth, one of Seligman's graduate students, set out to understand what makes a student become successful. Duckworth, who had spent some years teaching seventh graders in low-resource communities, had observed students who succeeded in learning were not those who had a high IQ. In fact, she had noticed some of her smartest students did not actually do well. She had a hunch non-cognitive abilities had more to do with achievement and success than intelligence or talent. As a doctoral student, Duckworth conducted several experiments with different groups of individuals, such as students at the military West Point Academy, high school kids in Chicago Public Schools, and newly hired teachers in low-resource communities. She found what predicted success in all of these groups—for example, for West Point cadets to endure their hard training and graduate or for novice teachers to stay in the field successfully—was not their intelligence, but rather, their *grit*, the ability to persevere despite setbacks and difficulties (15).

For Duckworth, grit is a means to an end, in that it is a necessary ingredient for achievement. Duckworth's formula for achievement is: *talent x effort = skill*; and *skill x effort = achievement*. Based on this formula, effort counts twice.

To achieve, one must gain mastery of skills, but to gain mastery, one must be gritty. The relationship between grit and resilience is obvious: Facing adversities; withstanding hardships; and not getting discouraged, weakened, or disappointed requires a higher purpose or a goal in mind and perseverance toward achieving it. Duckworth defines grit as a sustained passion and perseverance for especially long-term goals. Gritty children pursue their interests. They set long-term goals and purposefully work to achieve them; they do not leave a task unfinished. When they encounter a problem, they try different solutions instead of up with every small or large obstacle. They keep working until they learn and master the skill they are pursuing. Gritty kids are dogged in the pursuit of what interests them and are consistent in their efforts. They work hard and don't take learning for granted.

For gritty kids—and, in fact, any individual—to be successful, they should have a good degree of self-control to set long-term goals, resist impulses and immediate gratifications, and keep the course to achieve their small and large goals. They should also have a good working memory and mental flexibility in order to see problems from different angles. These happen to be the abilities related to executive functioning of the brain.

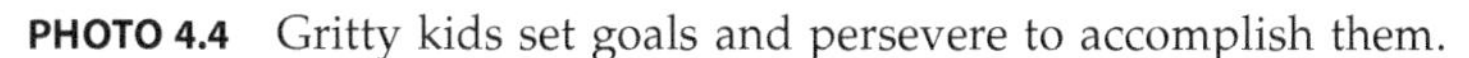

PHOTO 4.4 Gritty kids set goals and persevere to accomplish them.

Key Executive Functioning Skills for Resilience: Self-Control and Emotional Regulation

Executive functioning skills are brain processes that help us attend to and focus on something at hand, remember necessary information, and plan to perform a task. Executive functioning of the brain depends on three key functions and abilities: working memory, impulse- or self-control, and emotional regulation.

Working memory is part of our short-term memory and is necessary for learning and doing many simple and day-to-day tasks. It helps us hold new information in our head for a short time, and as we practice simple skills, it gets transferred into our long-term memory. The best example for seeing working memory in practice is when a teacher gives a child a simple direction to follow, and the child follows it without a problem.

Much as its name implies, *self-control* is our ability to set goals and priorities and, to achieve those goals, being able to resist impulses and temptations. (for clarity) Self-control involves delaying gratification and slowing down to think and plan. Although impulse control appears around age three or four, its foundations are built in infancy. Self-control is closely related to another foundational capability in young children and adults, *emotional regulation*. To regulate one's emotions, the person needs to understand the complex range of their own emotions and be able to express them appropriately at the right place and time. Emotional management doesn't mean the person keeps a stiff upper lip and does not express negative emotions such as anger. Instead, it's that the person knows where, when, and in what ways to express their anger. This also means the person is able to read and understand the emotions of other people and is able to manage people's emotions through appropriate communication. (Think back to Chapter 3, when we discussed the ways infants and their caretakers work to regulate each other's emotions. We're about to return to this idea.) These key emotional abilities happen to be the corner stones of *emotional intelligence*.

Jack Shonkoff, Professor of Child Health and Development and the director of the Center on the Developing Child at Harvard University, believes executive functioning capabilities are built through *serve and return* interactions between adults and children in the first three to five years of life (16). The concept of serve and return is similar to what Edward Tronick calls mutual regulation (described in Chapter 3), a process of emotional mirroring and responses that takes place during face-to-face interactions between the adult and infant. A stress-free serve and return (or mutual regulation process) primes the prefrontal cortex in the formation of attention, focus, and regulation of emotion and impulses, all of which help control our emotions and behavior when under pressure. So what if a child did not develop these key executive functioning skills early in life due to relational or neurobiological issues? The good news is executive function capabilities can be learned and reinforced in early childhood.

Control of impulses and emotions in preschoolers involves at least three important skills that must be explicitly taught and cultivated: *identifying the range of emotions*, both positive and negative; *understanding emotions in others*; and knowing when and how to *express emotions appropriately*. Without first building these skills, it is unrealistic for adults to expect three-year-olds to automatically know and follow directions that are all about self-control in preschool:

- "Keep your hands to yourself."
- "Sit 'crisscross apple sauce.'"
- "Wait until it is your turn."
- "Walk quietly in the hallway."
- "Clean up before you go to the snack table."
- "Ask your friend for a toy instead of snatching it out of her hand."

Furthermore, most preschool educators require children to slow down without first teaching them how to do so. Adele Diamond, a professor of neuroscience and developmental psychology at the University of British Columbia, researches activities that support and promote executive function in children in preschool and early primary grades. She believes two sets of activities are key to both directly and indirectly develop and support, as well as challenge and fine-tune, executive function skills in early childhood. First are those activities that directly help children to develop these skills, like literally slowing them down, making them wait, and having them reflect through play. In other words, these activities directly help children learn self-regulation and self-control. The second kind of activities are those that indirectly help children develop key skills of executive function. These are group music, dance, theatre, game-oriented and movement activities in which children share a goal with their peers and then plan, coordinate, and move to reach that goal (17, 18, 19, 20). We will discuss specific activities in Chapters 6 and 7. In the meantime, let's look at an equally important skill that resilient children need to learn: optimism.

Optimism: A Key Resilience Skill

In applying his findings from the learned helplessness experiments to humans, Seligman found when people experience learned helplessness, they begin to ask why, and then come up with an explanation that is both based on their past experiences as well as their own natural inclinations. Naturally, people who have experienced learned helplessness in the past tend to develop a negative way of explaining bad events, adversities, setbacks, or roadblocks.

I first learned about the phenomenon of "learned helplessness" in relation to the education of children with disabilities when I was completing a graduate program in early childhood special education in the early 1990s. The concept of learned helplessness in this context was used to describe a lack of motivation for learning in children with developmental and learning disorders. The explanation was that children with cognitive and learning impairments repeatedly experience failure in academic and adaptive areas in which their peers without a disability are usually successful. Their repeated failures result in developing learned helplessness. Therefore, when they are faced with a new task learning, they are not motivated to even try.

I don't buy this explanation any longer—the latest research on brain refutes this account of learned helplessness. As it turns out, helplessness is not learned at all! As far as children with developmental disorders are concerned (and all children, for that matter), we don't make tasks engaging, interesting, and relevant to their interests to ensure skill learning at the mastery level, nor, when their efforts end in a setback, do we encourage and teach children not to give up, try again, or try a different way until they get it.

—MB

Seligman believed helplessness is not only the reason for a lack of motivation, but also the cause of depression. For over thirty years, based on their experiments, Seligman and his colleagues had concluded that helplessness was learned. It turns out they were wrong. In his latest book, *The Hope Circuit*, published in 2018, Seligman writes, "It is gratifying to have lived long enough and to be in a vibrant enough science to find out you were wrong" (21, p. 376).

Steve Maier, who had worked with Seligman on the original helplessness studies of dogs, conducted a group of studies in rats and found the neurobiological underpinning of helplessness centered on a brain structure called the dorsal raphe nucleus (DRN). Maier and his team found inescapable shock activates serotonin-releasing neurons in the DRN (22, 23). Serotonin, a *neurotransmitter* or brain chemical, whose disregulation is implicated in a variety of psychiatric disorders, activates other brain regions implicated in the fight-or-flight and fear responses. In other words, when facing uncontrollable stressors (like the inescapable electric shock the dogs endured), the DRN releases serotonin onto the amygdala and other areas implicated in fear responses. By activating serotonin-releasing neurons in the DRN, even rats that received no shock displayed helplessness behaviors; by inhibiting or preventing these neurons from firing, helplessness was prevented. In this way, Maier and his team showed the activation of serotonin-releasing neurons in the DRN is necessary and sufficient for producing helplessness; that is, without the activation of serotonin neurons in the DRN, helplessness cannot occur.

These series of experiments eventually showed being helpless was a natural and unlearned default condition that occurred in response to prolonged and repeated failure. In instances where control exists, when the person thinks or learns they can control the situation by doing something, the DRN is inhibited/not activated, and so helplessness does not occur. In other words, *control* is learned; helplessness is not (22, 23, 24). Helplessness is a default condition our biology resorts to at times of repeated failure, but if we know or learn we can control the situation, our brain shuts off the mechanism that leads to "learned" helplessness (23). This is an amazing discovery of a solution for helplessness.

The solution, researchers believe, is in *optimism*. Seligman's studies have led him to conclude helplessness can, in fact, be prevented by not only teaching children skills to master various tasks, but also by helping them view and explain bad events in a more positive way (14, 25). In this way, they learn and understand they have some control over any situation in which they fail.

From 1990 to 2007, Seligman and his team, in a project called the Penn Resilience Program for Middle School Students, conducted over twenty controlled studies with several hundreds of fifth and sixth graders. They taught these children how to change their ways of explaining negative events from a pessimistic to an optimistic style. They wanted to see whether positive, hopeful, and purposeful ways of thinking and problem solving might prevent depression in these children in their adolescence (25, 26). Designing hundreds of games, videos, stories, and scenarios based on cognitive therapy principles, Seligman and his team of doctoral students taught the kids in their studies how to catch themselves when they were having negative thoughts about events, evaluate their own thinking objectively, and then come up with an alternative, more positive and optimistic way of thinking about situations. For example, they would have children complete a sentence like this:

> *You are walking to school and you notice a young group of kids whispering and pointing in your direction. You think to yourself* ______________ (25).

They worked with groups of children regularly for twelve weeks. They assessed children prior to the program, one week after its end, and every six months after that. They found that groups of children who participated in the intervention program were not only less depressed as compared to the control groups, but over time, these children continued to remain less depressed than their control peers. The major difference between the reasoning style of the intervention and control groups was that the intervention children explained events and setbacks in a hopeful, optimistic, and action-oriented way. Seligman believes that optimism is not only a key characteristic of wellbeing and resilience, but it is necessary to prevent depression in children later on (25).

It's not too late to learn optimism, even as an adult. When I was in my eating disorder treatment program, my therapists challenged my thinking in the same way Seligman challenged these children's. "What are other ways you can think about this?" they asked, whenever I told them of something that happened and my interpretation of the event. We would draw out diagrams of what it would mean if something were my fault versus circumstantial or situational. At first, I didn't really buy into their work; how could something *not* be my fault? I'd spent a lifetime internalizing the consequences of the world around me. But slowly, their way of thinking became my own. Over the years, the way I manage my depression has completely changed due to this optimistic explanatory style.

—NJ

Optimism is something children learn in early childhood from their parents, teachers, and other important adults around them. Children learn this through hearing how adults explain negative events and failures to themselves. Seligman calls a person's explanation of negative events as one's *explanatory style*. For example, if you have a pessimistic explanatory style, you are likely to tell yourself this event happened because of something that you directly or indirectly did, that there is not a whole lot you can do to change the situation, and that it is likely going to ruin everything for you. In other words, people with a pessimistic explanatory style think any negative event that happens to them is going to be forever (*it is permanent*), anything bad that happens is their fault (*it is internal*), and that it is going to permeate their entire life (*it is global*). Children who hear pessimistic explanation about negative events from adults are likely to develop similar types of reasoning and explanations when they are faced with an adverse event or a difficult task.

When a child or student faces a social emotional conflict, a setback, or is involved in a situation which the adult disapproves of, a teacher with a pessimistic explanatory style is also likely to use a negative type of reasoning to explain the situation and teach that child a lesson. The type of explanations below are examples of how many teachers talk to a child after a conflict:

- *Permanent*: "You never listen!"
- *Internal*: "Your friend is hurt. This is your fault."
- *Global*: "If you continue like this, you will never be successful."

If you're an optimistic person, you'll tend to explain a negative event or setback as something that is likely the result of collected circumstances. You'll be able to see not only your part in the occurrence of the setback, but also other factors that might have contributed to it. This will allow you to identify what part of this situation you have control over, which also means you believe whatever happened can be changed and prevented in the future. All of this will help you take action to change what you can and prevent a similar occurrence from happening again. In this type of reasoning, you have explained the setback to yourself as something that is *changeable, external*, and *specific*.

A teacher with this positive style of reasoning often looks at a conflict and setback as a challenging event to be solved and overcome. An optimist believes a setback is specific to one or more particular circumstance and does not necessarily affect all aspects of their life. A child who hears this kind of reasoning is apt to think positively, identify the problem, and take purposeful action without fear of future failure. A parent or teacher with an optimistic explanatory style is likely to respond to a conflictual situation in which a child is involved in in this way:

- *Changeable*: "You are not listening to me today."
- *External*: "It was a tough situation, and you lost control."
- *Specific*: "Next time, you will work harder, so this won't happen again."

As children observe teachers and parents' positive explanations of the situations, they learn to develop similar positive explanatory styles and gradually create a unique set of emotional, cognitive, and behavioral skills. When children learn to be optimistic, they not only think positively about a problem but also respond to it differently. Optimism directly influences how children face, cope, regulate themselves, and take steps to solve an issue or prevent failure. By the time they are in middle childhood, optimistic children are able to stop and think when a conflict or negative event happens, as opposed to jumping to a negative conclusion. When faced with a setback, they are able to identify their own mistakes and take responsibility for it. They also have learned to think hopefully for the next time around to do better, if this or a similar problem occurs again. Moreover, an important skill optimistic children develop is to understand what they realistically can and cannot do in a challenging situation and ask for help from a more abled person (26). This ability to reach out without embarrassment is something that can open the door to new opportunities and resources for children. Note here, then, that optimism does not mean the child is unrealistic—just hopeful instead of downtrodden.

Optimism, self-control, emotional regulation, and grit are some key resilience skills for children. Yet they are not sufficient to make a person resilient. A necessary component in resilience is having caring and positive relationships in life.

PHOTO 4.5 Optimistic children learn their explanatory style from adults and look at a failure or set back as something changeable and situational. They learn to take purposeful action to do better next time.

Positive Relationships: The Catalyst for Resilience

No one put it better than John Donne: "No man is an island." Relationships matter. It is not only that positive relationships are necessary for the formation of secure attachment in early childhood, but also for one's overall wellbeing and happiness in life. Having positive relationships is also directly and succinctly linked to the resilience of an individual. Emmy Werner was the first person who said a positive relationship was the most important protective factor in a child's resilience. Indeed, almost all stories of resilient individuals involve a positive relationship either in childhood or in adolescence.

As a human species, we might have evolved from hunter-gathering to designing sophisticated artificial intelligence, but we have not changed in our primary need to form meaningful relationships with other people and to have emotional support and companionship in our private and social lives. For us, the need to be connected and to belong is a deeply rooted psychological motivation (27). The need for attachment and belonging has an evolutionary basis that exists across all human cultures. Attachment secures our survival, motivates our reproduction, and gives us internal mechanisms to want to have friends and to be a part of a society or a group. Developmental and clinical psychologists have long argued our cognition, including our thought patterns and logic, are guided by a need to form interpersonal relationships (27–29). Our emotional responses, our feelings, our affect, and even our sense of happiness is closely linked to having close personal relationships (27).

Neuroscientists have presented evidence that without human interactions and relationships, our neurons will indeed wither and die (24). In fact, there are specific neurons in our brain that make up the neurological foundations of imitation, sympathy, empathy, and emulation. Research also shows in people who are lonely, there is considerable damage to the executive functions in the brain's prefrontal cortex and that lonely individuals seem to be less attentive and less flexible in their thinking and reasoning (19, 20).

Sometimes, I think about the way my grandmother looked at the world. She was a deeply lonely and unhappy woman who believed everyone hated her—and so she hated everyone right back. My mother and I could never convince her that no, people were not talking about her behind her back; no, people were not out to get her. I wonder, if I'd gotten a chance to look at her brain, would we have found her prefrontal cortex as damaged as the rest of her?

—NJ

As we explained in Chapter 3, early life relationship experiences and the related stress can affect how the brain circuitry related to our emotional processes is influenced. Just as distressed relationships decrease a child's health and development, a child's healthy attachment to adults not only keeps them safe and calm, but also increases their immune system health and resistance to stress (24). It should not be surprising to find healthy and positive relationships is, for children, the strongest factor of promoting their resilience. It is through these relationships that other skills of resilience are learned.

There are probably more than a hundred classic or contemporary stories or movies about a child on their way to destruction until a loving adult enters their life and redeems them forever. Dickens' *Oliver Twist* and *Great Expectations* are two of my favorite stories depicting just such relationships. Stories of child resilience prove to us that even if some children did not have an opportunity to form a healthy attachment with an adult early on, there are still opportunities for those types of relationships to be forged between them and other adults they meet later.

—MB

What this means for education is teachers have the power to become that secure and healthy attachment figure, one whom the child might have not had earlier on. Of course, connecting with a child who does not have positive relationships with others is a herculean task. These are usually the children who do not trust adults, whose perception of reality is affected by their early negative experiences, and whose learning is grossly influenced by their distorted early relationships with primary adults in their lives. Unfortunately, these are the same children teachers find hard to form relationships with. They are oppositional, defiant, mistrustful, and aggressive. And, not surprisingly, they usually do not show an interest or motivation in learning, particularly if a positive relationship has not been established between them and the teacher.

In early childhood education and special education, different metaphors have been used to convince teachers it is worth their efforts to establish positive relationships with all children, not just "the good ones." One is the metaphor of "making deposits" in a child's relationship piggy bank (22). With every effort to interact with a child in a positive way, to connect to the child, understand the child, and affirm the child's emotions and feelings,

PHOTO 4.6 Positive relationships forged between adults and children have buffering effects for children against risks and adversities.

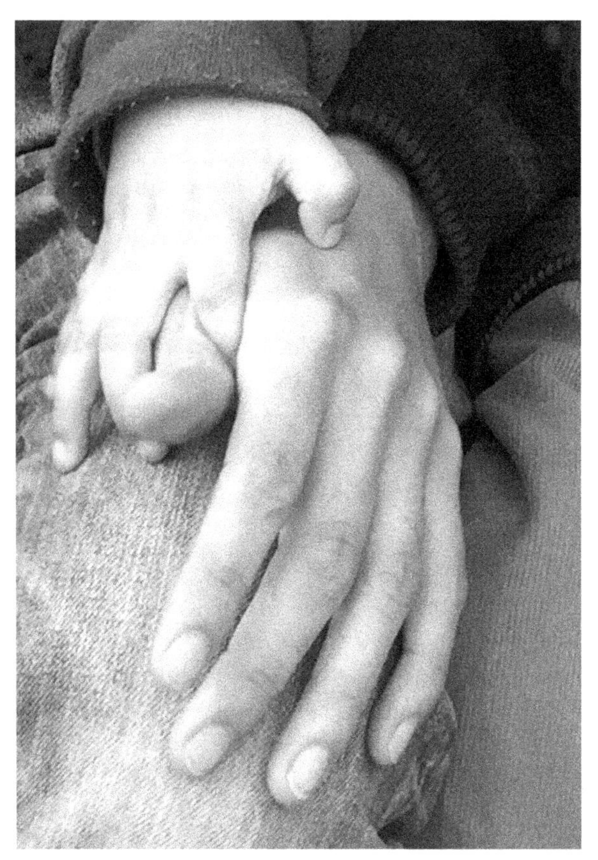

Photo credit: Liliana Bilbao

adults make emotional deposits in the child's piggy bank. With every negative interaction, there is a withdrawal from this bank. Too many withdrawals without enough deposits is like writing a bad check.

Final Thoughts

It is not necessary for every child or adult to be resilient. After all, the overwhelming majority of people live their lives from day to day without giving this concept a second thought. It is important, however, to help children who face adverse conditions in life to be resilient so they can withstand and overcome difficulties. This is particularly the case for children who deal with mental health issues. To help children cultivate skills of resilience, we need to make the effort and form positive attachment and relationship with them first, instead of expecting them to reach out.

References

1. Bayat, M. (2007). Evidence of resilience in families of children with autism. *Journal of Intellectual Disability Research, 51*(9), 702–714. http://doi.org/10.111/j.1365-2788.2007.00960.x
2. Werner, E. E. (2005). What can we learn about resilience from large-scale longitudinal studies? In S. Goldstein & R. Brooks (Eds.). *Handbook of resilience in children* (pp. 91–106). New York, NY: Springer.
3. Masten, A. S. (2014). Global perspectives on resilience in children and youth. *Child Development, 85*(1), 6–20. http://doi.org/10.111/cdev.12205
4. Rolf, J. E., & Glantz, M. D. (2002). Resilience. In M. D. Glantz and J. L. Johnson (Eds.), *Resilience in development: Positive life adaptation* (pp. 5–14). Boston, MA: Springer.
5. Masten, A. S., & Tellegen, A. (2012). Resilience in developmental psychopathology: Contributions of the project competence longitudinal study. *Development and Psychopathology, 24,* 345–361. http://doi.org/10.1017/S095457941200003X
6. Werner, E. E., & Smith, R. S. (1982). *Vulnerable but invincible: A longitudinal study of resilient children and youth.* New York, NY: McGraw Hill.
7. Werner, E. E., & Smith, R. S. (1992). *Overcoming the odds: High-risk children from birth to adulthood.* Ithaca, NY: Cornell University Press.
8. Masten, A. (2014). *Ordinary magic: Resilience in development.* New York, NY: The Guilford Press.
9. Masten, A. (2013). Afterword: What we can learn from military children and families. *The Future of Children, 23,* 199–212. Retrieved from https://pdfs.semanticscholar.org/8ef9/482fb284cfc84c5bf8419004d2e24dbdf29c.pdf
10. Unger, M. (2005). Introduction: Resilience across cultures and contexts. In M. Unger (ed.). *Handbook for working with children and youth: Pathways to resilience across cultures and contexts,* pp. xv–xxxix. Thousand Oaks, CA: Sage.
11. Rutter, M. (2013). Annual research review: Resilience-clinical implications. *The Journal of Child Psychology and Psychiatry, 48,* 17–30. http://doi.org/10.1111/j.1469-7610.2012.02615.x
12. Southwick, S. M., Bonanno, G. A., Masten, A. S., Panter-Brick, C., & Yehuda, R. (2014). Resilience definitions, theory, and challenges: Interdisciplinary perspectives. *European Journal of Psychotraumatology, 5*(1), 25338. http://doi.org/10.3402/ejpt.v5.25338
13. Seligman, M. (1991). *Helplessness: On depression, development, and death.* (2nd ed.). New York, NY: W.H. Freeman.
14. Seligman, M. (1990). *Learned optimism.* New York, NY: Knopf.

15. Duckworth, A. (2016). *Grit: The power of passion and perseverance*. New York, NY: Scribner.
16. National Scientific Council on Developing Child. (2015). *Supportive relationships and active skill-building strengthen the foundations of resilience: Working paper 13*. Retrieved from https://developingchild.harvard.edu/resources/supportive-relationships-and-active-skill-building-strengthen-the-foundations-of-resilience/
17. Blair, C., & Diamond, A. (2008). Biological processes in prevention and intervention: The promotion of self-regulation as a means of preventing school failure. *Development and Psychopathology, 20*, 899–911. http://doi.org/10.1017/S09545794080000436
18. Diamond, A., & Ling, D. S. (2016). Conclusions about interventions, programs, and approaches for improving executive functions that appear justified and those that, despite much hype, do not. *Developmental Cognitive Neuroscience, 18*, 34–48. https://doi.org/10.1016/j.dcn.2015.11.005
19. Von Hecker, U., & Meiser, T. (2005). Defocused attention in depressed mood: Evidence from source monitoring. *Emotion, 5*, 456–463. http://psycnet.apa.org/doi/10.1037/1528-3542.5.4.456
20. Diamond, A. (2014). Want to optimize executive functions and academic outcomes? Simple, just nourish the human spirit. In P. D Zelazo, & M. D. Sera (Eds.) *Minnesota symposia on child psychology. Developing cognitive control processes: Mechanisms, implications, and interventions* (Vol. 37, pp. 205–232). Indianapolis, IN: Wiley.
21. Seligman, M. E. P. (2018). *The hope circuit: A psychologist's journey from helplessness to optimism*. New York, NY: Public Affairs.
22. Joseph, G., & Strain, P. (2004). Building positive relationships with young children. *Young Exceptional Children, 7*(4), 21–28. https://doi.org/10.1177%2F109625060400700403
23. Maire, S. F., & Seligman, M. E. P. (2016). Learned helplessness at fifty: Insights from neuroscience. *Psychological Review, 123*(4), 349–367. http://dx.doi.org/10.1037/rev0000033
24. Cozoline, L. (2014). *The neuroscience of human relationships* (2nd ed.). New York, NY: Norton and Company, Inc.
25. Seligman, M. E. P. (2007). *The optimistic child: A proven program to safeguard children against depression and build lifelong resilience*. Boston, MA, & New York, NY: Houghton Mifflin Company.
26. Reivich, K. & Shatté, A. (2003). *The resilience factor: 7 keys to finding your inner strength and overcoming life's hurdles*. New York, NY: Three Rivers Press.

27. Baumeister, R. F., & Leary, M. R. (1995). *The need to belong: Desire for interpersonal attachments as a fundamental human motivation*. New York, NY: Routledge.
28. Karen, R. (1998). *Becoming attached: First relationships and how they shape our capacity to love*. New York, NY: Oxford University Press.
29. Stern, D. (1985). *Interpersonal world of the infant: A view from psychoanalysis & developmental psychology*. New York, NY: Basic Books.

5

Choosing What Works: Theories and Practices

PHOTO 5.1

Despite the popular definition, a theory is not just a hunch or an educated guess. A good theory is usually based on a hypothesis that is researched and backed by empirical evidence. In psychology, a theory provides a basis for understanding development of emotions, cognitive processes, and behaviors so a prediction can be made about people's future behaviors. There are a great number of old, modern, as well as emergent developmental and learning theories doing exactly that. To name a few, there are behavioral, maturational, social learning, cognitive learning, psychosocial, and systems theories, not to mention the theory of multiple intelligences and the emotional intelligence theory. There are also theories specifically used in counseling and therapy, like the humanistic theory, and there are others more commonly used in education, like the constructivist learning theory.

We are interested in more than one theory. We examine aspects of theories grounded in scientific findings, that can be applied both in therapy as well as in education. There is no single theory, nor an associated single method, that can do that, simply because there is not a single theory that can explain all the dimensions of biology, development, and learning in a holistic way. Therefore, we believe in borrowing practices from those theories grounded in science and which can be reliably applied in working with children. In this chapter, we briefly explain the theories and practices we borrow from to form a set of strategies to use with children as a way of promoting their mental and behavioral health.

On one side, we borrow from theories and practices grounded in emotional and relationship-based theories and practices. On the other, we borrow from behavioral and cognitive behavioral theories and therapies. Up to now, these theories have divided the fields of psychology as well as education. We believe they should not continue to do so. Indeed, we believe they can work together very well and in tandem to address all areas of developmental mental health and overall wellbeing in children.

A Theory Confusion

There is no doubt theories of development and learning have not only contributed to our knowledge about child development, learning, and behavior, but they have also resulted in the design of a multitude of models of practice in education, therapeutic treatment, and most of all, in our day-to-day parenting and interactions with children. But the sheer number of theories creates a lot of confusion about those couched in science versus pseudoscience, as well as what methods of practice are effective versus ineffective. Join in on one social media debate on education, parenting, or mental health to get a feel for this confusion, not to mention see the tension and sometimes the animosity and resentment that exists between the practitioners of one approach against the other. So which approaches can best promote child health and learning? We believe the answer is not in becoming a true believer in one particular theory and applying its practices rigidly, but rather, in taking what has proven to be effective from each theoretical tradition and use them in combination and based on the situational and developmental needs of each child.

One Side of Theories: Psychodynamic and Emotion-Centered Approaches

Freud is barely given a second thought in college-level introductory and advanced child development and psychology courses. Almost all of his ideas have been debunked, not to mention several—such as his ideas about sexuality and gender—of which are considered damaging and dangerous. By today's standards, he represents pseudoscience; his methodologies and conclusions are questionable and, to many, laughable. But even though he got a lot of things wrong, he did get some things quite right. In fact, some of his ideas are actually supported by research in neuroscience. So what are those?

Freud believed our experiences, thought processes, and behaviors are not only driven from our conscious rationalization, but from our unconscious memories. He took the idea of the unconscious mind from Pierre Janet, a psychologist/neurologist contemporary of his. Freud articulated that the unconscious mind is a place for past experiences, which we might not remember or might have repressed due to trauma or stressful emotional conditions. In this, he was correct!

There is ample evidence in neuroscience and psychology to support this assertion. Recall in Chapter 3, we covered how trauma causes the activation of the body's stress response through the HPA axis, and that long-term activation of the HPA axis causes a host of changes both in the body and in the brain. One clear example of this is in the hippocampus: Patients with PTSD—whose HPA axis is therefore overactivated—have reduced neural matter in the hippocampus, the area of the brain responsible for declarative memory (1). Declarative, or explicit, memory has long been thought to be an active and constructive process, such that new information—whether through an event or otherwise—is integrated into a mental framework of the world and is no longer available separately (2). This means recall of that information is never "true" but is instead through a lens of preexisting experiences and preconceptions. Furthermore, the neural pathways that underlie memory construction and consolidation include areas in the brain that focus on processing emotional input, such as the basolateral amygdala (3). (We'll discuss the amygdala in more detail below.) Thus, states of heightened arousal, such as fear, or other emotional states involved in stressful and traumatic situations are imprinted upon memories.

Interestingly, while anxiety disorders like PTSD are often associated with intrusive and triggering thoughts or recollections, many individuals who have dealt with trauma have the added complexity of not remembering much of their experience (2), thereby supporting Freud's theory. In fact, there are many documented accounts of traumatized individuals dissociating when triggered by something, such that others note they're "not all there" or "not themselves" (2, 4). In those states, they may reenact their actions during a traumatic event (if singular), but later have no recollection of it having happened.

The hippocampus is not the only area of the brain affected by trauma and certainly not the only center of memory. For our purposes, however, we want to focus on areas involved in emotional processing. Bessel van der Kolk, a psychiatrist specializing in trauma at Boston University, says the emotional brain is the heart of the central nervous system. It comprises the "reptilian brain" and the limbic system. The reptilian or "ancient animal" brain develops in the womb and works in conjunction with the hypothalamus (the H in the HPA axis) to address the body's basic needs and keep us in balance. The limbic system, or the mammalian brain, develops after birth and is central to emotional processing. Importantly, experience—both pleasurable and traumatic—literally shapes the limbic system, causing certain neural pathways to become more stable and others to degrade.

Key to the limbic system is the amygdala, a pair of almond-shaped regions nestled near the hippocampus. Since the 1990s, Joseph LeDoux, a prominent neuroscientist at New York University, has researched the amygdala in connection to emotions and memories. LeDoux explains the amygdala is an unconscious processor of experience—even before the hippocampus or our prefrontal cortex (PFC), which is responsible for conscious thought (5). All incoming stimuli to the brain first go through the thalamus, the brain's "switchboard," an area that integrates incoming information and sends it to the appropriate location. From there, this information goes to the area of the brain that needs to address it. Of course, two of those places are the amygdala and the PFC. LeDoux calls the pathway to the amygdala "the low road" and that to the PFC the "high road" (6). The low road is extremely fast, such that information reaches the amygdala several milliseconds before it reaches the PFC. In other words, our body has an emotional reaction to

PHOTO 5.2 The amygdala, the emotion center of the brain, plays a prominent role in our memory as well as our fast reactions to events.

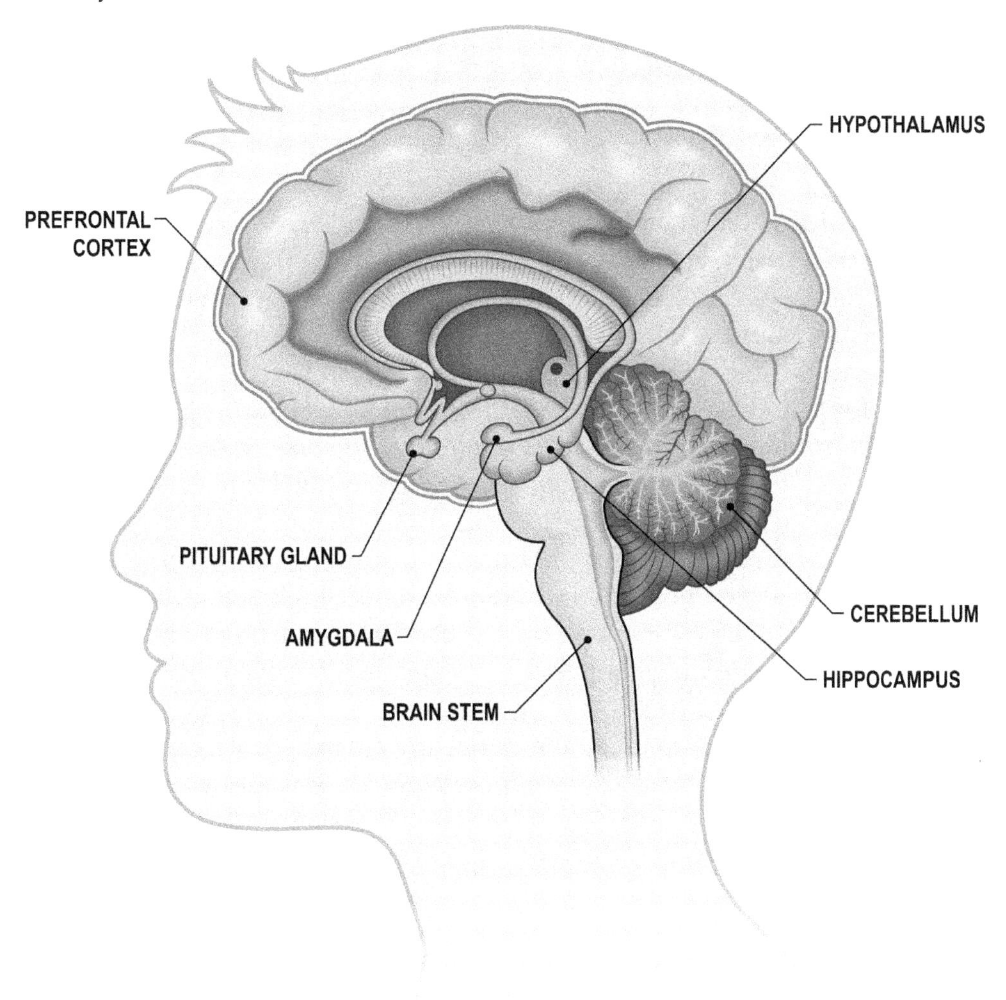

whatever is happening before we even have a conscious one. (To be clear, we're not discussing how we *feel* about something—that requires the PFC and consciousness! Rather, this conversation is in reference to our body's *unconscious reaction* to certain stimuli and the long-term effects.)

When we're faced with a stimulus, our emotional brain—and especially the amygdala—decides whether or not we're in danger. If we are, the amygdala, with input from the hippocampus, activates our HPA axis and corresponding fight-or-flight response. After a trauma, however, the brain may hyperactivate the amygdala and stress response—or shut down completely. Importantly, in both of these scenarios, the PFC shuts down, leaving the person incapable of language to describe what's happening or unable to use logic to explain the situation. Furthermore, the thalamus, the brain's switchboard, also shuts down. As a result, the brain cannot integrate further incoming information, even that which might show the situation is not dangerous. Without the integration of information across these various brain regions, memories of trauma are therefore often fragmented and sensory-based rather than narrative.

Some neuroscientists argue children are unable to form coherent narratives of traumatic events due to the physical structure of their brain; not yet fully developed, a child will not process a traumatic event the same way an adult would (2). Indeed, anecdotal and scientific evidence seem to suggest adults who experience trauma as children have worse overall memory for both personal and global (e.g. something that is happening in a larger cultural space, like a war) events (2). In one study, participants who had been abused as children were asked about their memories and lack thereof. Out of ninety participants, thirty-eight reported complete amnesia that persisted into adulthood (4). Furthermore, chronic trauma has a more pervasive impact on individuals than a single traumatic incident (4, 7). However, to be clear, being unable to form a coherent narrative does not mean children do not experience the same debilitating effects of trauma as adults.

In general, trauma changes the nervous system. "Being traumatized," van der Kolk writes, "means continuing to organize your life as if the trauma were still going on—unchanged and immutable—as every new encounter or event is contaminated by the past." In children, it's especially important to remember their emotional experiences are encoded on a neuronal level, regardless of their conscious realization of it or ability to articulate what is happening to them.

As we described in Chapter 3, early and modern attachment theories are founded on this same premise, that experiences—and hence memories—are shaped in the early years, that interactions and experiences between infants and caregivers not only matter but can determine future functioning. Erikson's psychosocial stage theory (8) and its modern counterparts, like Greenspan's theory of emotional development (9), also fall back on these fundamental ideas. Erikson's idea had a lot in common with attachment theory; he believed the early formation of trust between an adult and child is a pathway toward future development of cognitive processes, successful social emotional functioning and wellbeing, identity development, and self-fulfillment in life. Greenspan's stage theory, which became popular in the 1990s, is similar. Greenspan integrated the relatively more recent knowledge from perception, sensory, and emotional processing brain research into his idea and explained that early secure relationships are the foundation of not only healthy emotional development, but strong language and cognitive development.

Important lessons to learn from all psychodynamic, relationship-based, and emotion-centered theories is that emotional development and processes in a child has a prominent role in not just overall mental health development, but also in cognitive, language, and social development. Since the 1990s, research continues to verify that emotions underlie and are often intermingled with cognitive processes, that emotions drive behaviors, and that we cannot address cognition and learning before or without addressing child's emotional state. Though this seems intuitive, it is a relatively new understanding in early education, a field which is dominated by a focus on cognitive and early academic learning to guarantee future success.

A more modern theory of *emotional intelligence*, although not psychodynamic in nature, does build on the primacy of emotional development as the driver of future success in not only relationships, but in decision making, teamwork, and overall success in life.

Theory of Emotional Intelligence

In 1995, the book *Emotional Intelligence* by New York Times science reporter Daniel Goleman (10) revolutionized the way people defined success in life and the way businesses not only trained their leadership force but also evaluated their workers' job performance. Goleman persuasively argued it is not IQ, or the level of intelligence as we commonly understand it, but rather the emotional intelligence of a person that predicts a person's success in all areas of life—including academic, career, relationship, and personal achievements.

Five years earlier, Peter Salovey and John Mayer had synthesized a great amount of scientific research findings in different areas of psychology and neuroscience and had conceptualized a theory of emotional intelligence (11). However, it wasn't until Goleman's book that this concept became popular and found grounds, particularly in education. The influence of this theory and the wave of related research that followed has led to some states to integrate standards of Social-Emotional Learning (SEL) into their regular academic learning standards. Schools are beginning to catch on to the importance of social-emotional development. By now, a good number of curricula (e.g., Ruler Approach, MinUp, KidsMatter) have been designed according to this theory and are being used in early childhood, elementary, and high school programs. Some violence prevention programs (like Fast Track) also use emotional intelligence concepts to teach youth important skills like self-control, helpful responses to stress, empathy, self-motivation, and goal accomplishment.

So what are key elements of the theory of emotional intelligence? In their theory, Salovey and Mayer explicitly focused on skills for processing of emotions, as well as understanding emotion-related information (12, 13). They articulated a set of four essential skills for the development of emotional intelligence:

1. Perceiving, identifying, and expressing emotions accurately;
2. Using emotions to facilitate cognitive processing;
3. Understanding emotions; and
4. Managing emotions.

First, the ability to *accurately identify, perceive, and express emotions* is an important foundational ability that begins and should be taught in early childhood. It includes identifying and labeling emotions not only in faces, but in all other media like images, voices, and music. Though this seems like an ability anyone should inherently have, not all children nor adults have these skills or have them to the same extent. In fact, this ability is often missing or underdeveloped in certain disorders, like Autism Spectrum Disorder (ASD) and in children who have experienced trauma.

The correct recognition of emotions is the most basic level in emotional intelligence, as it drives our thinking and behavior. One of the issues we talked about in Chapter 3 was that maltreated children struggle to correctly read and identify emotions in the faces of others. In fact, some of these children tend to see people as being angry and hostile, even when anger isn't actually present. Seth Pollak at the University of Wisconsin-Madison has studied emotional processes in children, including those who have undergone trauma. In one of his studies, he had children play a computer game where they were shown pictures of people expressing different kinds of emotions. He measured their brain activities as he asked them to identify the emotions they saw. Pollak found children who were abused not only identified anger more quickly as compared with other emotions but also had much more brain activity—that is, they were more focused and hypervigilant when processing anger in the faces of others (14). This is just one aspect of emotional intelligence traumatized children have difficulty accessing.

The second set of abilities of an emotionally intelligent person is the ability to *harness emotional information to facilitate thinking and problem solving*. In other words, it is the ability to smartly use emotions. We all experience different feelings and moods in different times; the key is to use these to our advantage. For example, research finds positive emotions like happy feelings and excitement are conducive to motivation and creative problem solving, while other emotions like sadness or depression are likely to lead to a lack of energy and motivation (we will discuss this in more details in the next chapter). One way to use our emotions smartly, and to teach young children to similarly do so, is to promote our own positive emotions not only for its own benefits (we briefly discussed this in Chapter 4, but we'll come back to this later), but as a way to motivate us to persevere and accomplish our goals. This requires us to be actively attuned to our own emotional state and use it wisely.

The third set of skills in emotional intelligence is the ability to *understand emotions in ourselves and in others*. This ability is more involved than simply recognizing and labeling emotional states. A person with this ability can also see the subtle differences, similarities, and relationships between emotions, like the relationship between joy and happiness and between frustration and anger. The same person can see the signs of and understand how one emotional experience and state can transition into another and lead to a specific action. For example, frustration can easily turn into anger, which in turn can become aggression. Understanding our emotions enables us to recognize signs of emotional transitions in both ourselves and others and adjust our thinking and actions accordingly. This is especially important when working with children, especially children with disabilities, whose ability to regulate their emotions may be impaired or underdeveloped. (We will integrate this idea into our discussions in Chapters 7 and 8.)

When the term *emotional regulation* or *emotional self-regulation* is bandied about, many don't realize the complexity involved. The final set of skills involved in emotional intelligence uses this process; it is the ability to *manage emotions* in ourselves and others. It is one thing to understand emotions and adjust our own thinking and behaviors accordingly. It is quite another to manage the emotions and behaviors of others. In general, managing emotions involves displaying an emotion appropriate in a given situation and then using a verbal or behavioral action which is derived from that emotion to influence another person's emotions and behaviors. It sounds complicated, and it is! For example, we often teach children to control their negative emotions like anger or anxiety without showing them when and how they can actually use these negative emotions to galvanize them into appropriate actions. In fact, there are many situations where anger and outrage are called for. For example, when another child is being bullied, it is quite appropriate and effective to display anger and stand up to the bully to address that situation. Other unpleasant or negative emotions can also be

PHOTO 5.3 Children can learn to become emotionally intelligent by learning to identify emotions in themselves and others correctly, using their emotions in a logical way, understanding their own and others' emotions, and managing their emotions appropriately based on the situation.

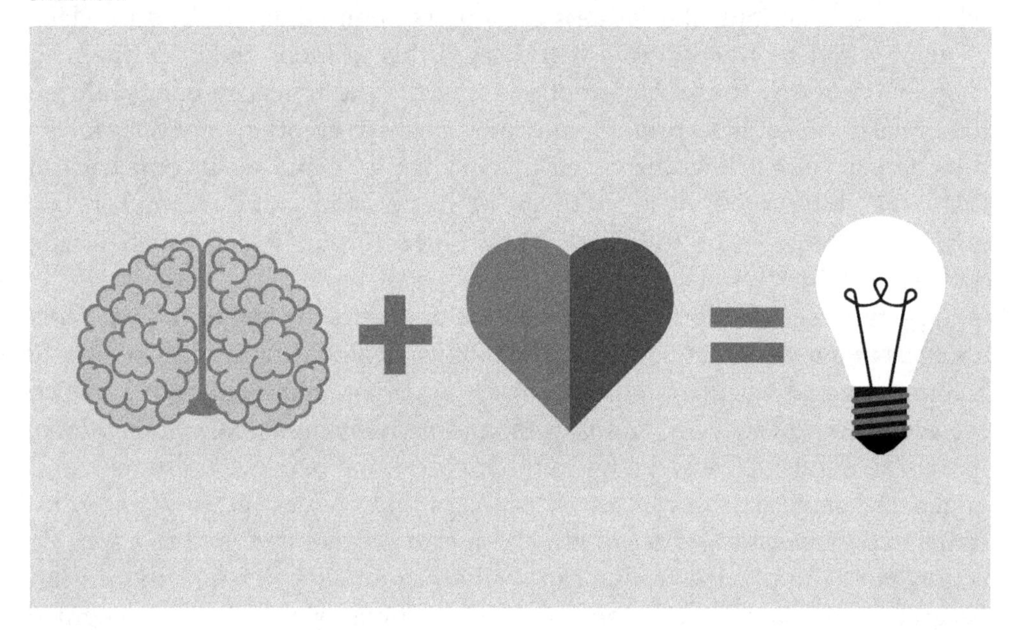

appropriate in a given situation; for instance, a logical amount of anxiety is similarly called for when an important event is coming up, prompting us into necessary action to be well prepared for the event.

The scientific evidence on the benefits of emotional intelligence is growing. There is now a body of research emerging which suggests emotional intelligence is linked to a range of positive physical and mental health outcomes (15–17). Because emotionally intelligent people have skills in self-expression, understanding, and managing emotions, they are adept at coping with everyday life stressors and making all-around healthy and smart decisions for themselves and others. There is also a growing number of studies linking emotional intelligence to resilience, as well as to life satisfaction (18–20).

So far, from what we discussed about the theories that focus on emotions, we can take away these points of understanding that are well supported by science:

- What happens early in life—for example, via relationships or events—affects not only our unconscious mind, but our emotional development.
- Emotions influence both our thinking processes and our behaviors.

- Supporting healthy emotional development in childhood builds the foundations for healthy developmental in other areas of development; all are also necessary for future academic success.
- Emotionally intelligent people are likely to be resilient, healthy, and satisfied with life.

Children Talking, Adults Listening: An Application of the Emotion-Centered Theories

The practice of psychotherapy originates from the Freudian psychoanalysis and later psychodynamic theories. Although psychiatrists and psychologists are trained psychotherapists, thanks to the gamut of psychotropic drugs, psychotherapy is not as commonly sought as medication alone. Nevertheless, psychotherapy or *talk therapy* is very much alive in psychology and counseling today. The practice goes back to the long-cherished act of seeking advice from an older, wiser person to whom one is attached and exists in virtually every culture around the world (21).

Psychologists, psychiatrists, school counselors, and social workers use talk therapy with older children and adolescents who can verbally express their thoughts and emotions. The idea is to create and provide a safe space in which children are encouraged to talk about their feelings, thoughts, and events that have happened to them, or freely discuss problems they face in their environments and with others. Although talk therapy is a problem-focused and time-limited solution, some neuroscientific evidence supports its effectiveness.

Brain research shows there are distinct emotional and cognitive benefits for children to have a trusting and supportive adult with whom they can regularly speak and approach. Here are some benefits when time is regularly spent engaging children in *conversations* in which children talk about issues they choose and adults do the listening (21):

- Children learn to develop a narrative about themselves and their experiences.
- Speaking about emotions, thoughts, events, and experiences activates the anterior cingulate cortex (ACC) and medial prefrontal cortex (mPFC), the regions of the brain essential for self-awareness. Listening to children encourages them to process and reflect on their own thoughts and emotions. This practice leads to self-reflection over time and that, in turn, helps them develop self-awareness.
- When children develop a narrative of self, they connect words to their feelings and can gradually create a story that has a beginning and an

end. As *listeners*, we can support them to edit and modify their own stories over time and in the ways they choose. This kind of storytelling can gradually help them associate their memories to their daily experiences and their reactions to events. Developing a narrative is also conducive to perspective about themselves and others. This will further encourage them to connect with others and to become more compassionate not only toward others, but toward themselves.

- Children who grow up with negative relationships with adults, or worse, experience daily stressors and unsafe environments, are usually anxious and fearful. (Anxiety is also a feature of certain conditions like ASD and ADHD.) Anxiety and fear in children inhibit executive functioning, emotional regulation, and problem solving. Furthermore, anxiety and fear prevent children from exploring new environments or materials and being open to trying new ideas and things. Allowing children to talk in a safe relationship will help them examine their anxieties or reflect on experiences that scare them. Over time, it can help them make sense of their anxieties and be open to learning and trying new strategies to address their fears.
- Early adult-child experiences that are negative, too restrictive, inhibitory, neglectful, and hence traumatic create lasting feelings of shame and helplessness in the child. Children who are encouraged to express their feelings and thoughts and are listened to in a safe and nonjudgmental environment learn to view themselves differently and develop skills to examine their maladaptive emotions and beliefs.
- In this process of speaking and listening, the adult listeners can help children co-create a new alternative and positive narrative about themselves, others in their environment, and about their relationships. In the new narrative, adults can create hypothetical situations in which children can face their negative emotions and anxieties. For example, adults can gently guide children to create behavioral solutions that are adaptive as opposed to their previous maladaptive ones. Children who learn to recreate a new positive and healthy narrative about themselves are able to use it as a blueprint to guide themselves in understanding and managing their emotions.
- Creation of a positive narrative with a help of an adult, when combined with using positive visual illustrations and imagery, is an amazing tool that promotes executive functioning capabilities in children. For example, in one study, scientists found when individuals look at positive images, specific brain regions involved in awareness, integration of sensory information, and action planning are activated (22).

PHOTO 5.4 When children talk and adults listen, children begin to reflect on their own emotions and thoughts, and gradually develop cognitive and emotionally intelligent skills to solve problems they face.

- Positive self-narratives in children open the pathways into productive imagination, optimistic thinking, and realistic self-reflection and self-awareness. This is where children begin to make more realistic yet positive alternative meanings about themselves, their environments, others in their lives, and the events that occur. In turn, this will give children a chance to develop the skills to evaluate a situation logically and try different solutions when faced with a problem.

Therapeutic Play

Play is the developmentally appropriate version of talk therapy for children who are younger and for those who are not verbal (either due to age or a neurodevelopmental disorder or other condition). As a therapy method, play has an interesting history which also originates from Freudian psychoanalysis.

Anna Freud and Melanie Klein were among the first people who used play in a therapeutic context in the 1940s. Anna Freud established the Hampstead Nurseries in London during World War II to offer a safe environment to infants and young children who were devastated by the war. She and her nursery staff observed and studied these children on a daily basis and used play as a way to help them develop secure attachments with adults and overcome the effects of trauma. Melanie Klein similarly used play with specific toys and art materials as psychotherapy with children. Since then, *play therapy* has progressed into several theoretical and methodological practices with a large following of mental health professionals around the world.

Despite what some proponents of play-centered early childhood education may claim, not every form of play is therapeutic nor would naturally result in emotional, mental, and behavioral health benefits for children. If this were the case, all children who attend play-centered early childhood programs, or those who engage in explorative or interactive play on a daily basis, would as a result be emotionally and behaviorally healthy. This also means practically most, if not all, children in developed countries who regularly attend preschool programs or play with peers and adults every day should, through play alone, overcome any mental health or developmental issues that they have. These are not sound assumptions.

Of course, regular play should be the staple of every early childhood program, and indeed, play should be the right of every child. But the kind of play that has emotional benefits for children and promotes their mental health has specific conditions that other types of play typically do not have. Play in a therapeutic context requires an adult to be present, but not to teach

PHOTO 5.5 Play therapy is the developmentally appropriate version of talk therapy for young children.

or correct; adults are there to be non-judgmental, encourage the child to build a play narrative, and validate the child's expressions throughout the play session. This type of play is used to encourage emotional expression and to help the child build a narrative about themselves, events they have experienced, and others in their environments. In fact, the techniques that are used in therapeutic play are equivalent of those in talk therapy, and so it has the same benefits for children as talk therapy has for older children and adults.

We've spent this chapter so far discussing the techniques involved in emotion-centric theories, theories that, at their core, center the emotions of an individual, whether in relationships or otherwise. However, other theories, have been just as if not more influential throughout the last century, especially in education. We'll spend the rest of the chapter discussing those and the possible middle ground between these two major types of theories.

The Other Side of Theories: Behaviorism

Behavioral theories are at the polar opposite of psychodynamic and emotional-centered and relationship-based theories. They dominated the field of psychology until the last quarter of the twentieth century, and their strong influence on the US education system and more particularly on our special education system continues solidly to this day.

Behavioral theories are not about emotions not the conscious or subconscious mind. Rather, they are about behaviors—which can be directly observed and measured. One of the best-known behaviorists is B. F. Skinner, the father of operant conditioning. He discouraged us from contemplating the human mind, since we couldn't see or measure anything inside our brain. Skinner believed that the mind was a "black box," sealed and inaccessible, so whatever was going on inside was, ultimately, irrelevant. In order to know anything about the mind, he argued, we must study and understand observable behaviors.

Many people understand operant behaviorism to be about the relationships between stimuli and responses. Skinner explained behaviors are the responses to what happens in the environment (the stimulus). Also, what takes place as a result of a behavior, or the behaviors' *consequences*, can be either positive or negative to us. Positive consequences determine whether we will learn to repeat the same behavior again (reinforcement), while negative or punishing consequences teach us to refrain from that action next time (extinction). (There is also negative reinforcement, in which a negative stimulus or outcome is removed in order to promote a desired behavior. We won't be discussing negative reinforcement in detail, but it is worth mentioning.) In other words, what increases a behavior is a reward, and what decreases it is a punishment. According to Skinner's theory, this informational chain of stimulus, behavior, rewarding or punishing consequences, and response gets stored in the black box of our minds, and so will further influence and shape our behaviors for the future.

Although simplistic, this is the basic premise of behaviorism and its modern iteration of Applied Behavior Analysis (ABA). ABA has a strong following in the treatment and education of children with neurodevelopmental disorders. Today, it is considered the most effective treatment for Autism Spectrum Disorder.

In special education, the basic operant learning strategies continue to be used as a way of teaching children with learning and developmental disorders, as well as addressing their challenging behaviors. Some examples are using tokens, points, or sticker systems as rewards, or using timeouts and restraints as punishment. Unfortunately, there are aspects of ABA that can be downright harmful; while we will only briefly mention its limitations in this chapter, we will expand on how ABA can be improved—thereby reducing the stress autistic children especially undergo when in ABA treatment—in Chapter 8.

Ivar Lovaas, the renowned UCLA clinical psychologist and researcher, brought ABA to the public's attention in 1987 with publication of his famous longitudinal study. In the 1960s and 1970s, Lovaas had seen some success using behavioral methods with children with communication disorders, intellectual disability, and ASD (whom at the time were diagnosed with *classic autism*). In the initial version of his model, he used behavioral principles to reduce self-stimulatory and aggressive and self-injurious behaviors. He used *positive reinforcements* (rewards), like toys and praise, to teach targeted skills, and *aversives* (punishment), like electric shock, spanking, or shouting to stop inappropriate behaviors. In later years, after a public outcry against punishment, he did away with aversives and only used positive reinforcers. This is the version of applied behaviorism we know as ABA. The ABA model today consists of a therapist teaching a child a simple skill in a discrete trial format. In each session, the therapist gives the child a direction (stimulus), waits for the child to answer (behavior response), and, following the child's response, the therapist either ignores and corrects (when the child's response is incorrect) or gives a positive reinforcement (when the child is correct). This trial lesson format can go on for hours in repeated sessions, until the child responds correctly to every presented discrete lesson. In that case, the learning of a specific skill has taken place, what behaviorists call *shaping*.

In the 1970s and 1980s, this approach was called *the Lovaas Method*, which was specifically designed for children with autism. Lovaas designed all discrete small lessons to address different areas of development, starting from the simplest of skills like eye contact and vocalization, to more complex skills in language, cognitive, adaptive, and social skills. Meticulous learning assessments and related data taking of the child's responses was and continues to be one of the hallmarks of this method. In a longitudinal experimental study, Lovaas and his graduate students used this model with an experimental group of nineteen children who had been diagnosed with autism. In 1987, Lovaas published the results of this study, showing that nine of the nineteen children in his experimental group had gained an average of thirty IQ points—putting them at the "normal intellectual and educational functioning" level—after two years of therapy, using his method for about forty hours per week with each child (23). In fact, these nine children had shown such a great degree of improvement that they no longer met the criteria for a diagnosis of autism, nor were they distinguishable from typically developing kids. After two years of Lovaas' intensive intervention, these nine children were enrolled in mainstream schools, and their parents did not divulge their child's previous diagnosis to unsuspecting school personnel.

When I entered the field as a parent of a child with severe autism and also as a graduate student, I was a *true believer* in behavioral theories and methods. I studied the Lovaas Method and used it with my son, first individually and later hiring a team of professionals whom I supervised. I saw great improvements, though not a thirty point increase in IQ! I attended many conferences to catch up with every new development. One of conferences in which I participated was in the late 1990s in a suburb of Chicago, in which Lovaas was the keynote speaker. Lovaas was quite an engaging and entertaining speaker. I took notes of everything he said. One of his memorable statements that day was a new version of Skinner's famous quote, "Give me a child and I'll shape him into anything." Lovaas said instead, "Give me any child and I promise to improve his IQ by at least twenty points after one year." It had been more than fifteen years after he had published the first result of his longitudinal study. The nine autistic children in his intervention group who had become undistinguishable from typical kids were now in their twenties. In that conference, he presented their progress to date. The result, he said, were mixed. Some of them continued to do very well, but others did not. In fact, some had lost their gains. Lovaas said that one child in particular had regressed a great deal a few years later. He explained this happened after the child's parents went through a divorce. Lovaas also said that all children who had undergone his treatment program continued to have certain social issues and "oddities."

For years afterward, I reflected on what Lovaas said that day about the kids who had regressed and those who continued to have social issues. Although ABA is often associated with claims of "recovery" from autism, to date, there is no actual proof that this is the case. In 2014, two separate studies released reports that showed there is in fact a very small group of children from those diagnosed with ASD in their early years who go on to "overcome" or "recover" from autism (24, 25). In one study, the researchers looked at a group of young individuals who had been diagnosed with autism in their childhood. Researchers examined their subject's autism history, diagnosis and medical records, types and length of interventions they received, and other family and social factors (23). In the other study, the researchers followed a group of autistic two-year-old children into adulthood (24). In both studies, there were a small number of children who were no longer considered autistic as young adults. Both studies searched to understand what might have contributed to the fact that some of these children were no longer diagnosable with autism, when other individuals in the study continued to meet the criteria for the disorder. They found no conclusive results as to the cause, but they did find some common facts:

- About 9 to 10 percent of children who are diagnosed with autism in childhood no longer meet the criteria for the disorder at some point later on.
- It is not clear what factors make the disorder "disappear." It is also not recognizable in childhood whom might "recover" from autism later.
- Children who, at the time of their diagnosis, have a nonverbal IQ of at least seventy are more likely to "overcome" their autism than those with a lower IQ. Those who recover are also more likely to have started intervention at an earlier age and at a more intense level (24).
- Not all children who "recover" from autism receive intense ABA or other forms of behavior therapy, nor do all children who receive ABA "overcome" autism. However, one of the studies showed children who "recovered" from autism were twice as likely to have received ABA or other forms of behavior therapy (25).

I am no longer a true believer of ABA. I find a major weakness of ABA to be its disregard for the emotional development of the child. ABA can only go so far. Without being paired with some positive relational approach to address their emotional and mental health needs, ABA's effects are short lived, and in some instances, where punishment is used, it is quite counter-productive to a child's emotional health.

—MB

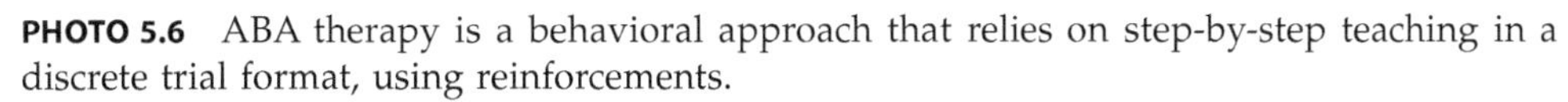

PHOTO 5.6 ABA therapy is a behavioral approach that relies on step-by-step teaching in a discrete trial format, using reinforcements.

There is no doubt behavioral theories have done a great service to psychology and to education, in that they established a scientific methodology for observing and studying human behavior. They also introduced using animal models of experimentation to understand human behavior, which now plays a prominent role in biomedical, neuroscience, genetic, and epigenetic research. More specifically, behavioral theories have influenced the field of education and special education by impressing upon teachers the importance of observational assessment methods and careful data-based intervention and methodologies. Today, in special education, creating a behavioral intervention plan that only uses positive reinforcements (also known as *Positive Behavior Support*; we will briefly discuss some of its principle elements in Chapter 8) is recommended for every child with a challenging behavior.

The success of behavioral therapy methods can be explained by evidence in neuroscience. We described earlier (in Chapter 3) that research shows what we learn behaviorally can change the wiring of our brain and be passed through to our children via epigenetic mechanisms. Recall that childhood maltreatment causes an increase in the body's stress response and can cause lifelong physical and emotional damage. Behavioral therapy methods are one way to counter such effects.

Despite these important contributions, behaviorism falls completely short in explaining and addressing our emotions and emotional processes. Human behavior is too complicated to be explained by Skinner's ideology. Behavior is influenced by a group of interconnected, complex factors that have as much to do with genetic and epigenetics mechanisms as with learning from the manipulation of the environment to reshape it.

The challenge many schools and classroom teachers face is that although behavioral approaches are effective in curtailing challenging behaviors in the short run, they are completely inadequate and ineffective in addressing the underlying emotional causes of the behavior in a child in the long run. Furthermore, as we discussed previously (Chapter 2), some behavioral strategies like timeouts and restraints verge on the point of being discriminatory, abusive, and doing more damage than any good. Indeed, adults on the autism spectrum who underwent ABA often report their experiences were stressful at best and abusive at worse—leading us to believe there must be a better way to address challenging behaviors.

The Middle Ground: Cognitive Behavioral Theories and Practices

In the 1960s, several theoretical developments began to change psychology and existing treatment applications, which were, up to that point, either psychotherapy or behavioral therapy. Emerging theories that focused on cognition and learning amounted to what is known as a *cognitive theory* "revolution" in psychology.

Albert Bandura's research in social cognitive processes introduced the influence of social learning and *modeling*. He expressed the importance of learning from other people's behaviors in the environment. The ideas of Jean Piaget and Lev Vygotsky started to dominate the fields of developmental psychology and early childhood education. Their theories led to the creation of *constructivism*, commonly known as hands-on learning in education, that focuses on play, exploration, experiential learning, and facilitating scaffolding and support from peers and adults. In later years, cognitive theorists used studies in neuroscience, perception, memory, language, and computer science to explain memory and neurological information processing mechanisms involved in learning.

The application of cognitive theories in addressing mental and behavioral health issues is known as *cognitive therapy* (CT). This practice is attributed to Aaron Beck with contributions from Robert Ellis. Beck and Ellis were two psychotherapists who, in the 1960s, studied and introduced a new therapeutic process different from both traditional psychoanalysis and behavior therapy.

Cognitive therapy relies on the premise that the way a person perceives and thinks of an event is connected to the way that person feels and therefore reacts to the event. In other words, it is not the event itself, but the meaning we make out of the event, that could upset us, and hence prompt us to act in a certain way. Cognitive therapy focuses on helping the person change their thinking by first noticing their automatic negative thoughts, then by looking at evidence for and against their thoughts. By doing so, the person reconstructs their distorted thinking and changes the way they view events, makes interpretations and/or inferences, and forms opinions and possible biases (26).

In the past thirty years, cognitive therapy has been blended together with elements of behavior therapy to form a family of interventions that we know today as Cognitive Behavior Therapy (CBT). In CBT, the person not only changes negative and dysfunctional thinking patterns, but also uses specific strategies to change their maladaptive behavioral responses to events. Unlike traditional psychotherapy which could take years, CBT is a short-term treatment, usually taking less than a year. There are many CBT forms and methods, and they continue to undergo change and further development. The most recent and popular form, known as "third wave" CBT, began to flourish in the 1990s. It includes *mindfulness*, an attitude of acceptance, non-judgment, and in-the-moment awareness of one's self and events (26, 27). We will come back to meditative practices and mindfulness in Chapter 8.

One form of therapy particularly effective for me, as I underwent my eating disorder treatment, was Dialectal Behavioral Therapy, or DBT. As CBT attempts to change thinking in order to address behavior, DBT attempts to change behavior in order to address thinking. The result of DBT and CBT are almost indistinguishable, but the methods getting there are a little different: In CBT, my therapist might have tried to address the concern of why I wasn't eating, but in DBT, my therapist was first concerned with getting me to stop restricting my eating, and upon ceasing or limiting that behavior, giving me tools to address my thinking.

I mention this because as various therapeutic theories change, they integrate research and methods from other theories. Functionally, CBT and DBT are very similar. Methodologically, they go about things in completely reverse orders. Ultimately, it's up to a therapist to understand which might benefit their patient.

In children, it's especially important to address and consider that various treatments may not have the intended effect as they would in adults. This is especially the case if the child has a neurodevelopmental disability or mental illness. In Chapters 7 and 8, we'll discuss an approach we believe is helpful in all children precisely because it picks the most general, evidence-based, and least harmful methods of these different techniques.

—NJ

Final Remarks: Making Sense of It All

Emotional, relationship-based, behavioral, and cognitive theories are all a result of what we, as researchers and practitioners, have learned over the years. As our understanding of human behavior and biology has increased, so have the varied methods we've created in order to address problems within them. Today, the most successful theories tend to be those that have a mound of scientific evidence backing them. However, keep in mind that scientists are not infallible, and as we have a better understanding of the mind and behavior, we also have more room to make mistakes. In other words, although research tells us one thing right now, in ten years, we might learn something entirely contrary.

The point in bringing this up is to understand that Freud, Piaget, Erikson, Skinner, and others were creating methods and theories that made sense given the evidence of their time. Much of older theories and practices have been debunked, either due to an increase in our overall knowledge or an understanding that those theories were harmful. As we move forward, we hope to present a theory that not only integrates our current scientific understanding but also considers the humanity of children that has been denied through the centuries. While we hope it ultimately continues to help children, we also will revisit and revise it as our evidence and understanding evolves.

References

1. Sherin J. E., & Numeroff, C. B. (2011). Post-traumatic stress disorder: The neurobiological impact of psychological trauma. *Dialogues of Clinical Neuroscience*, 13(3), 263–278. Retrieved from www.ncbi.nlm.nih.gov/pmc/articles/PMC3182008/
2. van der Kolk, B. A. (2002). Trauma and memory. *Psychiatric and Clinical Neuroscience*, 52(S1), S52–64. https://doi.org/10.1046/j.1440-1819.1998.0520s5S97.x
3. LaLumiere R. T., McGaugh J. L., & McIntyre, C. T. (2017). Emotional modulation of learning and memory: Pharmacological implications. *Pharmacological Reviews*, 69(3), 236–255. https://doi.rog/10.1124/pr.116.013474
4. Chu, J. A., Frey, L. M., Ganzel, B. L., & Matthews, J. A. (1999). Memories of childhood abuse: Dissociation, amnesia, and corroboration. *The American Journal of Psychiatry*, 165(5), 749–755. https://doi.org/10.1176.ajp.156.5.749

5. LeDoux, J. E., & Brown, R. (2017). A higher-order theory of emotional consciousness. *Proceedings of the National Academy of Sciences, 10*, E2016—E2025. https://doi:10.1073/pnas.1619316114
6. van der Kolk, B. A. (2015). *The body keeps the score: Brain, mind, and body in the healing of trauma*. New York, NY: Penguin Books.
7. van der Kolk, B. A. (2003). The neurobiology of childhood trauma and abuse. *Child and Adolescent Psychiatric Clinics of North America*, 12, 293–317. Retrieved from www.traumacenter.org/products/pdf_files/neurobiology_childhood_trauma_abuse.pdf
8. Erikson, E., & Joan, M. (1997). *The life cycle completed: Extended version*. New York, NY: W. W. Norton.
9. Greenspan, S. with Thorndike Greenspan, N. (1985). *First feelings: Milestones in the emotional development of young infant and child from birth to age 4*. New York, NY: Viking Press.
10. Goleman, D. (1995). *Emotional intelligence: Why it can matter more than IQ*. New York, NY: Bantam Books.
11. Salovey, S. D., & Mayer, J. D. (1990). Emotional intelligence. *Imagination, Cognition, and Personality, 9*, 185–211. https://doi.org/10.2190%2FDUGG-P24E-52WK-6CDG
12. Mayer, J. D., & Salovery, P. (1997). What is emotional intelligence? In P. Salovey and D. Sluyter (Eds.), *Emotional development and emotional intelligence: Educational implications* (pp. 3–31). New York, NY: Basic Books.
13. Mayer, J. D., Salovey, P., Caruso, D. R., & Sitarenios, G. (2003). Measuring emotional intelligence with the MSCEIT V2.0. *Emotions, 3*, 97–105. https://doi.org/10.1037/1528-3542.3.1.97
14. Pollak, S. D., & Tolley-Schell, S. (2003). Selective attention to facial emotion in physically abused children. *Journal of Abnormal Psychology, 112*, 323–338. https://doi.org/10.1037/0021-843X.112.3.323
15. Zeidner, M. Mathews, G., & Roberts, R. D. (2012). The emotional intelligence, health, and well-being nexus: What have we learned and what have we missed? *Applied Psychology: Health and Well-being, 4*(1), 1–30. https://doi:10.1111/j.1758-0854.2011.01062.x
16. Baudry, A. Grynberg, D., Dassonneville, C., Lelorain, S., & Christophe, V. (2018). Sub-dimensions of trait emotional intelligence and health: A critical and systematic review of the literature. *Scandinavian Journal of Psychology, 59*(2), 206–222. http://doi: 10.1111/sjop.12424
17. Schneider, T., Lyons, J., & Khazon, S. (2013). Emotional intelligence and resilience. *Personality & Individual Differences, 55*(8), 909–914. https://doi: 10.1016/j.paid.2013.07.460.

18. Jayalakshmi, V., & Magdalin, S. (2015). Emotional intelligence, resilience and mental health of woman college students. *Journal of Psychosocial Research, 10*(2), 401–408.
19. Di Fabio, A., & Saklosfske, D. (2018). The contribution of personality and emotional intelligence to resiliency. *Personality & Individual Differences, 123*, 140–144. https://doi: 10.1016/j.paid.2017.11.012
20. Liu, Y., Wang, Z, & Lu, W. (2013). Resilience and affect balance as mediators between trait emotional intelligence and life satisfaction. *Personality & Individual Differences, 54*(7), 850–855. https://doi:10.1016/j.paid.2012.12.010.
21. Cozolino, L. (2016). *Why therapy works: Using our minds to change our brain*. New York, NY: Norton.
22. Acevado, B., Aron, E., Aron, A., Sangster, M. D., Collins, N., & Brown, L. L. (2014). The highly sensitive brain: an fMRI study of sensory processing sensitivity and response to other' emotions. *Brain and Behavior*. Open Access: https://doi.1002/brb3.242
23. Lovaas, O. I. (1987). Behavioral treatment and normal educational and intellectual functioning in young autistic children. *Journal of Consulting and Clinical Psychology, 55*(1), 3–9. https://doi.org/10.1037/0022-006X.55.1.3
24. Anderson, D. K., Liang, J. W., & Lord, C. (2014). Predicting young adult outcome among ore and less cognitively able individuals with autism spectrum disorders. *Journal of Child Psychology and Psychiatry, 55*(5), 485–494. https://doi:10.1111/jcpp.12178
25. Oinstein, A. J., Helt, M., Troyb, E., Tyson, K. E., Barton M. L., Elgsti, I. M., Naigles, L., & Fein, D. A. (2014). Intervention for optimal outcome in children and adolescents with a history of autism. *Journal of Behavior Pediatrics, 35*(4), 247–256. https://doi.org/10.1097/DBP.0000000000000037
26. Thoma, N., Pilecki, B., & McKay, D. (2015). Contemporary cognitive behavior therapy: A review of theory, history, and evidence. *Psychodynamic Psychiatry, 43*(3), 423–462. https://doi.org/10.1521/pdps.2015.43.3.423
27. Lorenzo-Lucas, L., Keefe, J. R., & DeRubeis, R. J. (2016). Cognitive-behavioral therapy: Nature and relation to non-cognitive behavioral therapy. *Behavior Therapy, 47*, 785–803. https://doi.org/10.1016/j.beth.2016.02.012

6

Lessons From Positive Psychology

PHOTO 6.1

Jim Pawleski is a researcher and the director of education at the Positive Psychology Center at the University of Pennsylvania. During his lecture on the first of day of a course called *Positive Psychology: Applications and Interventions*, he asks his student to undergo this thought experiment:

> Imagine you find a magic lamp and after rubbing it, a genie pops out and tells you, "I have been so impressed by you as a human being that I want to transform you into a superhero. You have a choice to make, however. You have the option of either choosing a red cape or a green cape. If you choose the red cape, you will have the power to fight against all the negative things that we don't want in the world, like poverty, injustice, violence, and hunger. If you choose the green cape, you will have the power to fight for all the positive things in the world that we want, like understanding, harmony, and justice."[1]

Pawleski then asks his students to decide which cape they would like to choose and write down why. He explains the point of this experiment is not to find the right or wrong answer, but to demonstrate that these capes are different from one another. If you choose a red cape, you are apt to look for problems in the world, and if you choose the green cape, you will be looking for positive opportunities.

This exercise demonstrates the fundamental principle of *positive psychology*—that is, no one can flourish without the green cape of positivity. In other words, getting rid of risks or sources of adversity and problems doesn't necessarily amount to one's thriving and wellbeing.

In this chapter, we'll go into more detail about positive psychology theories (briefly discussed in Chapter 4) in order to apply it to our discussion of centering the mental health of at-risk children. The point of this discussion isn't to espouse every message in positive psychology; rather, it's to lay the theoretical foundations of our model, RIM, which we'll talk about in more detail in Chapters 7 and 8.

The Message of Positive Psychology

Positive psychology is a popular and relatively new movement described as the scientific study of what makes life worth living. It is concerned with human wellbeing and factors that contribute to a person's strength and health both mentally and physically. Positive psychology is interested in people's abilities, talents, motivations, and character strengths, as well as systems that empower people to have a good and positive life. In an interview, Christopher Peterson, one of the founders of the field, said, "I tell you what positive psychology is all about. Other people matter. Period" (1).

The concepts in positive psychology are certainly not new. Important researchers like William James, Abraham Maslow, Carl Rogers, and Albert Bandura have certainly contributed to development of concepts that are now central in positive psychology. It was not, however, until the beginning of this millennium that a movement took shape and gradually exploded into hundreds of research projects and applications. The founders of the movement are Martin Seligman, Christopher Peterson, and Mihaly Csikszentmihalyi. Seligman, who you might remember from Chapter 4, recounts an interaction he had with his daughter in his rose garden as the moment of epiphany for him to start this movement:

> "GET TO WORK, Nikki," I shouted irritably . . . We were supposed to be weeding. Nikki, however, was having a great time, throwing weeds in the air, dancing, and singing. She startled when I shouted at her, walked away, and slowly walked back. "Daddy, can I talk to you?" I nodded. "Daddy, do you remember before my fifth birthday I was a whiner, I whined every day?" I nodded. "Have you noticed that since my birthday, I haven't whined once?" I nodded. "Well, on my birthday, I decided that I was going to stop whining, and that was the hardest thing I've ever done. And if I can stop whining, you can stop being such a grouch" (2, p. 3).

In 1998, in his inaugural address as the president of the American Psychological Association (APA), Seligman criticized the field for having become solely concerned with healing pain and suffering and repairing psychological damage. He, who had devoted a major part of his professional life to the study of helplessness and depression himself, acknowledged the importance of such a mission. But he argued psychology as a science must include studying human strengths and wellbeing as well:

> When we become solely a healing profession, we forget our larger mission: that of making the lives of all people better . . . it is my belief that no medication or therapy holds as much promise for serving as a buffer against mental illness as does human strength. But psychology's focus on negative has left us knowing too little about the many instances of growth, mastery, drive, and character building that can develop out of painful life events . . . We have misplaced our original and greater mandate to make life better for

> all people—not just the mentally ill. I therefore call on our profession and our science to take up this mandate once again as we enter the next millennium (3, p. 561).

In the following year, Seligman mobilized hundreds of young scientists to attend the first conference of positive psychology in Akumal, Mexico. This ignited the movement, and since 2000, it has exploded not only in popularity but in research and application. The University of Pennsylvania established a Positive Psychology Center for research and practice, which has been offering a graduate degree in applied positive psychology since 2005. Today there are at least ten other universities around the world with degree programs in positive psychology.

Research in the field focuses on enabling positive conditions in humans, such as happiness, growth, love, gratitude, optimism, hope, meaning, mindfulness, spirituality, better relationships, and resilience factors. It is grounded in the premise that an increase in one's strengths and the positive elements in their lives will result in a decrease in illness. Applications of positive psychology theories have been researched and practiced on every population from teachers and kids in schools, to athletes, business people, drill sergeants and soldiers in the US army, and more recently on doctors, patients, and the elderly.

Though the message of positive psychology might seem straight-forward and intuitive, there has been a great degree of criticism and backlash toward it. Some critiques consider its topics soft, frivolous, and completely unnecessary (2–4). Others view its message to be Pollyannaish, and to some extent even harmful. Barbara Ehrenreich, a well-known journalist, has been a vocal critic of positive psychology and its proponents. She blames the economic downturn of the recent decade in the United States on a prevalent and broad, yet false, public optimism, such as those encouraged by positive psychology. She cautions people against taking this movement seriously, which she believes promotes unrealistic solutions for real-world problems (5).

Clearly, there are many problems—individual and social—that need to be tackled head-on, and admittedly, there are many existing issues which will not be resolved by simply keeping a positive attitude. This, in fact, is not what positive psychology suggests. Positive psychology says cultivating the positive is as important and necessary as fighting the negative. Fostering positive ways to think, feel, and act is a personal choice, and not everyone necessarily feels inclined to do so.

It is hard to ignore the studies that show the benefits of such actions, though. A thought-provoking example comes from *big data research*. Johannes Eichstaedt and his colleagues conducted a study in 2015, collecting social media tweets from over 1,300 counties across the United States (6). Just imagine the number of people and their tweets used in this study! They found the type of language—either negative or positive—people used on Twitter revealed not only the psychological state of the communities in which they lived, but it also showed the rate of health and disease in the same communities. In communities where the majority of its population used negative language in their tweets—for example, expletives or angry and hostile words like "hate," "jealous," "liars," "tired," "boring"—were hotbeds of heart disease and hypertension and had a high mortality rate. In contrast, communities where people mostly used positive language—like "wonderful," "friends," "company," "hope," "enjoy," "possibilities," etc.—had lower rates of the same diseases and a lower mortality rate. This is similar to what researchers have found in other, smaller-scale studies. For example, a study in Germany in 2011 showed people who had positive emotions and affect had higher life satisfaction and lower risk of heart disease (7). In two meta-analyses of health-related literature—one done in 2016 and another in 2018—researchers found people with attitudes and mental states of optimism, positive emotions, and life engagement are significantly at a lower risk for mental and physical illnesses, like cardiovascular disease (8, 9). They also found positive attitudes and mental states are predictive of reduced mortality rate in those communities (7–9).

The central goal of positive psychology is to understand human wellbeing—how it is defined, measured, and cultivated. But in order to do that, we must have a central definition or basis of measurement by which to compare these studies. In 2016, a group of scientists looked at ninety-nine studies on wellbeing to see how researchers defined and measured the concept (10). They found that though there was no single definition, all researchers agreed wellbeing is a single factor that consists of different dimensions (11). A widely used model of subjective wellbeing was developed in 1984 by Ed Diener. In Diener's model, there are three major elements for wellbeing: individuals having frequent positive emotions; having infrequent negative emotions; and regularly making a personal assessment of how their lives measure up to their aspirations and goals (12). The latest theory of wellbeing is PERMA, which was created by Seligman in 2011. PERMA stands for five dimensions or building blocks of wellbeing that we'll discuss below (13).

Building Blocks of Wellbeing: PERMA

Not every person defines wellbeing the same way, but everyone agrees that it's separate from health—that is, wellbeing is not simply the absence of physical or mental conditions, but the addition of specific elements (we'll discuss these shortly) in one's life. Seligman explains these elements of wellbeing are usually pursued for their own sake, and each contributes separately to the overall wellbeing of the person (13). PERMA is the acronym for these pillars of wellbeing, standing for *P*ositive Emotions, *E*ngagement, *R*elationships, *M*eaning, and *A*ccomplishment. Because wellbeing is a construct, it cannot be directly measured (13, 14), but PERMA can be. Studies which have looked at PERMA show that people who have one of the pillars of wellbeing tend to have roughly other dimensions to a similar degree (14, 15).

In our previous chapters, we discussed some factors for promoting mental health as well as resilience in children. These also happen to be some of the building blocks of wellbeing. For example, early positive relationships or promoting mastery for accomplishments, which we previously discussed, are two important dimensions of wellbeing. We can begin to see how these elements come together to promote both wellbeing and resilience in individuals. Let's look at each building block:

- *Positive emotions* are feelings like joy, gratitude, hope, and serenity. Having positive emotions is not about simply smiling, nor is it about seeking pleasure. While seeking pleasure is usually related to satisfying the body, experiencing a positive emotion is related to what make us feel inspired, creative, helpful, and connected (16).
- *Engagement* is a total immersion in an activity or a task. It takes place when we are interested in and fully enjoy an activity. In this situation, we might feel a sense of exhilaration and enjoyment while we're fully immersed. When engaged in a task we truly love, some of us may experience a state of intense concentration and optimal experience, also known as *flow*, in which nothing else seems to matter and we might not even notice the passage of time (17).
- *Relationships* are enduring connections. They are also necessary for human survival, for giving and receiving support. Having friendships, closeness, intimacy, and shared experiences are necessary for our wellbeing.
- *Meaning* is believing in or having a non-material purpose in life that is greater than our individual selves. This could be believing in a purpose or mission or having faith in something spiritual. A meaningful life can lead to increased positive emotions, positive relationships, and engagement.
- *Accomplishment* happens when we set goals and work to achieve them. Having accomplishments increases our sense of mastery and control. It's important for our sense of efficacy, usefulness, and pride.

PHOTO 6.2 Positive psychology is the scientific study of what makes life worth living. Identifying the factors of wellbeing is of special interest in this field.

All elements of wellbeing are interrelated with each other. For example, having positive emotions and attitudes provides opportunities for socialization with others during day-to-day interactions and events, which could in turn lead to forming close relationships. Engagement in work or some creative activities are necessary for mastery and accomplishments. Having a purpose and meaning in life can drive or reinforce the other elements of wellbeing. Since we have discussed some of these foundations previously, we are going to focus on those factors that we have not yet looked at.

The Power of Positive Emotions and Our Wellbeing

Emotions are fundamental in how a person acts. In children, the jump from an emotion to an action is almost immediate; in adults, that interaction is not necessarily immediate, because our thought processes and logic typically interact with our emotions—almost simultaneously—to propel us into action. In other words, our emotional reaction to an event or situation can be changed based on how we think about it.

As we touched on in Chapter 5, emotions are part of a system that has multiple biobehavioral components. They are momentary body-mind states activated in response to a change in our current circumstances (16). When this multi-component system registers something as "bad for us," a negative emotion occurs, and when it registers a circumstance as "good for us," a positive emotion arises (17).

Both negative and positive emotions have survival action benefits for us. As we've discussed, the amygdala, the emotional center of the brain, responds in times of stress to activate our physiological system to galvanize us into action to protect us from danger. Negative emotions, like anxiety, anger, sadness, hatred, or boredom, are therefore not necessarily bad things. They involve cardiovascular, endocrine, and muscular changes to motivate us to act—to flee from the danger, fight with an incoming offense, or freeze to preserve and rebuild our resources (the "fight, flight, or freeze response"). But negative emotions can also lead us into maladaptive and destructive behaviors that create problems in our social interactions and daily living (16). Similarly, negative emotions do not build or expand our cognitive resources. This means they are not designed to make us stop to think, reflect, or analyze the situation. Their primary function is to make us act immediately without stopping to think. From an evolutionary perspective, this is necessary for our preservation and survival.

If negative behaviors can defend, preserve, or save us, what then are the functions of positive emotions? Barbara Fredrickson is a professor of psychology at the University of North Carolina in Chapel Hill who has studied positive emotions since 1998. She is among a group of researchers who has shown positive emotions not only defend and buffer us against stress, but trigger lasting and durable changes in both brain structure and function that promote further adaptive thoughts and behaviors (17–21). Fredrickson's work has shown that unlike negative emotions, positive emotions build and expand our cognitive resources and lead to what she calls an *upward spiral* in our life (16).

Early in her work, Fredrickson researched the evolutionary role and benefits of positive emotions for humans. After conducting a series of laboratory studies, she articulated the *broaden-and-build* theory, which explains how positive emotions serve to expand people's existing cognitive capabilities and hence present new resources for growth and improvement of their lives. Since 2009, she and other researchers have conducted studies that explain the neurological processes in positive emotional experiences. One study found that the parahippocampal place area (PPA), an area in in the brain responsible for place processing (e.g. images of landscapes or cities), is activated every time a person experiences a positive emotion (19). Another study found positive emotions broaden the person's field of vision (20). Research involving stroke patients discovered the patients became more aware of their surroundings and others in their environments when they experienced positive emotions while listening to music (21). Fredrickson reasoned that increased activation of the brain in instances of positive emotions is the support for the *broaden* part of her theory—that is, when people experience positive emotions, they cannot help but to take in more of the context and information in their surroundings (17).

PHOTO 6.3 Experiencing positive emotions is one of the key elements of wellbeing in individuals. Cultivating positive emotions increases the activity of the brain, enabling it to take in more information. People who experience positive emotions frequently are more open to resources and have better coping skills.

So positive emotions momentarily broaden people's awareness, scope of attention, and their mindset. These in-the-moment effects are not the only functions of positive emotions, however. Fredrickson believes the second consequence of positive emotions is longer lasting, particularly when they are repeated experiences. These experiences accumulate, and over time *build* new resources for us that are long lasting. For example, when we are joyful or inspired, we are more apt to seek, explore, and learn about new people, places, and experiences—finding access to new resources. Therefore, just as negative emotions have evolutionary survival benefits for us, the evolutionary function of positive emotions is to increase our scope of awareness and mindset to eventually find and create new opportunities and resources for our growth.

Research also shows when people think in positive terms or engage in enjoyable and interesting activities, they experience positive emotions much more frequently. These experiences over time result in an increase in their positive (but not negative) affects and in long-term positive coping skills (22). Several of Fredrickson's experiments with college students show there is an upward spiral benefit as well. For example, students showed continued positive affect and coping five months after their initial positive emotional experiences. Fredrickson believes a healthy ongoing diet of positive emotions increases our mental and physical health and leads to improved lifestyle changes for us. She explains when people consciously make a healthy activity, like exercise or meditation, enjoyable and interesting for themselves, they begin to have repeated micro-positive-emotional moments during those activities. This in turn

TABLE 6.1 Barbara fredrickson's *broaden-and-build* theory applied to nine positive emotions

Positive Emotions	*Circumstances for Response Activation*	*Broaden Effects*	*Resources Built*
Joy	Activated when one has a good fortune, or receives good news.	Urges one to get involved, engage, and play.	Results in new skills acquired through engagement and experience.
Gratitude	Activated when one acknowledges the source(s) of a good fortune/event.	Urges one to consider new ways to be prosocial, kind, or generous.	Results in caring skills, loyalty, and additional social bonds.
Serenity/ Contentment	Activated when one recognizes a circumstance as cherished, right, or satisfying.	Urges one to savor the circumstances, and integrating them into new priorities.	Results in a more complex sense of oneself and one's values and priorities.
Interest	Activated when one observes a novel phenomenon in a safe context.	Urges one to explore, learn, and immerse in the novel phenomenon.	Results in gained knowledge, skills, and experiences in specific areas.
Hope	Activated when one fears the worst, yet yearn for better in a grim situation.	Urges one to draw on one's inventiveness and capabilities to turn things around.	Results in optimism and resilience to adversity.
Pride	Activated when one takes appropriate credit from some socially valued or good outcome.	Urges one to fantasize about even bigger accomplishments in a similar area.	Results in achievement motivation.
Amusement	Activated when one finds a situation to involve a non-serious social incongruity.	Urges one to share a laugh, and create continued joviality.	Results in building and solidifying enduring social bonds.
Inspiration	Activated when one witness human excellence.	Urges one to excel oneself to reach a higher ground.	Results in motivation for personal growth.
Awe	Activated when one encounters goodness or beauty on a grand scale.	Urges one to absorb and accommodate this new encountered vastness.	Results in new worldview, belief.

amplifies the enjoyment of these behaviors and compels them to repeat them and therefore develop healthy habits and lifestyle changes—hence, an upward spiral (21). This propels people into improved mental and physical health, fulfillment, and gradually an increase in capabilities that lead to their life's betterment (21). Table 6.1 displays examples of nine positive emotions and their momentary broaden (action) and long-term build (resources), described by Fredrickson (16).

There are several other interesting findings that Fredrickson and her team reached as they conducted their experiments on positive emotions. For example, they found when people cultivate frequent micro-moments of positive emotions, they take perspectives of others better and are able to connect and see each other as people much more (23). They also found these effects endure across race and class; frequent experiences of positive emotions make people think more in terms of "we" as opposed to "I" versus "you." This and other findings led Fredrickson to articulate a scientific concept of *love* with a unique broaden-and-build effect on physical and psychological health.

Wellbeing and Positivity Resonance: Love

The concept of love is one usually avoided in academic and professional literature and conversations. Love is usually associated with romantic relationships, familial love, physical intimacy, and sexual pleasure. However, from the perspective of emotion science, the concept of love differs from its popular definition. Fredrickson argues that from the positive emotion perspective, love is not a sexual desire, a special bond, or a commitment; nor is love exclusive, lasting, or unconditional (24). She explains just like other positive emotions, love is a micro-momentary experience and not an enduring event or a bond—although an enduring emotional bond or a commitment could be a long-term effect of a repeated experience of this emotion. According to Fredrickson, three interwoven events take place during this momentary experience of love (24):

1. There is a sharing of one or more other positive emotions (aside from this momentary emotional connection) between two or more people. This does not have to be the same positive emotion, but two or more people share a positivity element with one another.
2. There is a synchrony in biochemistry and behaviors, specifically of neural firings and heart rhythms as well as behaviors between the

parties. For example, Ruth Feldman and her colleagues looked at moments of connections between infants and their parents (25). They found when parents—mothers as well as fathers—connected with their infants, such as through affectionate touch, smile, and eye contact, both the parent and the infant had a synchrony of oxytocin surges and other neuronal firings.
3. There is a reflected motive to invest in each other's wellbeing that brings mutual care.

Fredrickson calls this trio of events *positivity resonance* (24). Preconditions for moments of positive resonance are feeling safe and being able to connect with another person (such as through shared eye contact, shared smiles, touch, etc.). In other words, if a person feels anxious, uncomfortable, or threatened, they are less likely to feel connected and therefore experience positivity resonance with another person(s). Fredrickson makes the case that over time, these micro-moments of positivity resonance experiences broadens a connection between people and builds the resources of social bonds, commitment, loyalty, and trust between them.

To understand the effects further, Fredrickson studied the physiological effects of repeated positivity resonance experiences. She found people who had frequent micro-moments with others had higher levels of cardiac vagal tone (24). Vagal tone is a measure of the slowness of one's heart rate. The vagus nerve is one of twelve cranial nerves that connect the brainstem to the abdomen through the heart and other organs. This nerve slows the heart rate down each time we exhale. It is particularly important in calming us down after a threat or danger has passed. People who typically have a high vagal tone have lower levels of heart problems, blood glucose, and inflammation. They also have a higher rate of attention, emotional regulation, and overall better social skills. The cardiac vagal tone is therefore a fair indication of physical and social-emotional wellbeing. Fredrickson found people who experience frequent positivity resonance instances had a higher vagal tone. She therefore concluded frequent micro-moments of positivity resonance drives love and links social to physical wellbeing (24).

We believe the broaden-and-build and positive resonance theory is not only fundamental to understanding positive emotions, but has direct implications for the relationship aspect of wellbeing. Positive emotion research makes a solid case for our ongoing argument that positive relationships with children are a catalyst for reversing mental health issues and promoting health and resilience. In the practice section of this book, we will look at specific ways to promote positive emotions in children through one-on-one time in play and conversations. With that said, let us turn our attention to another pillar of wellbeing: engagement.

PHOTO 6.4 Positivity resonance or love is formed with repeated small moments in which two or more people connect with one another. In these micro-moments, there is a sharing of positive emotions, biobehavioral harmony, and motivation on all sides to invest in the other's wellbeing.

Wellbeing and Flow: Being "In the Zone"

In 1992, Michael Jordan, after scoring his sixth three-pointer before the first half of the playoffs against the Portland Trailblazers, was asked how he felt after scoring thirty-five points in the first half of the game. He answered, "I can't explain it. It feels like time stands still . . . I am in the zone." In positive psychology, the state described by Michael Jordan is known as engagement or the state of *flow*.

Mihaly Csikszentmihalyi articulated the theory of flow after interviewing hundreds of people (musicians, artists, athletes, and others). They described their optimal performance when their work "flowed out of them," seemingly without much effort (26). Flow is a state of total absorption, in which we are so engaged and focused on the task at hand and our end goal that nothing else seems to matter, even an extreme challenge. The experience is so enjoyable that even if we may initially undertake an activity for other reasons, soon it will become intrinsically rewarding and we continue to do it for its own sake and not for any extrinsic rewards. The activity becomes an end to itself, and engagement in it lifts life to a different level. In his research, Csikszentmihalyi found people are most productive, creative, and even happier when they are in this state. Flow is universal and affects people the same way across races, cultures, genders, and developmental levels.

Flow is inevitably linked to the ability to set goals and also to having a balance between the skills and the challenges at hand. Csikszentmihalyi describes these specific characteristics for flow (26):

- The person has clear goals and immediate feedback about them.
- There is a balance between the challenge and the skill of the person.
- The person has complete concentration on the task.
- There is a degree of ease and effortlessness in the work process at some point.
- The experience itself is intrinsically rewarding.
- There is a feeling of control over the task.
- Time is transformed—it seems to either slow down or speed up for the person.
- Action and consciousness merge together—it seems that the person loses self or conscious rumination.

What happens in the brain during the process of flow has been somewhat of a mystery. Perhaps no one said it better than Edith Wharton, the turn-of-the-twentieth-century novelist. She wrote, "It is there that the central mystery lies, and perhaps it is impossible to fix in words, as that other mystery of what happens in the brain at the precise moment when one falls over the edge of consciousness into sleep" (27). Only recently have some studies begun to shed light onto what might be happening in the brain during the flow state.

In 2008 and 2012, two fMRI studies looked at the brain activities of jazz musicians and rap artists during memorized and improvisational or freestyle performance (28, 29). The researchers found that when these musicians improvised, a region of brain called the dorsolateral prefrontal cortex (DLPFC) became less active. The DLPFC mediates executive functioning like attention, planning, inhibition, and self-control. Its deactivation is linked to altered state of consciousness, like meditation, daydreaming, or REM sleep. One would think that during flow, we would need our wits about us, or for the DLPFC to be most active. As it turns out, it all depends on the task at hand.

Arne Dietrich, a neuroscientist at the American University of Beirut, explains that both events, either the deactivation of DLPFC or its activation, can happen based on what kind of task we are engaged in (30). In some types of activities, like jazz improvisation or in meditation, a phenomenon called transient hypofrontality may take place. This is a temporary downregulation of hyper-analytical and metacognition process in our brain; the latter process actually limits solution finding, so its downregulation is a plus in some activities we do. But the opposite can also hold in other activities. Dietrich explains flow in many instances occurs during activities that take many hours of trial and error, of systematically eliminating alternative possibilities; all of this requires an increased activation of DLPFC, and this is exactly what happens in activities that require intense problem solving (30).

An interesting finding comes from another brain scan study of jazz pianists in 2016 by Melinda McPherson and her colleagues. The findings of this study connect together our discussions about positive emotions and flow. The researchers found when creative tasks involve emotional experiences, it influences what brain regions are activated and to what extent. McPherson showed when jazz musicians improvised melodies intended to convey positive emotions, the activity in the DLPFC decreased. When these musicians played freestyle melodies to express negative emotions, like sadness, there was greater activation in the DLPFC. The reward regions of the brain were also activated in these latter instances, which reinforces behaviors that lead to greater connectivity to the DLPFC. In other words, the DLPFC is deactivated when we get in the zone with positive emotions; contrariwise we may need greater rewards initially when our task does not involve positive emotions. A reward in that instance is necessary until we get into the groove of things (31). This makes perfect sense according to the flow theory, in that we may initially need rewards—sometimes even artificial rewards—to complete many tasks which require practice and mastery to encourage ourselves to focus, until gradually engaging with the task itself becomes rewarding and carries us to the flow zone.

All in all, reaching a sense of accomplishment is related to having opportunities to be fully engaged in the work we are passionate about or, at the very least, interested in. Our engagement is also connected to our mastery level, opportunities to learn, and our goals and degree of determination to accomplish them. Both of these pillars of wellbeing, engagement and accomplishment, are necessary for our sense of wellbeing. The implications of this for our work with children may be clear at this point. It is important for children to:

- Be engaged in tasks that are interesting and engaging to them.
- Have some choice in the activities they undertake.
- Be supported to set clear goals related to their tasks, during which they receive feedback and are supported and encouraged to analyze and reflect on their own progress toward their goals.
- Be supported and taught to gain mastery—to build skills and to have tasks in which their skill and the level of challenge is balanced.
- Work in an environment in which distraction is minimized and pacing is according to their skill levels.

Meaning in Life and Wellbeing

Let's reflect on some of the world's mysterious archeological sites: the Seven Provincial Pyramids of Egypt, the Stonehenge of Wiltshire, the divination shrines of Armenia, or the Buddhist temple of Bangladesh. They remind us human beings across all times and cultures have believed in some higher meaning in life. The field of psychology often makes it out that meaning is an immeasurable entity, not to mention a luxury for only a few who have not themselves experienced any trauma or serious hardships in life. This, in fact, is not the case. Research shows meaning is not mysterious, infeasible, or immeasurable, and most people from all walks of life, with all kinds of experiences and across all times, have and do indeed attain meaning in their lives (32–35).

Meaning is a subjective experience. Whether or not one's life is meaningful is something that cannot be judged from the outside, because meaning can only be judged by understanding the quality of a person's inner state and inner life. Scientifically, however, meaning in life has been studied, measured, and researched, mostly through self-reporting, which is a reasonable method of looking at someone's subjective experience. From a scientific perspective, the definition of meaning is only understandable from the lived experiences of a meaningful life: "Lives may be experienced as meaningful when they are felt to have significance beyond the trivial or momentary, to have purpose, or to have a coherence that transcends chaos" (31, p. 180). In this definition, there are three aspects to meaning in life: *purpose*, *significance*, and *coherence* (33).

By and large, when people talk about meaning, they refer to having a sense of purpose, direction, or order in their lives. Cross-cultural studies show that around the world—the US and other nations, like Cuba, Kosova, Malawi, Sierra Leone, Sri Lanka—over 90 percent of people say on average, their lives are pretty meaningful (33). This may come as a surprise, since the common perception is that attaining meaning in life is next to impossible. These studies find there are several things that make people report their lives to be meaningful. For example, having positive and fulfilling relationships and emotional connections, belonging to or be included in groups, having a religious faith, and (not surprising to us) having positive emotions and affect are the common elements that make people describe their lives as meaningful (34–36). This latter factor, positive emotions and mood, seem to make life meaningful in equal measures as religious faith or social relationships put together, even for people who live alone (34).

People's sense of meaning is also related to experiences in which they transcend their sense of self, which is usually associated with spirituality.

These are experiences of momentary but powerful emotions in which one connects with something that is greater than oneself—for example, nature, other people or creatures, or God. In that state, there is a strong feeling of peace and wellbeing. David Yaden of the University of Pennsylvania is an expert on transcendence. He likens a *self-transcendent* experience to what astronauts experience when they view earth from orbit, called the *overview effect*, an intense state of awe and awareness, along with a unity with nature or the universe (37). Yaden and his colleagues explain two things happen in a self-transcendent experience: first, you completely forget about yourself—your problems, worries or desires; and second, you feel completely connected and united with what is around and beyond you (38).

Although self-transcendent moments are transient, research shows their repeated experiences leave a positive and indelible mark on the human psychological state. This includes an increased sense of meaning in life; increase in positive emotions, particularly in elation, compassion, admiration, gratitude, love, and awe; increase in altruistic feelings; increase in connectedness with other people—a universal brotherhood; and finally, an increase in one's overall wellbeing (38–40). Self-transcendent experiences can be induced and

PHOTO 6.5 Having a meaning and purpose in life is another cornerstone of wellbeing. Research shows meaning is not as unattainable or mysterious as it is commonly perceived. Most people do indeed have a purpose or meaning they strive for in their lives.

cultivated through healthy practices like mindfulness meditation or "loving kindness" meditation, in addition to the more traditional means, like mystical practices.

It is clear meaning in life is an important cornerstone of human wellbeing and not just a philosophical argument. Research on the connection between the meaning in life and wellbeing is extensive. They show the varying degrees and types of benefits:

- Longevity and lower mortality across adulthood (41).
- Higher quality of life and greater physical health (42).
- Slower age-related physical illness, like heart attacks, as well as cognitive decline, like dementia (43, 44).
- Lower incidence of mental health disorders and suicidal ideation, even within the context of depression (44–47).
- Adaptive coping skills, and pain and stress management strategies (48).
- Better adjustment at the work place and fewer occupational issues (49).
- More adept in social interactions and also being more socially appealing (49).

Like the other topics we've discussed in this book, our discussion of meaning has direct implication for our work with children. An important aspect of child development is developing a sense of meaning, so we will look at practices likely to promote healthy development in this sense in the last chapter.

Character Strengths and Virtues

Each child and adult has a unique character. What determines our character is not only our genetic inheritance and the environment and other people in it, but also what we do ourselves to develop our strengths. Research shows we can actually enhance and develop our character strengths and virtues not only from early childhood, but anytime during adulthood. Not only that, we can influence other people's characters through our relationships with them and by showing an appreciation of their strengths. From the perspective of positive psychology, *character strengths* and *virtues* are pathways through which wellbeing and its pillars can be reached. More importantly, scientists have shown character strengths have direct pathways to the happiness of not only adults, but children and adolescents (50, 51).

In 2004, Chris Peterson and Martin Seligman published a classification manual for human strengths of character and virtue. This manual is the result of perhaps the greatest project in positive psychology to date. The project was funded by the Values in Action Institute (VIA), which currently supports research, disseminates information, and conducts survey assessments of character strengths around the world (www.viacharacter.org/www/). In this project, Peterson and Seligman led 55 other renowned researchers to examine literature across cultures around the world and over two millennia. Their background research included collecting inventories of virtues and strengths from sacred texts and scriptures; literature in social sciences like psychology and sociology; creative literature, lyrics and poetry, and paintings; creeds and civic organizations; children's literature; catalogues; and virtue-related messages in cards, stickers, newspapers, etc. This arduous project resulted in a consensus on the categories of six major virtues: *wisdom, courage, humanity, justice, temperance,* and *transcendence*. These six virtues are organized and classified around twenty-four character strengths, which were tested via scientific criteria. This classification process is detailed in *Character Strengths and Virtues: A Handbook and Classification* by Peterson and Seligman in 2004 (52). In a way, this manual does the same for the classification and identifications of strengths necessary for human wellbeing as does the DSM for the classification and identifications of symptoms for psychiatric disorders. Table 6.2 displays this classification, called the VIA Classification of Character Strengths and Virtues.

Part of the work of Peterson and Seligman's team was to develop a measure for the assessment of character strength in adults and children. The result are two surveys, one for adults and one for youth ages ten to seventeen. Both can be taken for free from the VIA Institute website (www.viacharacter.org/www/Character-Strengths-Survey). To date, more than six million people have taken this survey, which enables individuals to identify their signature character strengths. Research shows character strengths can be learned, practiced, and cultivated in both adults and children with and without developmental or mental health disorders. In fact, the most recent research in this area includes identification of character strengths in children and youth with developmental disabilities, such as in autism (for examples see 53, 54). All character strengths have pathways to the pillars of human wellbeing, so the idea is to use signature strengths in novel ways to build new character strengths and pathways toward health and wellbeing.

Currently, there are no measures of character strengths or assessments for children younger than nine years, and there are not a lot of studies with young children. In 2006, Nassok Park and Chris Peterson conducted a study to identify character strengths in young children (50). They believed that

TABLE 6.2 Classification of character strengths and their virtues

Virtues	*Wisdom*	*Courage*	*Humanity*	*Justice*	*Temperance*	*Transcendence*
Character Strengths	➢ Creativity ➢ Originality ➢ Judgment ➢ Love of learning ➢ Perspective	➢ Bravery ➢ Perseverance ➢ Honesty ➢ Zest	➢ Love ➢ Kindness ➢ Social intelligence	➢ Teamwork ➢ Fairness ➢ Leadership	➢ Forgiveness ➢ Humility ➢ Prudence ➢ Self-regulation	➢ Appreciation of beauty ➢ Gratitude ➢ Hope ➢ Humor ➢ Spirituality

some character strengths, like kindness, can be identified in young children from an early age. Many character strengths emerge from infancy and solidify by age three. For example, the emergence of the strengths of love and kindness depends on the quality of attachment between the infant and the caregiver. Assuming there is a healthy attachment, the signs of love and kindness should be obvious as early as eighteen months. Think about a toddler who gives their own toy to another kid who is crying as a way of comforting.

Certain character strength begin to emerge during the third to fifth years of life, like friendship, self-regulation, and teamwork. Others, like gratitude, depend on a more advanced level of social-emotional and cognitive development and may not begin to emerge until age six or seven, despite the child's manners (for example, saying thank you appropriately). More complex and sophisticated character strengths, Park and Peterson believe, like open-mindedness, forgiveness, and spirituality, probably do not fully develop until adolescence; however, the capacity for most character strengths emerge from age one and solidify from age three to five.

A second study on young children and their strengths of character was conducted in 2014 (55). Its findings mirror what Park and Peterson discovered. Based on these two studies, ten character strengths are obvious in children during early childhood years:

- Love
- Kindness
- Creativity
- Humor
- Curiosity
- Love of learning
- Perseverance
- Self-regulation
- Social intelligence
- Bravery[2]

Character strengths can be taught and cultivated with young children through a variety of exercises, which we will discuss and present some examples of in the final chapter of the book.

Positive Education

The major reason why we devoted an entire chapter to positive psychology was that lessons from positive psychology can directly be applied to the education of children at all levels. In fact, there are currently several schools around the world—in the US, Australia, the UK, Bhutan, China, India, United

Arab Emirates, Saudi Arabia, Jordan, Israel, and Latin and North America—which are integrating positive psychology practices within their curricula (56). The application of positive psychology to education is called *positive education.* Programs of positive education have focused on elementary schools, middle schools, and high schools, and only more recently in select early childhood classrooms (55).

The goal of positive education is to integrate approaches that promote overall wellbeing in all children instead of only focusing on academic success. The way this goal is achieved is to first and foremost promote the wellbeing of teachers by preparing them to practice a group of core *positive intervention* techniques on a daily basis. Positive interventions are mental and physical exercises that have been studied and shown to be effective in enhancing and cultivating elements of wellbeing in a person. Teachers use a group of positive mental and physical exercises themselves and also learn and integrate the age-appropriate versions of these exercises into the school curriculum and in their own classrooms. So far, positive education programs in Australia, Mexico, and Bhutan have been researched longitudinally. They have shown promising results. For example, after the implementation of positive education for a year, students in these schools not only improved in their academic performance, but also in mental, behavioral, emotional, and physical health. The follow-up studies two years after the intervention showed the students' gains persisted in the long run (56).

Final Remarks

We are convinced cultivating positivity through mental, physical, and behavioral exercises will result in an increase in the health and wellbeing in all people. This holds true for young children as much as for adults. Based on existing research evidence, some of which we discussed in this chapter, positive approaches to intervention can address both our inner and outer world. In the final two chapters of this book, we will present examples of key positive approaches for children that our embedded in our model, called RIM.

Notes

1. Taken from James Pawleski's lecture in course: *Positive Psychology: Applications and Interventions*
2. The character strength of *bravery* was not identified in Park and Peterson's study for children in early childhood. It was, however, one of the strengths identified in a later study on this subject.

References

1. Peterson, C. (n. d.). What makes life worth living? (University of Michigan). Other people matter. Retrieved from https://positivepsychologyprogram.com/christopher-peterson-other-people-matter/
2. Seligman, M. E. P. (2018). *The hope circle: A psychologist's journey from helplessness to optimism*. New York, NY: Public Affairs.
3. Seligman, M. E. P. (1999). The president address (annual report). *American Psychologist, 53*, 854–857. Retrieved from https://ppc.sas.upenn.edu/sites/ppc.sas.upenn.edu/files/apapresidentaddress.pdf
4. Fredrickson, B. L. (2013). Positive emotions broaden and build. In P. Devine & A. Plant (Eds.), *Advances in experimental social psychology (Vol. 47)*, pp. 1–53. San Diego: Elsevier.
5. Ehrenreich, B. (2009). *Bright-sided: How the relentless promotion of positive thinking has undermined America*. New York, NY: Holt.
6. Eichstaedt, J.C., Schwatz, H. A., Kern, M., Park, G., Labarthe, D. R., Merchant, R. M., . . ., Seligman, M. E. P. (2015). Psychological language on twitter predicts county-level heart disease mortality. *Psychological Science*, *26*(2), 159–169. https://doi.org/10.1177/0956797614557867
7. Wiest, M., Schuz, B., Webster, N., & Wurm, S. (2011). Subjective wellbeing and mortality revisited: Differential effects of cognitive and emotional facets of well-being on mortality. *Health Psychology*, *30*(6), 728–735. https://doi.org/10.1037/a0023839
8. Cohen, R., Bavishi, C., & Rozanski, A. (2016). Purpose in life and its relationship to all-cause mortality and cardiovascular events: A meta-analysis. *Psychosomatic Medicine*, *78*(2), 122–133. https://doi.org/10.1097/PSY.0000000000000274
9. Hernandez, R., Bassett, S. M., Boughton, S. W., Schuette, S. A., Shiu, E. W., & Moskowitz, J. T. (2018). Psychological well-being and physical health: associations, mechanisms, and future directions. *Emotion Review*, 10(1), 18–29. https://doi.org/10.1177/1754073917697824
10. Linton, M. J., Dieppe, P., & Medina-Lara, A. (2016). Review of 99 self-report measures for assessing well-being in adults: Exploring dimensions of well-being and developments over time. *BMJ Open*, 6e010641. http://dx.doi.org/10.1136/bmjopen-2015-010641
11. Kashdan, T. (2017, October, 12). How many ways can we measure well-being. *Psychology Today*. Retrieved from www.psychologytoday.com/us/blog/curious/201710/how-many-ways-can-we-measure-well-being
12. Diener, E., Su, E.M., Lucas, R. E., & Smith, H. (1999). Subjective well-being: Three decades of progress. *Psychological Bulletin*, 125(2), 276–302.

13. Seligman, E. P. M. (2013). *Flourish*. New York, NY: Atria.
14. Seligman, M. (2018). PERMA and the building blocks of wellbeing. *The Journal of Positive Psychology*, *13*(4), 333–335. https://doi.org/10.1080/17439760.2018.1437466
15. Goodman, F., Disabato, D., Kashdan, T., & Kaufman, S. (2017). Measuring well-being: A comparison of subjective well-being and PERMA. *The Journal of Positive Psychology*, 1–12. https://doi.org/10.1080/17439760.2017.1388434
16. Fredrickson, B. (2013). Positive emotions broaden and build. In P. Devine & A. Plant (Eds.), *Advances in experimental social psychology* (Vol. 47), pp. 1–53. Burlington, NJ: Academic Press.
17. Garland, E. L., Fredrickson, B., King, A. M., Johnson, D. P., Meyer, P. S., & Penn, D. L. (2010). Upward spirals of positive emotions counter downward spirals of negativity: Insights from the broaden-and-build theory and affective neuroscience on the treatment of emotion dysfunctions and deficits in psychology. *Clinical Psychology Review*, *30*(7), 849–864. https://doi.org/10.1016/j.cpr.2010.03.002
18. Garland, E. L., & Howard, M. O. (2009). Neuroplasticity, psychosocial genomics and the biopsychosocial paradigm in the 21st century. *Health and Social Work*, *34*(3), 191–199. https://doi.org/10.1093/hsw/34.3.191
19. Schmitz, T. W., De Rosa, E., & Anderson, A. K. (2009). Opposing influences of affective state valence on visual cortical encoding. *The Journal of Neuroscience*, *29*(22), 7199–7207. https://doi.org/10.1523/JNEUROSCI.5387-08.2009
20. Schrammel, F., Pannasch, S., Graupner, S. T., Mojzisch, A., & Velichkosvsky, B. M. (2009). Virtual friend or threat? The effects of facial expression and gaze interaction on psycho-physiological responses and emotional experience. *Psychosociology*, *46*(5), 922. https://doi.org/10.1111/j.1469-8986.2009.00831.x
21. Fredrickson, B. L. & Joiner, T. (2018). Reflections on positive emotions and upward spirals. *Perspectives on Psychological Science*, *13*(2), 194–199. https://doi.org/10.1177/1745691617692106
22. Kok, B. E., Coffey, K. A., Cohen, M. A., Catalino, L. I., Vacharkulksemsuk, T., Algoe, S., B., Brantley, M., & Fredrickson, B. L. (2013). How positive emotions build physical health: Perceived positive social connections account for the upward spiral between positive emotions and vagal tone. *Psychological Science*, *24*(7), 1123–1132. https://doi.org/10.1177/0956797612470827
23. Waugh, C. E., & Fredrickson, B. L. (2006). Nice to know you: Positive emotions, self-other overlap, and complex understanding in the formation of a new relationship. *Journal of Positive Psychology*, *1*(2), 93–106. https://doi.org/10.1080/17439760500510569

24. Fredrickson, B. (2013). *Love 2.0: How our supreme emotions affects everything we feel, think, do, and become*. New York, NY: Hudson Street Press.
25. Feldman, R., Gordon, I., Zagoory-Sharen, O. (2010). The cross-generation transmission of oxytocin in humans. *Hormones and Behaviors, 58*(4), 669–676. https://doi.org/10.1016/j.yhbeh.2010.06.005
26. Csikszentmihalyi, M. (1990). *Flow: The psychology of optimal experience*. New York, NY: Harper & Row.
27. Wharton, E. (1933, April). Confessions of a novelist. *The Atlantic*. Retrieved from www.theatlantic.com/magazine/archive/1933/04/confessions-of-a-novelist/385504/
28. Limb, C. J., & Braun, A. R. (2008). Neural substrates of spontaneous musical performance: An fMRI study of jazz improvisation. *PLOS One*. https://doi.org/10.1371/journal.pone.0001679
29. Liu, S., Chow, H. M., Xu, Y., Erkkinen, M. G., Swelt, K. E., Eagle, M. W., Rizik-Baer, D. A., & Braun, A. R. (2012). Neural correlates of lyrical improvisation: An fMRI study of freestyle rap. *Nature, Scientific Reports, 2*, 834. https://doi.org/10.1038/srep00834
30. Dietrich, A. (2015). *How creativity happens in the brain*. London, UK: Palgrave Macmillan UK.
31. McPherson, M. J. Barrett, F., Lopez-Gonzalez, Jiradejvong, P., & Limb, C. (2016). Emotional intent modulates the neural substrates of creativity: An fMRI study of emotionally targeted improvisation in jazz musicians. *Nature, Scientific Reports, 6*, 1860. https://doi.org/10.1038/srep18460
32. King, L. A., Hicks, J. A., Krull, J. L., & Del Gaiso, A. K. (2006). Positive affect and the experience of meaning in life. *Journal of Personality and Social Psychology, 90*(1), 179–196. http://dx.doi.org/10.1037/0022-3514.90.1.179
33. Heintzelman, S., & King, L. A. (2014). Life is pretty meaningful. *American Psychologist, 69*(6), 561–574. https://doi.org/10.1037/a0035049
34. Baumeister, R. F., & Vohs, K. D. (2002). The pursuit of meaningfulness in life. In C.R. Snyder & S. J. Lopez (Eds.), *Handbook of positive psychology* (pp. 608–618). New York, NY: Oxford University Press.
35. King, L. A., Heintzelman, S. J., & Ward, S. J. (2016). Beyond the search for meaning: A contemporary science of the experience of meaning in life. *Current Directions in Psychological Science, 25*(4), 211–216. https://doi.org/10.1177%2F0963721416656355
36. Mattiuzzi, P. G. (2015). Meaning and purpose in life: Commonplace or hard to come by? *Everyday Psychology*. Retrieved from www.everydaypsychology.com/2015/01/meaning-and-purpose-in-life-commonplace.html#.W1iG8i-ZNTY
37. Yaden, D. B., Iwry, J., Slack, K. J., Eichstaedt, J. C., Zhao, Y., Vaillant, G. E., & Newberg, A. B. (2016). The overview effect: Awe and self-transcendent

experience in space flight. *Psychology of Consciousness: Theory, Research, and Practice*, *3*(1), 1–11. http://dx.doi.org/10.1037/cns0000086

38. Yaden, D. B., Haidt, J., Hood, R. W., Vago, D. R. & Newberg, A. B. (2017). The varieties of self-transcendent experience. *Review of General Psychology*, *21*(2), 143–160. http://dx.doi.org/10.1037/gpr0000102
39. Esfahani Smith, E. (2017). *The power of meaning: Finding fulfillment in a world obsessed with happiness*. New York, NY: Broadway Books.
40. Hill, P. L., & Turiano, N. A. (2014). Purpose in life as a predictor of mortality across adulthood. *Psychological Science*, *25*(7), 1482–1486. https://doi.org/10.1177%2F0956797614531799
41. Krause, N. (2007). Longitudinal study of social support and meaning in life. *Psychology and Aging*, *22*(3), 456–469. https://doi.org/10.1037/0882-7974.22.3.456
42. Boyle, P. A., Barnes, L. L., Buchman, A. S., & Bennett, D. A. (2010). Purpose in life is associated with mortality among community-dwelling older persons. *Psychosomatic Medicine*, *71*(5), 574–579. https://doi.org/10.1097/PSY.0b013e318a5a7c0
43. Steger, M. F. (2012). Experiencing meaning in life: Optimal functioning at the nexus of spirituality, psychopathology, and wellbeing. In P. T. P. Wong & P. S. Fry (Eds.), *The human quest for meaning* (2nd Ed., pp. 165–185). New York, NY: Taylor and Francis.
44. Mascaro, N., & Rosen, D. H. (2005). Existential meaning's role in the enhancement of hope and prevention of depressive symptoms. *Journal of Personality*, *73*, 985–1014. https://doi.org/10.1111/j.1467-6494.2005.00336.x
45. Heisel, M. J., & Flett, G. L. (2004). Purpose in life, satisfaction with life, and suicidal ideation in a clinical sample. *Journal of Psychopathology and Behavioral Assessment*, *26*(2), 127–135. https://doi.org/10.1023/B:JOBA.0000013660.22413.e0
46. Kleftaras, G., & Psarra, E. (2013). Meaning in life, psychological wellbeing and depressive symptomatology: A comparative study. *Scientific Research*, *3*(4), 337–345. http://dx.doi.org/10.4236/psych.2012.34048
47. Thompson, N. J., Coker, J., Krause, J. S., & Henry, E. (2003). Purpose in life as mediator of adjustment after spinal cord injury. *Rehabilitative Psychology*, *48*, 100–108. https://doi.org/10.1037/0090-5550.48.2.100
48. Littman-Ovadia, H., & Steger, M. F. (2010). Character strengths and well-being among volunteers and employees. *Journal of Positive Psychology*, *6*, 419–430. http://dx.doi.org/10.1080/17439760.2010.516765
49. Stillman, T. F., Lambert, N. M., Finchman, F. D., & Baumeister, R. F. (2011). Meaning as magnetic force: Evidence that meaning in life promotes interpersonal appeal. *Social Psychological and Personality Science*, *2*(1), 13–20. https://doi.org/10.1177%2F1948550610378382

50. Park, N., & Peterson, C. (2006). Character strengths and happiness among young children: Content analysis of parental descriptions. *Journal of Happiness Studies, 7*(3), 323–341. https://doi.org/10.1007/s10902-005-3648-6
51. Park, N., & Peterson, C. (2006). Moral competence and character strengths among adolescents: The development and validation of the Values in Action Inventory of Strengths for Youth. *Journal of Adolescence, 29*, 891–905. https://doi.org/10.2202/1940-1639.1042
52. Peterson, C., & Seligman, M. E. P. (2004). *Character strengths and virtues: A handbook and classification*. Oxford, UK: Oxford University Press/New York, NY: American Psychological Association.
53. Niemiec, R. M., Shogren, K. A., & Wehmeyer, M. L. (2017). Character strengths and intellectual and developmental disability: A strengths-based approach from positive psychology. *Education and Training in Autism and Developmental Disabilities, 52*(1), 13–25. https://doi.org/10.1371/journal.pone.0192323
54. Shogren, K. A., Shaw, L. A., Raley, S. K., Wehmeyer, M. L., Niemiec, R. M., & Adkins, M. (2018). Assessing character strengths in youth with intellectual disability: Reliability and factorial validity of the VIA-Youth. *Intellectual and Developmental Disabilities, 56*(1), 13–29. https://doi.org/10.1352/1934-9556-56.1.13
55. Lottman, T., Zawaly, S., & Niemiec, R. M. (2017). Well-being and well-doing: Bringing mindfulness and character strengths to early childhood classroom and home. In C. Proctor (Ed.), *Positive psychology interventions in practice* (pp. 83–105). Cham, Switzerland: Springer.

Seligman, M., & Adler, A. (2018). *Positive education*. Retrieved from www.researchgate.net/publication/323399593_Positive_Education

7

Resilience-based Interaction Model (RIM): Introduction

PHOTO 7.1

In the previous chapters of this book, we laid the foundations for our recommendations for practice in early childhood by describing the theoretical principles that inform them. The social-emotional wellbeing of a young child is the solid foundation for their mental/cognitive and behavioral health. Early childhood education must be about healthy emotional development and socialization of the child. Throughout this book, we have presented scientific research that supports this belief. In the last three chapters, we borrowed from several theoretical foundations to lay the grounds for practices that, in our opinion, will promote not only mental health and wellbeing, but also will set the stage for future academic well-doing. In this and the next chapter, we bring together principle elements of theories that historically have competed and worked against one another within a positive approach, called the Resilience-based Interaction Model (RIM). We describe its basic premises and some of its elements in details in this chapter and will present the remaining components in the next and final chapter of this book.

RIM is not a curriculum or a group of prescriptive lessons, nor a curriculum to be used on certain days of the week in your classroom. It is a philosophical model with guidelines to inform your/our (teachers') daily interactions not only with children, but with adults. It is about us adults because it revolves around our verbal and body language, our attitudes and behaviors, and the responses and feedbacks we give to children and one another. When used regularly, the example practices of RIM can promote our own wellbeing. Our positive approach is the result of years of teacher training, including trial and errors, success and failures in the field. We use this approach with all children—with and without diagnosed conditions. Teachers who use RIM practices tell us of positive and transformational changes in their own attitudes and behaviors as well as in the behaviors and attitudes of their students.

Conceptual Framework of RIM

In previous chapters, we presented attachment theories, studies in resilience, neuroscience, other emotion-based theories, behavioral theories, and positive psychology, all of which inform the RIM framework and example practices. Here, we will first describe the conceptual framework of RIM, then proceed to guidelines for practice.

RIM is grounded in resilience science and the relevant protective factors for children. The circular graph at the bottom of the model shows the foundational elements of our resilience-based model: forming and maintaining

FIGURE 7.1 The conceptual framework of the resilience-based interaction model (RIM)

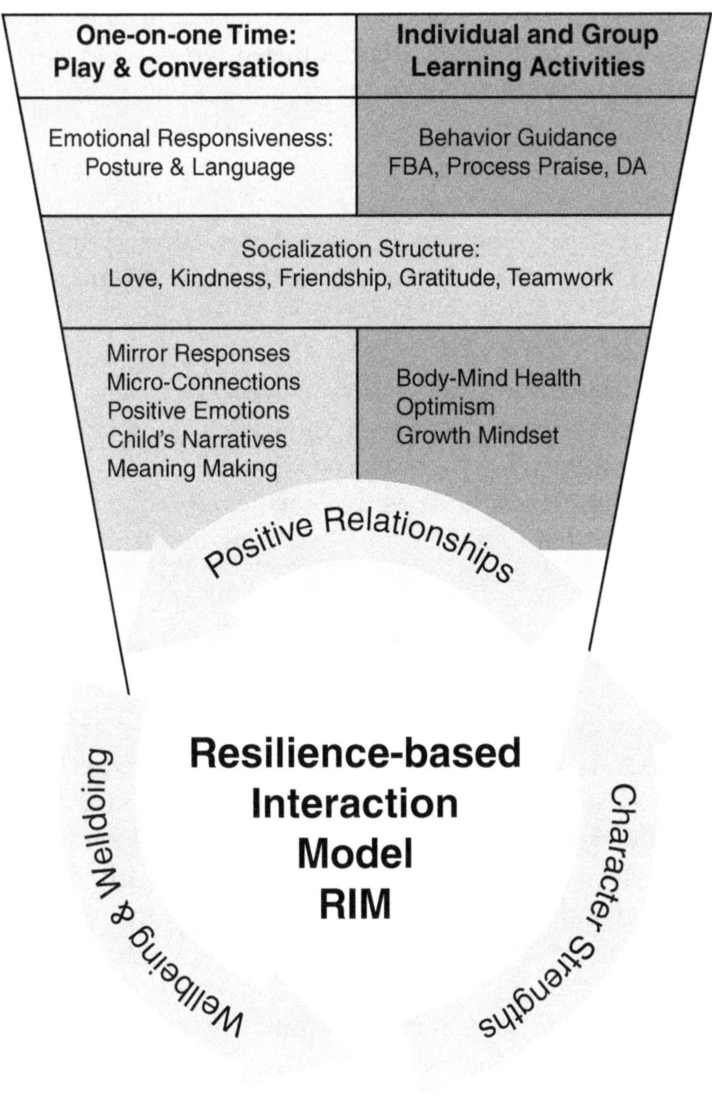

positive relationships with children, reinforcing *character strengths*, and promoting *wellbeing and well-doing* in children.

The first element (arrow) of RIM is forming positive relationships with children, which is the strongest promotive factor of resilience in children. We have at length described the importance of secure and positive relationships in resilience, emotional health, and overall wellbeing of all children (Chapters 3–6). This is particularly important for children who deal with high stressors—those come from homes in which their relationships with their caregivers are compromised due to negative environmental influences like poverty, parental stress, parental mental health, negative parenting, or maltreatment. This is also the case for children whose own development is compromised due to vulnerabilities or diagnosed conditions. Truly, where do we *not* find kids who face one or more of these issues?

To form trusting and positive relationships, we must spend individual time with children. The left hand-side panel of our RIM diagram details the principles and practical elements of our relationship-building approach in one-on-one time. We particularly recommend specific techniques to be emotionally responsive to children. These are:

- Making repeated micro-connections with children;
- Cultivating positive emotions in ourselves and in children;
- Mirroring children's emotions and thoughts;
- Helping children build a positive narrative of themselves; and
- Helping children build positive meaning about themselves and the world.

We will go into more detail about these individual techniques as we continue our discussion.

The second premise of our model is promoting a child's strengths of character. Again, here, we focus on the character strengths that promote resilience. We also focus on the strengths that already exist in young children by the time they're toddlers and preschoolers, such as love and kindness, as well as characteristics which are likely to emerge throughout early childhood years, such as optimism and teamwork (1). The goal of our model is to encourage children to use their existing strengths in novel ways so they can develop additional ones.

We target building their strengths through two means. First, we create a classroom environment that not only values the community as a whole, but also respects an individual's needs and strengths. Depicted in the middle of the diagram, the structure we recommend for an early childhood classroom should promote socialization as well as cooperation and teamwork among all children. The structure not only should have clear, enforceable, and realistic rules of citizenship, but should promote character strengths like love, kindness, friendship, gratitude, and teamwork, which are principle character strengths for socialization.

The third arrow of our model is about promoting children's wellbeing and well-doing. Parents want their children to be physically, mentally, and behaviorally healthy (1–3). But we also want children to do well and be successful. In the US, schools have a broad mission of ensuring the academic success or cognitive well-doing of children. Schools do not necessarily and/

or overtly concern themselves with the social-emotional wellbeing. As you may have realized, in our opinion, this focus misses the mark completely. How can a child *do* well if they *are not well* in reality?

In RIM, to promote the behavioral health of children, we recommend the use of select principle techniques of Applied Behavior Analysis, depicted in the top right hand-side panel of Figure 7.1. These behavioral principles are used to guide children to change their maladaptive and challenging behaviors into adaptive ones. The basic behavioral principle of conducting a functional behavior analysis (FBA) is used (when and if necessary) to assess environmental triggers and consequences that contribute to challenging behaviors. Second, the appropriate and correct use of process praise and differential attention (DA) supports children in developing adaptive behaviors. This is a top-down approach. Behavioral methods, however, can only go so far. We also have a bottom-up approach, in that we regularly engage children in certain mental and physical exercises called *body-mind activities* (meditation, yoga, physical exercise) to help them with self-regulation and the reduction of anxiety.

During group and individual activities, we not only help children learn social-emotional skills, but we also encourage them to engage in healthy cognitive habits necessary for successful peer socialization and individual work habits and learning. For example, we help children modify the ways in which they think about and respond to learning setbacks and negative events. We do this by first monitoring our own responses and feedbacks and then embedding key positive messages in targeted social-emotional activities and lessons we typically deliver to groups or for individual children, such as in stories, lesson activities, and games.

The well-doing element of our model is about learning to learn—to find new solutions, persevere, and ask for help to find alternative solutions. We achieve this through the promotion of a growth mindset in children.

All together, we encourage a set of collective practices based on the following principles:

- *Body-Mind Health* includes daily short breaks for meditation, yoga, and physical exercises to help with self-regulation and executive functioning skills.
- *Optimism* includes modifying the ways we respond to children's questions, daily work, and during one-on-one time, as well as using targeted stories to promote an optimistic explanatory style.
- *Growth Mindset* centers around our responses, reflecting and modifying our mindset, and giving feedback to children in such a way to encourage their perseverance. We also recommend teaching targeted lessons to children about how the brain works.

First Things First: Our Own Wellbeing

Putting Our Oxygen Masks On

Years ago, when my son was a toddler and my husband and I suspected something was wrong with his development, we participated in a renowned and award-winning early intervention and parent education organization in Chicago to help us work with our son successfully. This program was not only elemental in the diagnosis of my son and securing appropriate early intervention and special education services for him, but was also transformational for me. Four years later, I became the executive director of the same organization.

The program we ran was designed for children who had challenging behaviors and was behaviorally oriented. Most children had been expelled from one or more preschool programs. Some had diagnosed conditions, like ADHD, ASD, or ODD. Others did not, but their parents had serious concerns. Most parents who came to our program were at their wits' end. They had just about had it, either with the school system and teachers who had previously worked with their children, with their children themselves, or with both. In short, they were exhausted on all fronts.

Our program had a two-pronged approach. While children were placed in classrooms with expert professionals, the parents themselves met with veteran parents who had previously completed a training period. After completing the program, these parents themselves became experts on behavior management of their children—and other children, for that matter. As a part of requirements of our program, each parent agreed to mentor another parent before they and their kids graduated and left the organization. The program was more about helping to change parental behavior than about changing the child, in that the adult's behavioral change was a catalyst for supporting children to change their maladaptive behaviors.

One of the great features of this program was a weekly group session with a clinical psychologist at the helm. These sessions usually took place around a very large table with anywhere between ten to twenty parents and mentors. Our resident psychologist facilitated this session and gave feedback to everyone around the table. The group was a place for sharing ideas, receiving and giving support, as well as for brainstorming and problem solving. On occasion, when parents seemed exhausted—which was very often—or shared some of their ongoing stressors with the group, our psychologist gave this advice:

Think about one of the very first things that a flight attendant tells you to do when there is a lack of oxygen in the air cabin. They tell you to first put on your own oxygen mask before you put the mask on your child. They tell you this because unless you are able to breathe first, you can't help your child to breathe.

I learned a lot from this wonderful program, and I hope this advice is as helpful to others as it was to our parents.

—MB

In its essence, RIM is a philosophical framework that embraces positive education at its core. Positive education is not just about children; it is also about educators. We cannot empower children to cultivate positive emotions, strengths, and health if we ourselves are not positive thinkers or feel healthy. Despite its noble purpose and daily joys of success, being a teacher is one of the most demanding and stressful jobs in the world. We cannot expect children to be and do well unless we are well enough to weather the stressors of our job with zest and energy. Our own wellbeing comes first and foremost, because without it, there is no way we can support children or promote their wellbeing. Similarly, we are barely able to model positive emotions and adaptive cognitive skills for children unless we ourselves use them in our day-to-day personal interactions and socialization. Therefore, we recommend that you try principle practices for stress reduction and cultivating positive emotions and cognitive skills yourselves as often as you can outside work and/or at the same time with children when you implement them in your classroom.

In the following sections, we will describe two other components of our approach, relationship building with children and behavior guidance.

One-on-One Time with Children in RIM

The guiding principle of our one-on-one approach, *emotional responsiveness*, along with its five core principles, are depicted in the left-hand side panel of our model (Figure 7.2).

No matter how busy we are, how important our teaching agenda is, and how little time we have, we must put aside a portion of our day to

FIGURE 7.2 Principles of one-on-one time during play sessions or in conversations with children

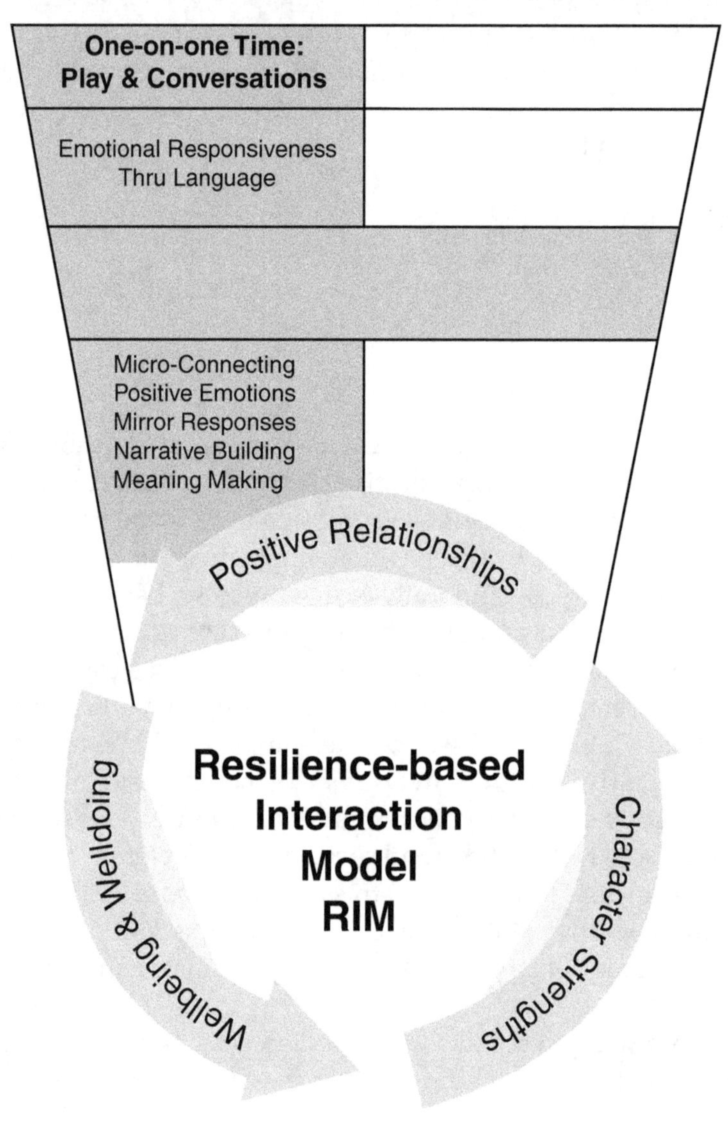

spend in one-on-one time with children. We believe in early childhood classrooms, it is crucial to spend one-on-one time with every child in a non-academic context. Depending on the age and developmental level of the child, this time alone should preferably be spent during play, or if the child is older, verbal, and prefers it, in a conversation with the child. Because most young children prefer to play, we will describe this type of one-on-one time.

In RIM, we recommend setting aside between ten to fifteen minutes per day to spend with each individual child in a session during the child's play. There should be time for every child to spend with you at least once in a week. This session could take place anytime during the day: early in the morning, as children arrive in your classrooms; later throughout the day, at strategically well-placed periods; or at the end of the day, when children are getting ready to leave.

We have seldom found teachers to be receptive to our recommendation to spend one-on-one time with children aside from what is prescribed by the school curriculum. First, as early childhood teachers, we think we are actually playing with children when we use toys and other materials to teach children academic or cognitive concepts in a Piagetian tradition. We are, in fact, not playing when we guide children (albeit indirectly) to discover new cognitive concepts; we are teaching. Second, our time is precious; we have a teaching agenda, and we must spend every minute we can carrying it out. When there is hardly enough time in a day for us to finish all we have to do, how can we set aside time for additional individual sessions with kids? However, teachers are often amazed how well these sessions

PHOTO 7.2 In Rim one-on-one sessions, the child directs the play or a conversation. The adult is there not to teach, but to pay close attention and responds to the child in a non-judgmental way.

work when they are strategically placed in between small and large group times or during the arrival and departure of children. They often tell us this time alone with children helps them learn so much about their students' capabilities, which in turn helps modify their lessons and the children's overall behavior and learning.

In RIM's one-on-one sessions, the child must make the choice about what they want to do during this period and what materials they want to have—whether they want to play, do an art activity, or they want to just talk about something. Our job is to follow along, forgetting for this duration that we should teach. Instead, our entire effort should be on being in the moment with the child, attuning to their emotions and thoughts, and giving our entire attention to them. In other words, there are three things to remember in these moments: listen, observe, and be aware.

This time alone with every kid is even more crucial for children deal with various stressors or who come from adverse conditions. This is particularly important for children who have challenging behaviors, those who always get in trouble or have/are suspected of having diagnosable conditions. These are children who usually do not have healthy and sustaining positive relationships with their caregivers or their peers. Despite teachers' reluctance, these children are the very same kids who need this time alone with you.

Teachers frequently tell us how futile it is to spend their time individually with children who have challenging behaviors. They usually have a knee jerk reaction the minute we recommend spending this type of one-on-one time. This is for a couple of reasons. First, despite our goodwill efforts, often the relationships we have with children who have behavioral or developmental issues are actually negative, stressful, or, in some cases, uncomfortable. One teacher told us a particular child she had worked very hard with for many months made her feel inadequate and a failure as a teacher whenever she spent time with him. She told us no matter what she did to help him, it was unsuccessful. She was quite jaded, convinced it was outside of her expertise and skillset to deal with him. Second, in a typical course of a school day, our time is monopolized by the kids who have either challenging behaviors or have learning and developmental issues. These children demand extra time and attention away from other children who are also in our charge to teach—so is it fair to give them even more time in this context? Short answer: It's not only fair but necessary. In reality, when teachers have one-on-one sessions with children who have challenging behaviors, these children become less demanding and monopolizing, more compliant and cooperative throughout the day, and ready to learn.

This time alone with a child is as important in a special education or inclusion classroom as it is in a general education classroom. Special educators spend most of their instruction time in a one-on-one format with their students anyway. If you are a special educator, we ask that you set aside these ten to fifteen minute periods to spend with every kid in a very different context from your typical instruction. Spend this time not instructing, but following the lead of the child and becoming part of what the child decides and likes to do.

Andrew

Andrew is an eight-year-old boy with learning disabilities in my self-contained special education classroom. Aside from his learning issues, Andrew gets frustrated and angry easily and has a hard time calming down and regulating himself. My work with Andrew has had mixed results until I tried one-on-one play sessions with him.

The one-on-one play session was quite a revelation to me. I had not fully realized the extent to which my normal interactions with children involved so much judgment. For example, I had to constantly remind myself during the play session to not add remarks like "Good job" or "I liked the way you did that," which I realized I say almost constantly to children as a way to direct and motivate their actions. Although our interaction at first seemed a bit awkward and strange, by removing my judgment and just being with Andrew in a non-directive way, I could literally see him taking in the attention and enjoying it for its own sake. This came as almost a relief to me as I let go of the need to teach or direct behavior and let the play session unfold on Andrew's terms. It was equally amazing to me that I could sense this shift in my perspective and the power of the play session in only one fifteen-minute session. What might be the benefit of more consistent play sessions for Andrew over time? I believe it could be very powerful for him. Later the next week, Andrew approached me to see if he could stay inside again to "play with the toys." Although I have not yet had a chance to have another play session with him, I plan to do so. I am convinced it is the simplest and most effective way I can help him. By building our relationship on his terms, I am confident I will discover a way we can move forward together.

Intrigued by the shift in my own ability to interact with children in a different way and the positive impact it had had on Andrew in such a short time, I decided to try some of these techniques later in the day. After finding a library book on world records, another student, Nathan, began to tell me about some of the amazing things he had found. I don't think he had ever talked to me so much! After a few minutes, I noticed that other students who were near our conversation, but not directly participating, began to do something very interesting. They began to clean up the room without being asked by organizing supplies on the classroom tables. It was as if the bubble of our interaction felt safe or grounding in some way and they responded in turn by acting in a grounded, but non-verbal way. I realized that this happened without me once saying, "Stop, clean up, do this or do that."

—Laura Knotts, Special Education Teacher

In Chapter 3, we discussed the concept of the internal working model in attachment theory. As a reminder, internal working models are the understanding that children develop about themselves and their attachment figures, which is formed based on their relationships and repeated interactions with those adults. Recall that children who tend to have impaired relationships with their caregivers have negative internal working models of many adults in their lives, believing these figures to be untrustworthy and unsafe. More importantly, they have formed an understanding about themselves as being unworthy of an adult's love and attention.

The purpose of spending one-on-one time with children is not to teach, guide them to discover new concepts, or learn new facts. The purpose is to help children form new and healthy positive internal working models of themselves and of adults—in this case, their teacher. This can only happen when we devote the space and time to build a trusting relationship in a context that is safe for the child. It is in this space that the child can begin to build a new internal working model of themselves and other adults. The reason we ask you not to teach during play sessions is because the learning environment can, by nature, be stressful, particularly for a child who has problems with self-regulation. Learning can also be anxiety producing for children who experience stress in their home lives regularly or who have learning difficulties. In times of anxiety and stress, no person can feel safe to relax, connect with others, or take in information. In fact, as you may recall, we presented research in earlier chapters supporting the idea that emotional connections are only positive when the people involved in the interaction feel safe (4, 5).

Giving the child the choice of activity and material is one way to create a safe space, but it is not enough. What makes the child feel safe is to have the teacher's full attention without being afraid of being judged—which includes being taught, corrected, lectured at, told they are wrong, or worse, being shamed or blamed. When children feel safe, they are not hypervigilant as a way to escape from stress. They are able to relax, play, talk, interact, and express their thoughts and emotions freely. It is in this way that we can understand who these children really are, what their capabilities are, and how we can harness these capabilities for growth and learning. Our next step is to be emotionally available and responsive to the child during these one-on-one sessions.

Emotional Responsiveness and Its Core Principles

We borrow from the rich tradition of play therapy to inform our practice of one-on-one time with children. Play therapists are experts in being emotionally responsive to children. Their purpose is to build a trusting relationship in a completely non-judgmental/non-blaming, non-invasive, and safe space. For young children, an emotionally responsive person should be an adult, teacher, or parent. Becoming emotionally responsive not only depends on our willingness to give our attention completely and positively to the child in that time period, but also to be fundamentally willing and ready to form a new, healthy understanding of the child. It also completely depends on the amount of effort we put into building and establishing this new trusting relationship and/or being willing to repair a previously impaired relationship.

Emotional responsiveness is having a posture—this includes our nonverbal language, facial expression, and body posture—and language that are empathetic to the child. Our body language and facial affect should convey to the child, "I am interested in you," "I pay attention to you, to what you say and do," and "I am here to understand you." Simply put, an emotionally responsive posture is sitting across, leaning toward, having a pleasant affect, and being ready to see, listen, pay attention to, and be open to everything the child does and says in this short period.

From brain research supporting the benefits of talk therapy and findings in emotion research, we understand talking and listening to children in an emotional responsive posture does in fact help them begin a process of self-reflection and gradually develop a healthy narrative about themselves and their experiences (6). Our non-blaming and non-judgmental responses during these one-on-one sessions are also crucial for us to make genuine connections with children.

Emotional responsiveness also includes the verbal language we use. In the next sections, we will articulate the specific ways to comment on children's behaviors during the play session. For now, it is important that we explain the core principles inherent in this approach.

Mirror responses are verbal and nonverbal responses to a child's behavior or a statement they make. Our response should mirror the emotional state of the child in a healthy way. For example, when the child expresses sadness during play or in a conversation, mirroring sadness could be saying something like, "This made you sad." When the child expresses anger in an explosive way, the way we mirror their anger could be *downregulating* or *upregulating*. Responding with something like "I see you are very angry" in a calm voice downregulates the child's emotion by showing our understanding of the child's emotion, but at the same time indirectly helps the child regulate their anger through imitating our calm manner. On the other hand, upregulation occurs when we mirror the anger emotion—or any other emotion, such as excitement—in such a way as to show we are angry or excited along with them. While upregulation is a good strategy to help a child experience a positive emotion like joy and excitement, it is not appropriate to use for mirroring negative emotions like anger.

Mirror responses and being attuned to the child's moods and behaviors will result in both parties (you and the child) making many *micro-connections* together. These short spats of repeated connections are opportunities in which we and the child can experience shared *positive emotions*

PHOTO 7.3 When children talk and adults are emotionally responsive, they are able to help children regulate their emotions through many moments of connection in which they share positive emotions and form trust.

together. Over time, these will become the building blocks of our positive relationships.

Recall our discussion in Chapter 6 about broaden-and-build and the upward spiral capabilities of cultivating positive emotions. It is for this reason that we want to have connections that build positive emotions. Looking together at the research on positive emotions and talk therapy (6–8), we can reasonably conclude if we spend time with children individually, using emotional responsive body and verbal language in a safe space, we will have multiple micro-connections with the child. Having mirror responses in order to make micro-connections and cultivate positive emotions in ourselves and children are the first three core principles of emotionally responsive one-on-one time with children.

The fourth core principle of our approach is to help the child build a healthy *narrative*. We don't mean for you to become narrative therapists. Rather, we mean to be good listeners of the stories that children tell and retell us through their play scenarios or through what they say. When we listen to children, we allow them to develop a healthy way of telling us the events, and often problems, that surround them and their families. Children are resourceful; when we listen to them, we allow them to reflect and modify their stories. Let's look at an example.

We met with Xavier in the first chapter of this book. He was the preschooler who introduced himself as "the bad kid." He had completely frustrated his teachers and other professionals. He was uncooperative, oppositional, aggressive toward other kids and adults, and often destructive toward classroom equipment and materials. His teacher and her assistant had grown somewhat resentful and were not initially willing to spend individual time with him in a one-on-one session, so our early childhood coach decided to conduct play sessions with Xavier herself.

Play Sessions with Xavier

My notes for the first three sessions with Xavier all look very similar to this: I introduced the rules for our play session (keep yourself and me safe, keep materials safe) and told him that he could choose to play with whatever he wanted to. He chose the action figures and acted out a fighting sequence with them. I tracked his behavior [described his actions] aloud: "These guys are fighting so hard with one another," etc. He threw the toys on the ground and at me, and tried to climb the loft walls. I ended the session, and he went back to class with almost immediate aggressive behavior.

My notes for the next four sessions all look very similar to this: I introduced the rules for our play session (keep yourself and me safe, keep materials safe) and told him that he could choose to play with whatever he wanted to. He chose the action figures and acted out a fighting sequence with them. I tracked his behavior. The fighting grew more and more aggressive. He threw the toys on the ground, then sat in my lap until he calmed down. I talked quietly with him, acknowledging and validating his feelings: "I can see you got all excited, playing with your action figures," "You are now trying to calm yourself . . ."

My notes for the eighth play session look very differently: Xavier chooses the action figures and plays out a fighting sequence with them. The fighting sequence gets more and more aggressive. He stops his play, sets the figures down, and sits in my lap (for almost fifteen minutes). I ask him if he wants to go back to class now. He says no and picks up the baby doll. He roleplays with the doll. He sits the doll up and puts on a bib. He pretends to prepare the doll food and takes the food to the doll. He tells the doll, "You can't have any food. You are a bad baby." He then pretends to eat the food. He repeats this pattern three more times. I talk about the doll's feelings and about Xavier's feelings: "The doll must be sad to be hungry. You are angry at her for something she did." Xavier says yes to this. Then he ends the session by sitting in my lap again. This time, he takes my arms and wraps them around him.

—Heather Little, Graduate Student and Teaching Coach

Xavier's play narratives are quite revealing. This is one example that when we allow children to tell their stories in a safe and non-blaming environment, their anxieties decrease, and they begin to develop a sense of trust with us. It is at this point that the child begins to reflect on their own actions and narrate a story. Listening to children's stories directly through what they say or through observing their play narratives not only informs us about their feelings and the issues in their lives, but connect them to us. It allows for them to share their feelings and experiences with us and gradually sort out and understand their own feelings. Over time, as they organize their thoughts and feelings, and as we support them during these one-on-one sessions and throughout the day in other activities, they learn to make positive meanings about themselves and the world around them.

Through making multiple connections with children, we are not only able to share in their emotions and promote their positive ones through shared experiences, but we also help children write new and more positive narratives and therefore *make meaning* about the world and themselves in it.

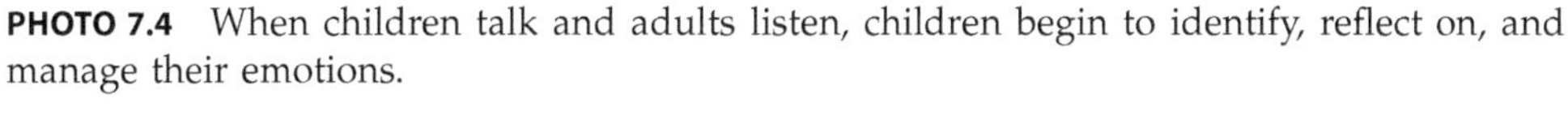

PHOTO 7.4 When children talk and adults listen, children begin to identify, reflect on, and manage their emotions.

Meaning making is the final principle of our approach. It does not happen overnight. By being emotionally responsive to children, we help them develop the cognitive and emotional tools to begin this process. There are also four side benefits for children when they have emotionally responsive adults around them (9):

- Children begin to perceive, understand, and express their own emotions accurately;
- Children begin to reflect on and manage their emotions;
- Children begin to express their emotions in a healthy way; and
- Children begin to form cognitive solutions to conflicts and problems, using their emotions accurately.

What to Do and What Not to Do in One-on-One Sessions with Children

It helps when there is a designated time period of the day which is set aside in a specific space far from the hustle and bustle of the classroom for one-on-one time. We have found when teachers label this time something like "A Special Time with the Teacher," children respond very enthusiastically. Play or conversation are two common and convenient modes for children to engage in during one-on-one sessions. However, essentially any other activity the child chooses to engage in is also appropriate. The key is the child is the one who chooses what to do.

Teachers tell us they are initially afraid other children in the classroom might react negatively or interrupt the sessions. But once they begin, they often find other children learn to view these one-on-one sessions as a regular part of their classroom schedule and observe the privacy of these sessions without interrupting.

If you have had previous negative interactions or an impaired relationship with a child, we suggest you begin by first spending one or two brief five-minute periods with the child in the following way:

- Choose a time that the child is engaged in an activity and is calm.
- Sit close and across from the child.
- Do not interfere with the child's activity. Simply sit across and pay attention to and look at what the child is doing.
- Be present in the moment with the child.
- Give eye contact when and if the child looks at you.
- Have a positive affect; smile genuinely.
- Make occasional comments on what the child is doing:
    - "You are coloring your flower." "You are making a robot." "Oh, my goodness, that looks kind of tough to do!"
- Use your natural voice instead of a singsong tone.

In many instances, children will respond by looking, asking a question, or making a statement. In those instances, look back, listen to what they have to say, and respond to their questions honestly. If the child invites you to join in their activity or play, you should do so.

If the child is non-verbal, simply be present in the moment and make comments on the child's actions as we recommend. If the child looks at you, give eye contact and smile. You can also muse aloud about what the child might be thinking. This might feel awkward at first, like a one-sided conversation, but in time, you will feel natural making comments. For example, you can say something like, "Hmm, looks like you thought pushing the ring through the small hole would be easier than taking off the lid!" If an opportunity arises and you notice an emotional expression label it appropriately: "I see that you really enjoy squeezing this Koosh-ball." Brief five-minutes of togetherness are effective ways of reversing any existing negative dynamics and begin to connect with the child in preparation for the longer play sessions.

In longer sessions, the child can choose any materials (toys, books, or art supplies) available in the classroom for their preferred activity. Everything we suggested above for the short period of connecting stands also for the play session. Additional guidelines for what to do in the play sessions are as follow:

- Announce it is a "special time" to spend together with the child.
- At the very beginning, set the limits clearly: "In this time together, there are three safety rules:
  - "Keep yourself safe, keep me safe, keep the materials safe—no hitting, breaking, throwing, etc."
  - "When you follow the safety rules, you can play in any way you like. If you break the rules, you choose to end the play time with me."
- Be present, pay active attention to the child with your body language, and observe closely what the child is doing.
- Join in the play only if invited to participate. Otherwise, continue to sit in close proximity to the child.

There are things that you must not do during the RIM one-one session with children:

- Do not teach, correct a mistake (whether verbal or behavioral), say what to do, or what not to do. For example, if the child showed you a rectangular block and said, "This is a circle," *do not say*, "No. This is a rectangle." Instead say, "You say this is a circle." You are stating what you heard. There will be enough time for you to teach the correct shapes to the child.
- Do not insert yourself into the child's activity or play unless the child invites you to do so.
- If the child begins conversing with you, do not make the conversation about you (for example, your thoughts, likes or dislikes, etc.).
- Do not talk about something negative the child did earlier, if any.
- Do not express any judgment about what the child does or says.
- Do not say "no" to something the child is doing. If the child breaks any of the rules, such as throwing toys around or becoming aggressive toward you or themselves, simply announce you are ending the session and do so. You can say something like, "We are ending our time together because you did not follow the rules. Next time we play together, you will remember not to break the rules and will do better to keep us safe." You should then follow up and promptly end the session.

We consistently find when the limits are set at the beginning of the session, and when they are followed through immediately, children learn to respect the rules of the session.

Use Emotionally Responsive Language

Emotional responsiveness has a language of its own. Psychotherapists and play therapists are especially adept at using this language. In play therapy, there are three types of language techniques: 1) commenting on what the child is doing, called *tracking behavior*; 2) repeating what the child says, called *restatement of content*; and 3) musing on what the child might be feeling as reflected in the child's behavior or expressions, called *reflection of feelings* (10). To simplify this technique, we call it three emotionally responsive languages that convey the following messages from you:

1. *Commenting*: By commenting, you are saying to the child that you are paying attention to what they do without judgment. For example, "You are putting the red magna tile on the blue one."
2. *Repeating*: By repeating, you are saying to the child that you are paying attention to what they say. You are also asking for clarity. This helps the child reflect, or revise and modify, if needed. For example,
   a. Child: "This car is going over the bridge." Teacher: "You are driving your car over the bridge."
   b. Child: "She took my doll." Teacher: "She took the doll when you were playing."
3. *Musing Out Loud About the Child's Feelings*: By musing about the child's feelings, you are telling the child you understand how they feel without any judgment. The child will correct you if your musing is incorrect. It will also help the child to identify their own emotions.
   a. Child: "This doll keeps crying. I don't like her crying." Teacher: "You don't like to see this doll sad and crying." Child: "She makes me angry." Teacher: "You are angry at her."

Teachers usually get uncomfortable when children express anger or use hostile words. It is important to keep in mind that children must have a safe space where they can express their anger without fear of being judged or shamed. Your downregulating and relabeling what the child says can help them express their anger appropriately, which is an important component of emotional intelligence (9). Unless the child is allowed to express their emotions freely first, they cannot later begin to reflect on their emotions, make sense of them, and control them in an appropriate way.

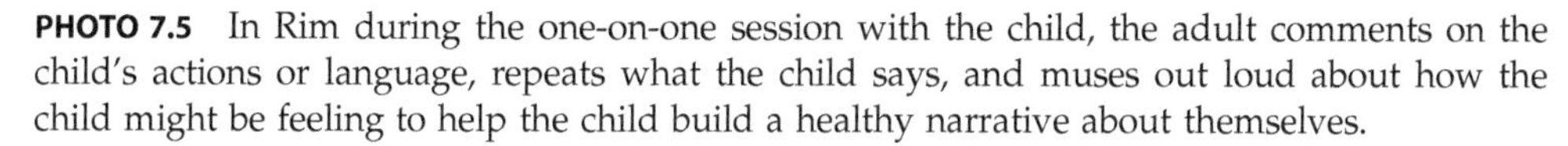

PHOTO 7.5 In Rim during the one-on-one session with the child, the adult comments on the child's actions or language, repeats what the child says, and muses out loud about how the child might be feeling to help the child build a healthy narrative about themselves.

Similarly, teachers have a strong stance against children playacting aggressive themes, and for good reasons. Thanks to the increasing incidence of violence and mass shootings in the community and schools, play themes of aggression, guns, and weapons provoke strong emotions on many sides. We believe, however, it is okay for children to playact aggressive themes with toys and materials as long as they respect the safety rules—that is, to keep themselves, others, and the materials safe. When and if the child breaks any of the rules, for example by throwing the toys, you should end the session immediately as we suggest in the guidelines. There are certain materials that also help playact aggression safely. For example, beanbags and cushions are good materials for children to punch and play out their anger and aggressions. You can say something like, "I see you are angry. You can hit the cushion to show me your anger."

Children will not need to resort to aggression when they have a safe place in which they can explore their negative emotions and playact socially inappropriate behaviors under the guidance of an adult. In most children, like Xavier, once we form a positive relationship with them and help them explore and understand their own thoughts and emotions, they are capable of finding appropriate solutions and replace their maladaptive behaviors with adaptive ones. Once Xavier's teachers understood some sources of his unsettling behaviors, they were able to form positive and enduring relationships with him through play sessions, limit setting, positively reinforcing his appropriate behaviors through attention and praise, and targeted social-emotional lessons. As soon as they understood some issues within his home environment, the teachers gave him access to nourishing food as soon as he arrived so as to alleviate his hunger, which he was not able to articulate prior to the one-on-one sessions. Xavier graduated from kindergarten successfully, having received the "Classroom Leader" award of the year from his school.

Concluding Remarks

We are aware of the difficulties some children with mental and behavioral health issues create in the classroom environment. Teachers have a lot to contend with in a typical school day. They are often tired, stressed, and discouraged. We understand some teachers face repeated failures in whatever techniques they use with these children. We are also aware there are many elements in a child's life that contribute to a child's emotional and behavioral difficulties in a classroom, such as issues at home and community environments, that are outside of teachers' hands. We, however, believe children should be viewed separately from the issues and problems they deal with. Whether they have a developmental or mental disorder or come from stressful and traumatic home backgrounds, children are not the same as their disorders or their problems. They are children. We believe a respect for the personhood of a child begins with our willingness to get down to that child's level and begin to see the world from their eyes. We believe we can do that through listening to them, seeing them, feeling their feelings, and connecting with them at a common human level during one-on-one sessions.

References

1. Park, N., & Peterson, C. (2006). Character strengths and happiness among young children: Content analysis of parental descriptions. *Journal of Happiness Studies*, 7(3), 323–341. https://doi.org/10.1007/s10902-005-3648-6
2. Seligman, M., & Adler, A. (2018). *Positive education*. Retrieved from www.researchgate.net/publication/323399593_Positive_Education
3. Seligman, M. E. P. (2007). *The optimistic child: A proven program to safeguard children against depression and build lifelong resilience*. Boston, NY: Houghton Mifflin Company.

4. Waugh, C. E., & Fredrickson, B. L. (2006). Nice to know you: Positive emotions, self-other overlap, and complex understanding in the formation of a new relationship. *Journal of Positive Psychology, 1*(2), 93–106. https://doi.org/10.1080/17439760500510569
5. Fredrickson, B. (2013). *Love 2.0: How our supreme emotions affects everything we feel, think, do, and become*. New York, NY: Hudson Street Press.
6. Cozolino, L. (2016). *Why therapy works: Using our minds to change our brain*. New York, NY: Norton.
7. Fredrickson, B. (2013). Positive emotions broaden and build. In P. Devine & A. Plant (Eds.). *Advances in experimental social psychology* (Vol. 47), pp. 1–53. Burlington, NJ: Academic Press.
8. Zeidner, M., Mathews, G., & Roberts, R. D. (2012). The emotional intelligence, health, and well-being nexus: What have we learned and what have we missed? *Applied Psychology: Health and Well-being, 4*(1), 1–30. https://doi.org/10.1177/1754073916650494
9. Mayer, J. D., & Salovery, P. (1997). What is emotional intelligence?. In P. Salovey and D. Sluyter (Eds.), *Emotional development and emotional intelligence: Educational implications* (pp. 3–31). New York, NY: Basic Books.
10. Landreth, G. L. (2012). *Play therapy: The art of relationships* (3rd ed.). New York, NY: Routledge.

8

RIM: Behavior, Body-Mind Health, and the Strengths of Character

PHOTO 8.1

In this final chapter, we articulate the remaining elements of the Resilience-based Interaction Model (RIM). Here, our focus is on our daily interactions with children, the way we encourage them, and the messages we give them, all of which can promote positive work habits and character strengths. In our concluding remarks, we will briefly look back at the major points we made throughout this book about development and resilience and our role as teachers in promoting their wellbeing and well-doing.

As a reminder, Figure 8.1 presents the RIM diagram with the concepts we will discuss in this chapter.

FIGURE 8.1 RIM diagram with principles governing individual and group activities

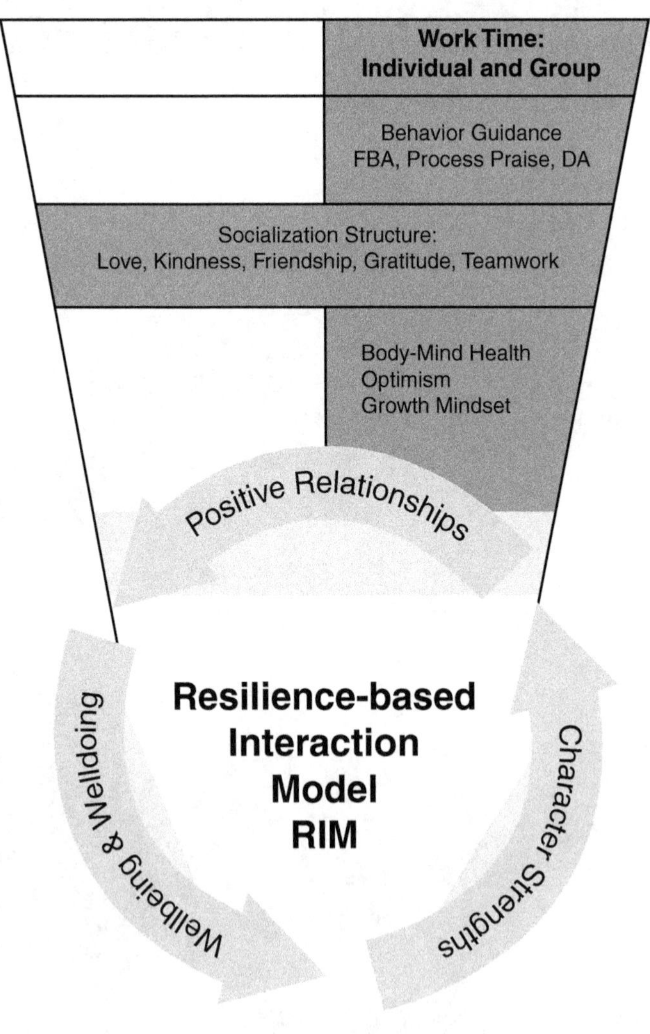

The Other Side of RIM: Children's Work in Individual and Group Activities

Children spend the majority of their time in small and large group learning activities. With the exception of individualized lessons in special education, most lessons teachers deliver in early childhood and beyond are designed for small and large group activities.

Group lessons—whether in a structured, teacher-directed format, or in an unstructured, free-play or activity format—should, in an ideal world, incorporate activities that allow for teamwork and cooperation, as well as opportunities for conflicts and resolution. This is, in fact, far from reality. In early childhood classrooms, there are few group lessons or projects designed intentionally for children to complete with partners or in collaboration with one another. Children are simply left to play alongside each other. This is where children who have self-regulatory and/or developmental and mental health issues usually fall apart and have a hard time functioning adaptively. The alarming statistics about the rate of expulsions in preschools, which we presented in Chapter 1, is a strong indication that the typical classroom environment in early childhood programs is not conducive to the well-functioning and appropriate socialization of children, particularly those with developmental and social-emotional vulnerabilities.

In recent years, most early childhood teachers and special educators have become adept in modifying the environment for children who have sensory and regulatory issues. Creating a "cozy corner" or a "calm center" is one common modification. Children who lose self-regulation are guided to go to this area as teachers model deep, calm breathing. Sensory vests, wrist weights, seat gels, and stress balls are common materials teachers give to children with tactile sensory issues during large group activities. Sound muffling headphones are also useful and effective for children with ASD who have auditory and sound sensitivity; it allows them to participate in many group activities they would otherwise find sensory offensive. These types of modifications are necessary and should be a given for every classroom, not just to special education classrooms. However, they are not always sufficient to address the maladaptive behaviors of many children. In the following section, we will discuss our approach for behavior guidance in including the remaining principles related to the daily work the classroom.

PHOTO 8.2 Children not only develop skills necessary for self-control and socialization, but values of democracy and citizenship through participating in group learning activities.

Behavior Guidance

Our approach to behavior guidance is first and foremost grounded in building a positive relationship with the child who shows maladaptive behaviors. As we've discussed, we do that through regular one-on-one sessions. In most cases, relationship building with individual children is extremely effective in changing any existing negative dynamics and alleviating the child's anxiety and many of their maladaptive behaviors. In some children, however, relationship building alone may not be sufficient. For these children, in addition to one-on-one time, it may be necessary to also use a behavioral approach that includes conducting a *functional behavior analysis* (FBA). Conducting an FBA is necessary in order to understand why the child resorts to the maladaptive behaviors and what should be done to help them replace these behaviors with adaptive ones.

Our behavior guidance approach and procedure for addressing aggressive behaviors, along with other strategies like praise and differential attention (DA), have been described in detail in *Addressing Challenging Behaviors and Mental Health Issues in Early Childhood* (1) Therefore, we will not go into too many details; rather, we'll briefly describe these procedures in the next sections.

Functional Behavior Analysis (FBA)

Depicted in the right hand-side panel of our RIM diagram in Figure 8.2 are the principles we have borrowed from Applied Behavior Analysis (ABA) to help children form adaptive behaviors. These are FBA, praise, and DA. When and if appropriate, we use an FBA to assess where, when,

FIGURE 8.2 Behavior Guidance Principles in RIM: These include conducting functional behavior assessment, and appropriate use of differential attention and praise to change maladaptive behaviors

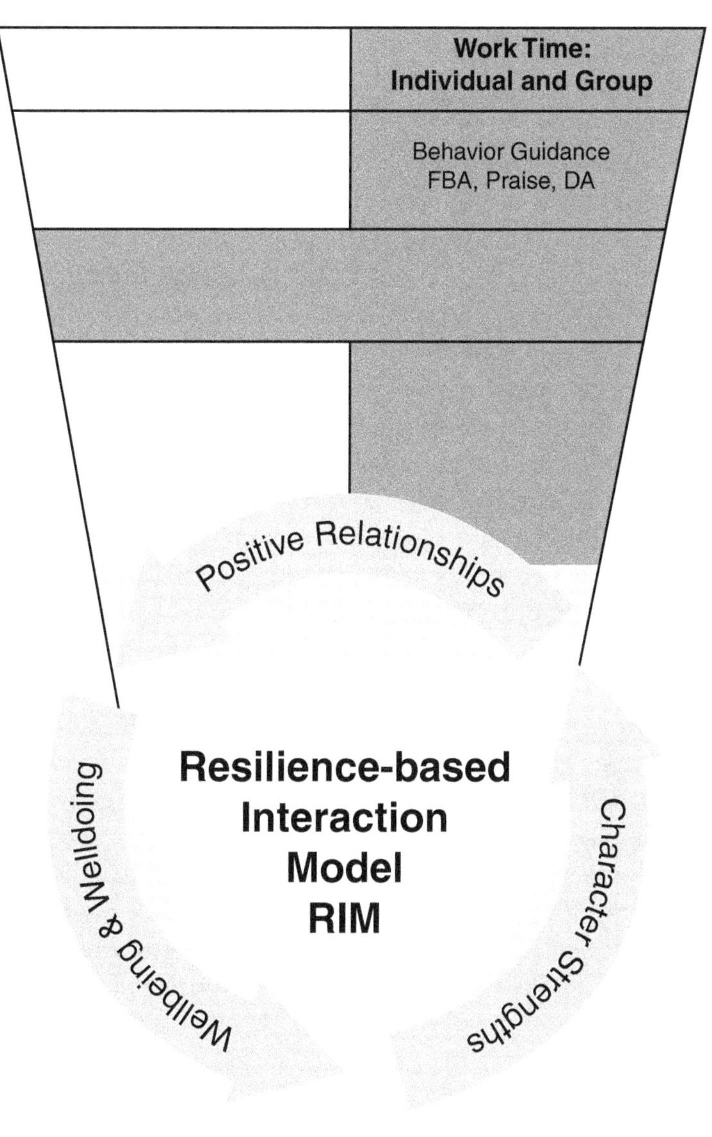

and under what circumstances a child resorts to a maladaptive behavior (2). We also pay special attention to what is happening in the environment and how teachers and peers respond to a child's maladaptive and challenging behaviors, which directly or indirectly contributes to maintaining those behaviors. We use simple *ABC* (*Antecedent, Behavior, Consequence*) note-taking on these occasions. This will help us assess the function of the child's behavior—that is, we identify for what purpose the child resorts to maladaptive behaviors and what function(s) that specific behavior serve(s) for the child.

Almost all special education professionals and teachers have strong backgrounds in behavioral methods. They are very adept in taking observational ABC notes and assessing the functions of a child's maladaptive behaviors. Unfortunately, general early childhood educators are not typically trained in behavioral methods and often have a hard time correctly observing and isolating circumstances before and after a behavioral episode. To our knowledge, very few early childhood teacher preparation university programs include training in basic FBA, which is necessary for all teachers to identify the purposes behind a child's maladaptive behaviors. These simple principles should be part of basic skill training for all teachers.

Taking good ABC data requires that teachers observe everything occurring before and after a maladaptive behavior episode (e.g. aggressive behavior, temper tantrums) and record them in a simple table format. In ABC data, *A* stands for antecedents, anything that happens before the child resorts a challenging behavior, which includes anything the teacher or peers say and do, the schedule of the day, the overall noise level and sensory stimulation in the classroom, the activity or type of materials presented, or something said to the child. Antecedents are not straight-forward to figure out and require several careful observations of the visible or removed environmental circumstances that could trigger a behavior. In the language of positive behavior support, antecedents are referred to as the *setting events* in order to include all sorts of occurrences in the environment. *B* stands for behavior, what the child does or says (in our case, the challenging behavior). Behaviors that are recorded should be observable and concrete. A good rule of thumb is to put down exactly what the child says or does, not what intention we think were behind the child's action. *C* stands for consequence, what the adults (and peers) do in response to, and as a result of, the child's behavior. This includes any disciplinary procedures, teacher's redirections, and verbal reprimands, as well as what other kids in the environment do in reaction to the child's behaviors.

After a series of ABC data taking, we should be able to see a pattern in the child's behavior, with a direct link to specific antecedents and consequences that are similar and, in many cases, repeated. Usually, the child resorts to specific maladaptive behaviors under similar circumstances (antecedents) and similar consequences. Understanding antecedents are often the key to the reasons behind a child's behavior.

If you recall Xavier from the last chapter, the most important antecedent for his behaviors (issues surrounding hunger and eating) was not apparent in his daily aggressive episodes. After the play session, the coach and the teachers met with Xavier's grandmother. They found out Xavier's father was in prison and his mother had left him in the care of his grandmother, who was also raising six other cousins of different ages. Conflicts around mealtime was a common occurrence in this home, with Xavier getting punished by his older cousins for being a "bad boy" and therefore not getting the food he wanted. His teachers didn't help matters with consequences they enforced, which were highly punitive and had no teaching value: constantly reprimanding, shaming, putting Xavier in timeouts, and referring to him as a "child with behavior problems."

Good ABC data taking (along with our one-on-one sessions with the child) should help us determine the correct function of the child's behavior—what the behavior does for the child. Behaviorists believe maladaptive behaviors usually serve three possible functions for the person:

1. The child gains something they desire; this could be an activity, food, a sensory input, or (more importantly) attention from adults (and even peers);
2. The child gets to escape from something they don't like; this could be a disliked learning activity, action, object or sensory input, or a person; and/or
3. The child receives an automatic sensory input—pleasure. This usually concerns behaviors that in and of themselves are reinforcing to the child, behaviors which feel good to do without necessarily resulting in any additional gains. For example, self-stimulatory behaviors, like hand flapping, or other similar actions, like doodling on a paper or tapping a pen on the table, are automatically reinforcing behaviors.

PHOTO 8.3 Conducting an FBA is necessary to appropriately understand the functions of a child's maladaptive behavior and design a plan that addresses them.

A typical behavioral intervention plan in schools today usually consists of using positive reinforcers (activities and things the child likes) that are given only when the child is prompted and resorts to an appropriate behavior instead of a previous maladaptive behavior. Many schools also use strategies like restraint and timeouts (previously discussed in Chapter 2) when maladaptive behaviors occur to eliminate aggressive behaviors harmful to the child themselves or others in the environment.

As previously discussed, we do not believe in nor use restraints or any other punishing methods to stop a child's maladaptive behaviors. We don't think restraining or giving electric shocks to children is effective in the long run. On the contrary, as we explained (Chapters 2, 3, 4), based on research, restraint can only create helplessness and anger. We cannot say this enough: Even if restraint doesn't result in any physical harm, it is, without any doubt, emotionally abusive and harmful to the child.

We use a specific procedure for addressing challenging behaviors like self-harm or aggression toward others. Basically, it consists of guiding the child to a quiet and calm area, free from equipment and materials. While children are in such a state of dysregulation, we stay nearby without engaging with the child or touching them, nor do we have a conversation with the child or lecture them about their behavior and its consequences. This is counterproductive, gives the child attention for aggression, and is useless when the child is in such a state of anxiety and escalation. We don't give direct eye contact or make any gestures. We simply stand by to make sure the child is safe and others around do not come nearby. Once the child shows signs of de-escalation, we signal to the child by holding our hands up with five fingers spread, asking the child in a low tone and calm voice to count to ten and take very deep breaths while ticking our fingers as a visual reminder and model taking deep breaths. Because in our RIM approach we regularly exercise meditation, deep breathing, and calming activities with children throughout the day, children typically have learned and practiced calm breathing exercises and know what these signals mean. When teachers use this approach to aggression, children gradually learn ways to calm themselves when they get angry, frustrated, and anxious.

In our work with teachers and children, we repeatedly find after regular body-mind practices, children learn very quickly to calm themselves at times which they lose self-control and regulation. We also find children who are normally prone to tantrums and loss of self-regulation no longer or very infrequently have those episodes of anger and aggression. We'll discuss body-mind activities in more detail later in this chapter.

Differential Attention for Attention-Seeking Behaviors

Most inappropriate and challenging behaviors have an attention-seeking function in addition to other reasons that may underlie them. This is particularly the case for young children. Adults' attention and regard for young children is a powerful reward (positive reinforcer), even if that attention is negative, like reprimands, negations, or yelling. Examples of typical attention-seeking behaviors are speaking out of turn, disrupting the class, whining, crying, throwing temper tantrums, or being oppositional. These behaviors are generally more annoying than they are harmful. Interestingly enough, they turn out to be the hardest things for teachers to ignore, particularly when a teacher is stressed or tired. However, ignoring a child at times of attention seeking is actually the best deterrent. When done consistently, the child learns, "This is not the way to get the teacher's attention."

The term differential attention (DA) is modified terminology, taken from Differential Reinforcement of Other Behaviors (DRO), a technique in ABA. In DRO, a behaviorist only reinforces an appropriate response or behavior and applies extinction to any undesirable response. In RIM's version, DA is a strategy we use to only address attention-seeking behaviors. DA consists of ignoring a child's inappropriate behavior consistently and without fail, no matter how insistent the child is in their maladaptive behaviors. Once the behavior stops, we immediately turn our attention back to the child; for example, we acknowledge the child and their appropriate behaviors (for details see Ref. 1). We use DA only for harmless, non-aggressive, and persistent inappropriate behaviors. It's a very effective strategy if and when used consistently. Inconsistency in using DA only teaches the child to persist longer in their maladaptive behaviors, because they know at some point, the adult will give in and pay attention to them.

Socialization Structure of the Classroom

In Ms. Lisa's Toddler Room, there are six children from twenty-two to forty-one months old. Ms. Lisa sets clear limits in a firm tone, so the children know what to expect. It makes them feel safe. During a surprise fire drill, she had six rambunctious toddlers swiftly out the door and quietly sitting in a row outside. I feel in awe of her quiet authority.

Yet, after a few days, I sense there is something missing in this room. Austen, twenty-two months old, picks up a block and puts it on the stack Kylin, twenty-five months old, has built. But Kylin doesn't want to play this game; he takes Austen's block off. Austen seems confused; Kylin won't let him touch any blocks, so Austen wanders away to play alone. When Harley, twenty-five months, practices walking along a board like a balance beam, Jordan, the oldest, decides she wants to try this, too. But Harley wants the board to herself and pushes Jordan off. Jordan squawks and pushes back. They are quickly pulled apart to play on opposite sides of the room. Both cry and are told, "You're OK!"

Watching, I wish Ms. Lisa had helped Austen and Kylin learn to stack the blocks together, or helped Jordan and Harley learn to take turns. Perhaps their tears should not have been so quickly dismissed. Ms. Lisa wants the kids to be self-directed; she doesn't want conflicts in the room. Independent toddlers keep the room calm and require less teacher intervention.

> What I miss in Ms. Lisa's room is the sound of children giggling at silly games or impromptu dances together. I miss hearing words like "helping," "our friends," or "Do you feel sad?" Ms. Lisa knows how to control the room. But I miss the messy, joyful moments when toddlers are learning the tricky skills of sharing and the simple words of kindness.
>
> —Julie Parson Nesbitt, Graduate Intern

Having a structure in place to promote socialization and strengths of character is at the heart of the RIM model (Figure 8.1). Many early childhood teachers are afraid of putting structures in place which are conducive to children's interactions and teamwork. Teaching appropriate social skills is only possible when children have opportunities to intermingle, cooperate, and collaborate with one another and in teams. Despite common misperception, creating such a structure is not just about designing learning centers or organizing materials and equipment in a particular way. It is rather about designing learning activities and lessons to promote teamwork and opportunities for socialization. A well-structured classroom is one which is full of engaging, relevant, meaningful, and practical learning activities, with a balance of independent activities as well as those which requires collaboration and partnership in both small and large groups.

For younger children like toddlers and early preschoolers, these learning activities and lessons usually target early social cognitive skills like togetherness, emotional regulation, turn taking, sharing, and working alongside one another with regular interactions. In older preschoolers, kindergartners, and primary grade students, lessons and learning activities should require them to learn to lead and follow, cooperate and collaborate, divide and share, and complete assignments and projects together.

What often works against this type of social structure is a teacher's misconception and, in some cases, fear of losing control of the classroom and its management if they allow too much freedom of movement and intermingling during structured lessons. Some teachers believe a social classroom equals chaos and disorder, while a structured classroom equals a well-managed, quiet, and strictly controlled environment.

There are similar attitudinal patterns in most special education classrooms, particularly in classrooms designed for children with ASD. In most self-contained classrooms, except for meal or snack times, children are barely engaged in any activities which require them to work in team formats. It is far easier for many teachers to work with individual children than to teach and assist them to work with each other.

One evening, over dinner at our house with our friend Donna, my husband and I shared with her how our son had enthusiastically followed a visual, step-by-step set of instructions for a woodworking project. Together with my husband, my son had successfully built a beautiful wooden fruit bowl, which he was very proud of. Donna is an occupational therapist (OT) working in public schools with different groups of six- and seven-year-olds in self-contained special education and inclusion classrooms. Most kids she works with have ASD, but she also works with kids with other developmental disorders.

That evening, my husband enthusiastically shared how he had designed visual instructions using an engineering software, which could be used to design other learning activities/projects for children of various abilities. We shared with Donna our thoughts on mundane, repetitious, unchallenging, and boring learning activities that most children seem to be doing in special education classrooms. Our belief was when learning activities are interesting, relatable, meaningful, engaging, practical, and sufficiently challenging, even children who are deemed to be "low functioning" rise up to the occasion and show their true potential.

Being an innovative and enthusiastic professional, Donna was inspired by our woodworking conversation. She showed up in her school the next week having purchased some basic woodworking materials (wood, nails, saw, hand tools, paint, etc.) to work with children on her caseload. She had reasoned many of the fine motor goals she had written in their IEPs should be easily achievable through activities required for completing a woodworking project. Her colleagues and the school principals in which she worked were skeptical and even alarmed at first, but Donna managed to convince them the activities she took to classrooms would be safe, and she would target every kid's fine motor IEP goals with her lesson plans and activities.

Within a short period, Donna's woodworking project got expanded. Under her supervision, her students, in collaboration with one another, completed several interesting projects, such a dog house for a teacher's dog, several dog feeders for a greyhound dog breeder, and wood planters as Mother's Day presents. Children learned to work as a group, cooperating and collaborating with one another, making decisions about what projects they wanted to do next, and how and with what specifications they wanted their products to be completed. Most of these children are considered to have "behavior problems," are "hard to work with," or are considered "low-functioning."

—MB

Healthy socialization can be taught and learned, along with values necessary for success in our communities, such as working together, resolving conflicts, problem solving, and working towards a common goal. It is in this context that we have an opportunity to teach other character strengths—e.g. love, kindness, friendship, teamwork, etc.

FIGURE 8.3 RIM Socialization Structure: Important strengths of character can be promoted and taught through group activities

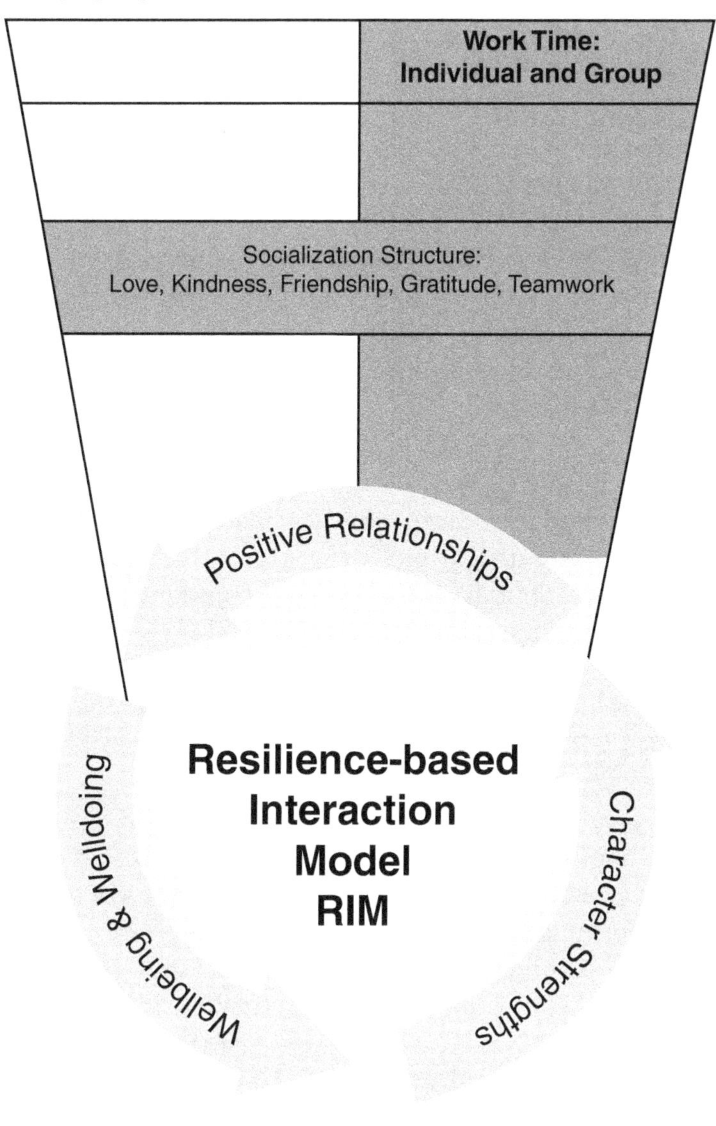

Character Strengths of Love and Kindness

Love, kindness, and social intelligence are the strengths of character that fall under the virtue category of humanity, based on the classification of character strengths (3). These three strengths are related to interpersonal development and relationships between and among individuals. The character strength of love includes parent-child attachment and love, compassionate and altruistic love, companionable love between friends, and romantic love (4).

The strength of *love*, the capacity to love and be loved, should be present and visible in children from toddlerhood. The development of this strength depends on the quality of the attachment formed between that child and their caregivers. In the absence of a secure attachment, there are usually problems with development of this capacity. Love is one of the strongest strengths that has the emotional capability to move individuals in an upward spiral (discussed in Chapter 6).

In our RIM approach, our efforts to help children develop and strengthen this character are through one-on-one positive relationship building between (Chapter 7), as well as through encouraging kindness, friendships, and teamwork among and between children. Friendship formation is particularly important and can easily be cultivated among children through targeted social activities. For example:

- At the beginning of the year, do a "getting to know you," activity. Have each child introduce and say something about themselves (e.g., what they like to do, eat, etc.).
- Read stories about friendships. Have students talk about what a "friend" is and does.
- Have students roleplay scenarios of friendship. For example, "How does a friend respond" when a friend shares happy and exciting news versus sharing sad news, or "How do friends help one another?"

Kindness is another strength dependent on the formation of a secure attachment between a child with a caregiver and should be present by age two. It's the belief that others are worthy of attention for being themselves and not based on responsibility or duty (4). The strength of kindness has three other characteristics embedded within: having empathy and sympathy, moral reasoning abilities, and a strong sense of social responsibility (4). Kind individuals are caring, helpful, and friendly. They are apt to err toward caring than not. Examples of activities with kids are:

- Have a large group discussion with children about kindness. Read a story about kindness with children.
- Have students come up with examples of "acts of kindness." Have groups of two roleplay with each other a scenario of an "act of kindness" for the whole class.
- Have students come up with "kind" and "kinder" words, and then use them with each other throughout the day.

Teamwork, a Strength of Character Important for Socialization and Citizenship

In the classification of character strengths, the strength of *teamwork* belongs to the virtue category of justice (3). This character strength contributes to fairness in judgment and improves interactions between the person and their community or group. Teamwork depends on the development of the cognitive concepts of citizenship: responsibility toward a person's community; loyalty, trust of the group, and patriotism; and loyalty toward one's home without animosity against another (4). This character strength begins to emerge around three to five years of age. Its cultivation occurs best through team projects, group games, and fun races among children starting in preschool.

One good example for building teamwork skills is the *marshmallow challenge*, developed by Peter Skillman, a creative software and engineering product designer. To gauge the teamwork abilities in individuals, Skillman has different teams of four individuals build a tower in eighteen minutes, using only twenty strands of spaghetti, one yard of string, one yard of rope, and one marshmallow. The goal for each team is to build the tallest structure with the marshmallow on top. Skillman has tested this experiment with hundreds of different groups of people around the world, including engineers, technological designers, architects, business people, and CEOs. He's found kindergartners have the best performing teams. They consistently have the highest average score on every objective measure (5). This experiment is the best example for what we discussed earlier: Early childhood classrooms are the best places for doing project-based lessons and learning activities.

- Try the marshmallow challenge in your class in teams of four in the fall. Have students do this same challenge three months later to see how they have improved their skills.

The Importance of Cultivating Gratitude in Ourselves and in Children

Robert Emmons from the University of California, Davis has done extensive work on the concept of gratitude. He defines it is as a cognitive-affective state that occurs when an individual has received personal benefit that was not intentionally sought after, deserved, or earned, but rather received because of the good intensions of another person (6). Studies on this topic link gratitude to overall wellbeing, life satisfaction, decreased depression, positive emotions and affect, low level of stress, and strong interpersonal relationships (7–14). In school research, gratitude is linked to principals' and teachers' job satisfaction, work wellbeing, and reduced burnouts (7, 8).

Feelings of gratitude require higher cognitive functioning that has not yet emerged in early childhood (three- to eight-year-old children) (10). Even though young children learn basic appreciation manners like saying "thank you" early on, it does not indicate that they understand or feel gratitude. Feelings of gratitude are grounded in two essential information processing abilities: 1) an affirmation of goodness or "good things" in a person's life, and 2) recognizing the sources of goodness lie at least partially outside of the self (12). Gratitude is also a state related to spirituality and transcendence, and its quality is recognized in almost every religious and spiritual tradition. Therefore, gratitude requires advanced cognitive and processing abilities which emerge later in childhood and through adolescence (12, 13).

Studies show cultivating gratitude has inevitable psychological benefits (10, 12, 13). Because gratitude always occurs in relationship to an "another," its healing power occurs in response to being esteemed and affirmed by someone else, which leads to expression of love and tenderness toward them (12, 13). Psychological healing effects therefore happen when we feel recognized, affirmed, and esteemed, which in turn helps us do something (albeit an adaptive behavior) which we might have otherwise been reluctant or anxious to do before (10, 12).

We believe cultivating gratitude in ourselves and children is important and should be a value in the classroom community. In RIM, gratitude is one of the character strengths we encourage teachers and students to cultivate through simple exercises during the day. In young children, these emerging feelings can be cultivated through helping them become aware of and acknowledge positive events or things that exist around them, such as remembering the positive events of the day, appreciating the beauty and goodness in nature, and becoming aware of kind acts. Many of children we work with come from adverse conditions, in which daily stressors make it difficult for them to be aware of any good event they might encounter. We think there should be hundreds of emotionally positive experiences in a classroom, and we can encourage children to become aware of these events and acknowledge them. Gratitude exercises with children not only help us recognize and appreciate positivity in our own daily lives, but prime children to develop gratitude. Some examples include:

- Describe the concepts of thankfulness, appreciation, and gratitude to children, and read stories about these concepts with children.

- In the morning, have kids sit in a large circle and share with them one to three good things that happened to you or went well for you yesterday or this morning that you are grateful for. Have each child describe one to three good things that happened to them either yesterday or this morning.
- Take children on a nature walk. Have them stop, look around, and find something in the nature that they really like. Have them savor the experience—smell a flower, take a deep breath and enjoy the fresh air, look and appreciate a beautiful tree.
- Have children either dictate to you or write a thank you card to someone they want to thank for something nice that person did for them.

Encouraging the Development of a Growth Mindset in Children

As depicted in our diagram, optimism and growth mindsets are two other characteristics we focus on in RIM. Because teaching these strengths are most productive during individual and small group lesson planning, we address them during targeted small group and/or individually designed lessons. We have at length described (Chapter 4) why optimism is a resilience factor and how it contributes to the prevention of depression and helplessness and the promotion of grit and perseverance. Optimism and a growth mindset are closely related to one another. But, first, what is a growth mindset?

The valuable work of Carol Dweck at Stanford University has popularized the concept of a growth mindset in education. Since the 1970s, Dweck has studied motivation for learning in children, including helplessness and mindsets (14–18). Her studies have resulted in the articulation of two concepts: *fixed* versus *growth mindsets*. Growth mindset is now a buzzword, and many schools and educators use it to describe their curricular goals and daily work with children. Let's look at some important findings relevant to our discussion here.

Dweck did some of her earlier work with young children (14, 15). She found most young children in preschool and kindergarten didn't much care when they made a mistake, but they did care when adults criticized their mistakes. In instances of an adult's criticism, many children showed aspects of helpless reactions. These children said things like they felt they were "bad," and they failed to or said they "could not" correct their mistakes, even when the solution was obvious. Dweck and her colleagues also found many young children believed badness was a fixed trait (14–18). It is important to consider here that these conditions occurred only when adults criticized children.

Later work by Dweck on older school-aged children showed when children were praised for their intelligence or other attributes, it created a fixed mindset in them about themselves. When faced with any difficulties, these kids couldn't handle them and showed a helpless reaction. They, of course, loved to be praised, but they also learned that their ability (intelligence) was fixed: "I am smart, so I should be able to solve this problem." They had a *fixed mindset*. Dweck and her team gave these children several math problems that were slightly harder than what they were typically used to. They found that as soon as they hit upon hard problems—where solutions were not obvious to them—their fixed mindset turned on them and they stopped even trying to find the solution: "I can't solve this problem because I am not smart enough." In later studies, a number of older children with a fixed mindset, when asked, told adults they would do anything to get the right answer and win, even if it meant cheating (17–20).

Dweck and her team gave the same more difficult math problems to a second group of children who were praised differently: "You are working so hard," "You tried so many different ways to solve this problem." This group had a different mindset and hence a totally different reaction. When they faced with problems, they tried different solutions and persevered until they finally got the right answer. In other words, when children were praised for the process of their work, their effort, and their perseverance, they showed a mastery reaction to an obstacle. Dweck concluded that when children are praised for their perseverance, they learn to think that their intelligence can be developed (a growth mindset) (17–20).

It should be obvious how a growth mindset (having a flexible way of thinking about our intelligence) and optimism are related to one another: Having a growth mindset means we can control the growth of our intelligence and learning, and being optimistic means we can take purposeful action to

PHOTO 8.4 In a fixed mindset, the individual believes their intelligence cannot be changed. In a growth mindset, the individual believes with perseverance and work, their abilities and intelligence can grow.

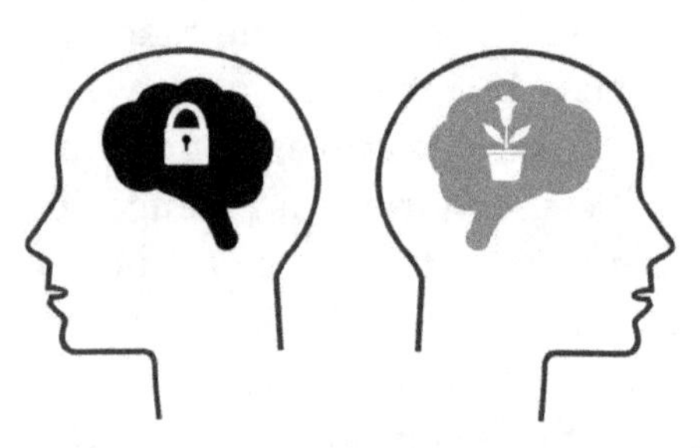

control what we can in bad events. Optimism includes our mindsets (explaining to ourselves that our capabilities can grow), and it also includes how positively we explain events in relationship to ourselves. Optimism and a growth mindset are both the opposite of helplessness. Like optimism, a growth mindset can be taught and learned.

The reason we promote these in early childhood through RIM is first to prevent helplessness and other internalizing emotional issues that are present or may arise later, like anxiety and lack of self-worth, by giving children simple cognitive tools to use. Second, both growth mindsets and optimism are foundations for building more advanced cognitive-based and emotion-based character strengths that children need for wellbeing and well-doing. For example, having a growth mindset promotes perseverance and brevity, which are needed for goal setting and accomplishment (an important element of wellbeing, as we discussed in Chapter 6). Optimism underlies hope and other positive emotions and is connected to gratitude, kindness, and love.

Both optimism and growth mindsets can be taught to children through ways we use our praise, respond to children's questions, and give them feedback about their work: "You are almost there," "Try a different solution," "It's not done yet; let's see what else you can do to make it better." What we say to children and how we say it to them is important. All character strengths we want to inculcate in children can also be explicitly taught through storybooks, activities, games, roleplay, and simple lessons are embed in their typical curriculum. Positive messages of optimism, growth, hope, gratitude, love, kindness, and the like are not hard to give when we modify our language and responses.

Teaching children the science behind intelligence is also important. There are hundreds of good books in young children's literature about brain elasticity, how neurons connect, and how learning can improve our intelligence and talents. Lesson plans for early childhood grade levels (preschool-3rd grade) about character strengths and how the brain works are available online through hundreds of educational organization and teacher preparation universities.

A couple of additional things about promoting a growth mindset: Although it's important, teaching children a growth mindset is not just about encouraging and praising their efforts. For many children, particularly those who have developmental and learning disorders, making repeated efforts when they get stuck in a problem doesn't necessarily end in their finding a solution or in improved/newly learned skills. Many teachers of young children are, in fact, very good at praising or rewarding a child's effort. It is common to give children stars and certificates for "good effort." We might want to be careful about exactly when and how often we dispense this kind of rewards. Think about this question: Does it make sense to constantly reward a child's effort, when, in fact, that child has not demonstrated improvement? We think not! You can, however, praise and reward efforts when there are signs of progress.

In situations where a child has a learning or developmental issue, it is absolutely necessary that, along with encouragements, the teacher actually steps in to give feedback, show different strategies to try, and provide prompts and scaffolding in novel ways so the child learns the actual process of discovering new strategies via their efforts. Often, we have seen the opposite. When students fail, the teachers may say something like, "He's just lazy," "He knows the answer but is not trying hard enough," or "He's not putting effort into it." We've even heard a modern version: "He has a fixed mindset." We ought to be careful not to get into the trap of banning a fixed mindset versus a growth mindset or using every new buzzword as an explanation for why some children "can't learn". The truth is that we work with children with all kinds of developmental needs, learning abilities, and mindsets. In fact, most children have a mix of growth and fixed mindsets; so do we as adults. We can work on ourselves and children to improve our ways of thinking—for growth, perseverance and grit, mastery, and optimism.

Right Ways of Praising Kids

There are three right ways we can praise children. First is process praise, which is praising hard work: "I see how hard you've been working," "Good work finding a new way," or "This is good, but not yet complete. Let's see if we can try it a different way." This is the type of praise we should give children during work time—independent or cooperating team work—including academic or daily living and adaptive skill tasks (e.g. tying shoes or getting dressed). Process praise in young children should be paired with good teaching and be used to promote persistence and mastery.

Another form of praise is used to encourage more adaptive behaviors. In this type of praise, we praise the exact behaviors we want *for* the child to have: "I like the way you're sitting so quietly," "I see you're working hard to calm yourself down," and "Good job following rules so nicely." When children are praised and receive positive attention for behaviors that are sanctioned, they feel good about themselves and learn to cultivate those behaviors in themselves.

The third kind of praise we like to encourage is praising the child for demonstrating universally valued character strengths. Looking at Figure 8.1, we can see these values in the middle section of our RIM diagram. These are early character strengths that emerge in toddler years and become firm in the subsequent two to three years. They are also values that surround democracy, citizenship, and healthy socializations among children. These are love, kindness, friendship, and teamwork. To promote these characteristics, we praise children in an appreciative way when they demonstrate them: "I appreciate the way you took turns and shared this toy with your friend," "I am proud of you for helping your friend get up when he fell down," "Thank you for telling the truth," or "Excellent job cooperating so nicely to complete this tower."

Despite teachers' perceptions of their own frequency of praising children, in reality, teachers actually do not praise children enough. As part of our research with teachers, we ask them to record how many times they appropriately praise children. This data has almost always showed us that in reality, teachers either do not praise children at all, or do it the wrong way (e.g. "Good job," "Excellent," "Awesome"). This type of praise is often ingeniousness, is meaningless because it does not tell the child what they are

PHOTO 8.5 There are three right ways to praise kids: their work process, their appropriate behaviors, and demonstration of their character strengths.

being praised for, and can actually create a fixed mindset in children. In fact, NAEYC (National Association for the Education of Young Children) bans praising children for the same reason. This ban has caused an erroneous belief in most early childhood programs that "praise is bad for kids." Let's be clear here: We do not believe praise is bad for children. Based on research evidence, we believe the right kinds of praise teach children grit, adaptive behaviors, and character strengths.

Teaching Children Realistic Optimism

Many adults (parents and teachers) are weary of the term optimism and what they think it teaches children. Optimism is not about giving children empty promises like "Everything will be well" when things go wrong. It's not about making repeated excuses for their mistakes or teaching them not to take responsibilities for their actions: "It's okay; you're only four."

Optimism requires a set of four rather advanced cognitive abilities that must be present and applied when faced with a problem (11). These abilities are not present in children between the ages of two to five years, but they are learned in early childhood and begin to emerge in elementary school years. Children learn optimism early on from how the adults around them handle and explain negative events. More importantly, optimism is taught to children when adults themselves are optimistic and show a positive explanatory style not only in what they say, but in their own behaviors. Let's look at a hypothetical situation.

Imagine you have worked really hard in your school for several years and have been an exemplary teacher. There is a newly opened leadership position in your school for which you are qualified. You apply for it and get an interview with your school principal for the position. There are also other applicants, including another teacher from your school, who also gets an interview along with a couple of others. The person who gets the position is the other teacher from your school.

If you are a pessimistic thinker, you explain this setback with this explanatory style: "It was all my fault. I didn't work hard enough. I'm just a failure. This ruins everything. I know I can never get another promotion." You may also explain the whole thing negatively in another way, like being suspicious of other people involved, blaming them or circumstances to have conspired against you, seeing yourself as having absolutely no control in this and other upcoming job promotion opportunities. As a pessimist, you are likely to catastrophize and ruminate in this setback for a long time: "I always fail; I can never do anything right," or "Others won't let me succeed," etc.

If you are an optimist, you have four cognitive abilities. These cognitive abilities are (11):

1. *Recognizing* the thoughts that flow through your mind: "It's all my fault," or "It's all this other person's fault."
2. *Evaluating* your thoughts in a realistic way and recognizing if your thoughts are not accurate: "The way I'm thinking is not accurate or helpful."
3. *Generating a more accurate way of thinking*: "I think I did work hard, but the other person might have worked harder," or "The other person had prior experience in a leadership position."
4. *Decatastrophizing* the situation; that is, you stop ruminating about the worst-case scenario that could have happened or could happen. Instead, you direct your energies to identify what you can and cannot change in this situation next time. You think of a realistic solution and begin to take steps toward it: "I should talk to my principal to see what I could have done better, or how I can improve my skills to have a better chance if and when a similar position becomes available next time around," etc.

As we discussed in Chapter 4, optimism is an important factor of resilience. Although teaching optimistic thinking has not been researched in early childhood, it's not unreasonable to think we can teach foundations of optimism to young children not only through our own way of explaining and talking about setbacks, negative events, and failures, but also through teaching them fundamental skills. In this book, we have at length talked about all of these. As a reminder, we'll quickly summarize the skills that directly underlie optimism in children (11):

- Teaching children *mastery*. This means matching children's skills to challenges; making tasks engaging and interesting; scaffolding their learning; encouraging their efforts through feedback and appropriate praise; creating playful explorations in one-on-one and group team formats; and teaching and supporting them to have adaptive behaviors through guidance, appropriate positive attention, and praise. Mastery teaches children that they have control over their behaviors and their learning. It prevents helplessness.
- Cultivate in yourself and teach children *positivity*; share positive feelings with children like love, kindness, smiles, joys, pride, and happiness unconditionally. Praise children correctly, on their work effort, their appropriate behaviors, and demonstrations of strengths of character. Do not give empty, meaningless, and ungenuine praise.

Finally, we can teach an optimistic explanatory style through reading and telling stories, such as giving hypothetical negative situations and asking children to come up with different solutions. Creating stories for children based on specific situations for individuals or large groups is a very useful strategy. Carol Grey, a social worker in Michigan, developed social stories in 1990 as a strategy to teach children with ASD appropriate social-emotional skills. Social stories are wonderful and effective ways of teaching all children—particularly children with intellectual and developmental disorders—social-emotional skills, work skills, and strengths of character, all of which will help them be and do well in their communities.

Although many teachers write social stories for their students, in our experiences, most of them write them incorrectly or for purposes other than social-emotional skill teaching. There are also thousands of websites as well as many social story apps. Unfortunately, there are many incorrectly written stories that are not necessarily useful for social-emotional skills.

Writing a social story correctly can be tricky. It requires understanding the four types of sentences necessary for the story,[1] as well as structuring those sentences correctly. Carol Grey's website provides the history of social story development and has valuable resources, such as sample social stories for educators.[2] Social stories can be illustrated by using the child's picture, line-drawing pictures, or using images from the internet.

Illustrated social stories can be used with any one or more of these four goals in mind:

1. to describe an important and advanced concept, a social or emotional event/skills, or a situation that is typically stress- producing or problematic for the child;
2. to make clear the child's own perspectives, thoughts, and emotions, and/or to make clear the perspectives, thinking, and emotions of others who are involved in a situation;
3. to clarify that the present behavior or solutions the child uses is/are not effective and to suggest specific other alternative effective solutions;
4. to give the child control of the situation by suggesting strategies to use so the child can and will use the alternative positive and productive solutions successfully.

We suggest you write social stories having these four goals in mind. You may see keeping these in mind will let you easily teach emerging as well as advanced skills, like teaching children to think differently about and explain negative events, handle stress, try different solutions, ask for help, and to keep trying when faced with setbacks.

Body-Mind Activities: Educating the Heart and Mind Together

One of the most important elements of our model is promoting body-mind health through daily exercises that involve specific physical activities as well as mindfulness, meditation, and calming exercises. We rely on the extensive and growing body of literature in these areas to argue for the necessity of physical as well as meditative practices for children on a daily basis.

There are over 49,000 research articles and policy statements published by the American Academy of Pediatrics about the benefits and necessity of regular physical exercise for children of all ages and abilities. The health benefits of regular exercise for children (and adults) are numerous: strengthening the heart, keeping arteries and veins clear, strengthening the lungs, reducing blood sugar levels, strengthening bones, preventing cancer, regulating blood pressure, improving energy levels, improving the immune system, better quality of sleep, and recovering faster from illnesses. (For research examples see Ref. 18–23.) The list goes on.

There is also an increasing number of studies since the 1990s that link physical exercise to emotional and mental health and to overall wellbeing of children and adults (across all age-groups). For example, simple movement exercises (like dancing, walking, running):

- increase levels of serotonin, dopamine, and norepinephrine in the brain, which are associated with improved mood and energy (22, 23);
- reduce the level of and help us manage stress better and relax more (22);
- prevent depression and reduce the symptoms of depression (23–27);
- prevent and reduce anxiety (25–28);
- improve mental clarity, attention, cognitive functioning, learning, judgment, insight, memory, and other executive functioning skills like self-regulation and planning (28, 29);
- reduce symptoms and treat more serious mental disorders, like panic disorder, generalized anxiety disorder, obsessive compulsive disorder, post-traumatic stress disorder, schizophrenia, and bipolar disorder (26, 27).

It is unfortunate that despite all the existing and increasing amount of scientific evidence proving the benefits of physical activities and exercise,

PHOTO 8.6 Body-mind activities include short body movement segments as well as mindfulness and meditation activities.

it's one of the last things schools, including early childhood education programs, invest time and effort in. In many states, recess time has been restricted or completely taken away in favor of academic tasks. This problem is even more compounded in special education. Children with disabilities seldom and almost never have physical education (PE) as a part of their curriculum. Adaptive PE is almost nonexistent in public schools for students with disabilities. Even in private and day schools, exercise is seldom an option or part of daily education of children with developmental disorders. To make matters worse, teachers themselves are reluctant to incorporate simple physical exercises (dancing to music or simple in-place movements) in the daily routines of their classrooms in favor of their own teaching agendas. In addition, they often don't buy the notion that all children, including children with disorders such as ADHD, ASD, and cognitive impairment, embrace physical exercise readily and with zest, especially once it occurs every day and becomes part of their daily classroom schedule. These children feel the benefits themselves and become very good at it.

In RIM, we recommend physical exercise paired with calm, relaxing, and meditative practices and done in tandem—first a short movement activity, like dancing to music, then a five-minute meditative, calming exercise. We believe pairing these together has great self-regulatory benefits, particularly for children who deal with mental and behavioral health issues. We call it *body-mind* for this reason. It should take no more than ten to fifteen minutes and should be done with the entire class. We recommend teachers implement one to two body-mind exercises throughout the school-day period—once in the morning and once toward the end of the day. We highly recommend that teachers join in and participate along with children in these exercises. This is an important part of RIM we ask teachers to consider adopting in and outside of their own work. We have seen the amazing results of this practice in classroom after classroom. Teachers are themselves incredulous about the immediate positive effect of body-mind exercises on children and themselves.

Research shows meditative practices, such as mindfulness, meditation, and yoga, have strong benefits on emotional and mental health, as well as cognitive functioning and attention of children and adults alike (30–34). Meditative practices have their roots in Eastern traditions, and they are usually attached to spiritual and transcendent practices. In the West, meditation forms have been isolated from their transcendent context. Schools and educational organizations have been particularly receptive in adopting simple meditative practices for children. Mindfulness and yoga are now quite popular in early childhood and elementary programs.

Research on meditation is relatively new, with most of it having been conducted in the last decade. There has been a certain interest on the benefits of meditation for children who have mental health issues and developmental disorders. A recent review of studies concluded that meditation (including yoga and mindfulness) is particularly effective in reducing ADHD symptoms in children (33). Meditation improves focus and attention, reduces externalizing and internalizing behaviors, reduces stress, and improves adult-child interactions and overall relationships (32–34). Effects of meditation on children who have been the subject of maltreatment and trauma has also been examined (for a review, see Ref. 35). When meditating regularly, children who have been traumatized are able to regulate their emotions better, gain confidence in their abilities, lower their stress level, reduce depression, increase positive emotions, and decrease PTSD symptoms (35, 36).

There are different kinds of meditative practices. Mindfulness is focusing on being in the present by bringing our full mind to an object: for example, focusing completely on taking in the scent of a flower while smelling it, the taste of milk (truly tasting it) while drinking it, or the sound of a wrapper when opening a box. These focus exercises are usually while the person tries to remove any overpowering emotions from their mind. Being mindful of the breath is another important exercise. This technique is important to help build awareness and be present in the moment.

PHOTO 8.7 Children can learn to do mindfulness, meditation, and yoga exercises in early childhood.

Other forms of meditation include visualization, loving kindness meditation, and other forms of contemplation. Mindfulness can be and is often recommended to be combined with visualization or contemplation. Loving kindness meditation is a guided meditation done to bring awareness and cultivate positive emotions about creation—nature, people, etc. Research shows loving kindness meditation has tangible results in increasing positive emotions (37–39). Simple loving kindness meditation can be done in classrooms with young and older children. Stanford University's Center for Compassion and Altruism Research and Education (CCRE) is a good resource for more information, like sample guided meditations and research publications. The CCRE also provides teacher training in this area.[3]

We recommend experimenting with a combination of mindful breathing and guided visualization. Once children are acclimated to simple meditative practices, loving kindness and compassionate simple meditation will be an excellent option for cultivating positive emotions and affect in children.

Guidelines for Body-Mind Activities

When we introduce body-mind activities to children, it is important that we explain the benefits of physical exercise and meditation through large group activities like reading, sharing ideas and discussions, and roleplaying.

Like adults, children always respond better when they know why they do what they do.

Any movement for children is appropriate: dancing to music, following the leader, or other energetic movements. A typical exercise should last from three to five minutes, followed by another three to five minutes of meditation. It may be easier to begin with shorter segments of body-mind activities and move to longer periods. For meditative practices, it is useful to have children first prepare for meditation by practicing thirty seconds of simple guided meditative techniques first. Here are some examples of simple meditative practices for children:

- Model breathing from the stomach and practice with children, taking deep, calming breaths. Once they have learned how to breathe for calmness, have them take deep slow breaths (while you count to ten and hold a visual sign, like holding up your fingers). Repeat this exercise frequently throughout the day.
- Point to sounds children can hear in or outside of their classroom (clock ticking, cars going by, wind rustling through the trees) and have them close their eyes and focus on one sound for one minute. Repeat with another sound.
- Have students sit on the floor cross-legged. Play a recording of instrumental music for two to three minutes (extend to longer period later), and have children listen to the music/sound with their eyes closed while taking deep breaths. Ask them to be still, to empty their minds, and only listen to the music.
- Play a short, recorded sound of nature (water fall, river, ocean, wind). These are usually available with instrumental accompaniments or alone. Ask students to close their eyes and imagine the picture of the sound in their mind. Showing a picture of nature that matches the sound before the start of this activity is also an option.
- Have students practice simple yoga poses, holding them for several seconds as you count. Have children practice standing in rejuvenating poses in the morning after their movement exercise. Have them do floor, relaxing poses in the afternoon.

Concluding Remarks

In this book, we discussed the importance of mental health in children as the foundation of early childhood education. We brought together different, often opposing theoretical foundations by providing research to support the effective practices and elements of each theory. We built a case for the importance of forming positive relationships with children as the foundations of our work, cultivating positive emotions in ourselves and children, and promoting strengths of character. Finally, we presented the Resilience-based Interaction Model (RIM) and example practices and guidelines as one approach to build resilience, wellbeing, and well-doing in all children.

Notes

1. There are four types of sentences in Carol Grey's social stories. These are: descriptive, perspective, directive, and control sentences.
2. Carol Grey's website provides the history and philosophy of social stories and has valuable resources, including sample social stories: https://carolgraysocialstories.com/social-stories/. This website is the best place to start from to learn writing effective social stories for children.
3. See their website: http://ccare.stanford.edu/

References

1. Bayat, M. (2015). *Addressing challenging behaviors and mental health issues in early childhood*. New York, NY: Routledge.
2. Alberto, P. A., & Troutman, A. C. (2017). *Applied behavior analysis for teachers* (Interactive 9th ed.). Upper Saddle River, NJ: Pearson
3. Peterson, C., & Seligman, M. E. P. (2004). *Character strengths and virtues: A handbook and classification*. Oxford, UK: Oxford University Press/New York, NY: American Psychological Association.
4. VIA Institute for Character. (2018). *Humanity*. Retrieved from: www.viacharacter.org/www/Character-Strengths/Love
5. Skillman, P. (2006). Peter Skillman marshmallow design challenge. Retrieved from: www.youtube.com/watch?v=1p5sBzMtB3Q
6. Emmons, R. A., & McCullough, M. E. (2003). Counting blessings versus burdens: Experimental studies of gratitude and subjective well-being in daily life. *Journal of Personality & Social Psychology*, 84, 377–389. https://doi.org/10.1037//0022-3514.84.2.377
7. Rusk, R. D., Vella-Brodrick, D. A., & Waters, L. (2016). Gratitude or gratefulness? A conceptual review and proposal of the system of appreciation functioning. *Journal of Happiness Studies*, *17*(5), 2191–2212. https://doi.org/10.1007/s10902-015-9675-z
8. Waters, L., & Stokes, H. (2015). Positive education for school leaders: Exploring the effects of emotion gratitude and action-gratitude. *The Australian Educational and Developmental Psychologist*, 32(10), 1–22. https://doi.org/10.1017/edp.2015.1

9. Park, N., & Peterson, C. (2006). Character strengths and happiness among young children: Content analysis of parental descriptions. *Journal of Happiness Studies, 7*(3), 323–341. https://doi.org/10.1007/s10902-005-3648-6
10. Emmons, R. A., & Stern, R. (2013). Gratitude as a psychotherapeutic intervention. *Journal of Clinical Psychology: In Session, 69*(8), 846–855. https://doi.org/10.1002/jclp.22020
11. Park, N., & Peterson, C. (2006). Moral competence and character strengths among adolescents: The development and validation of the Values in Action Inventory of Strengths for Youth. *Journal of Adolescence, 29*, 891–905. https://doi.org/10.2202/1940-1639.1042
12. Emmons, R. (2007). *Thanks: How the new science of gratitude can make you happier*. Boston, NY: Houghton Mifflin Company.
13. Russell, E., & Fosha, D. (2008). Transformational affects and core state in AEDP: The emergence and consolidation of joy, hope, gratitude and confidence in the (solid goodness of the) self. *Journal of Psychotherapy Integration, 18,* 167–190. https://doi.org/10.1037/1053-0479.18.2.167
14. Haimovitz, K., & Dweck, C. S. (2017). The origins of children's growth and fixed mindsets: New research and a new proposal. *Child Development, 88* (6), 1849–1859. https://doi-org.ezproxy.depaul.edu/10.1111/cdev.12955
15. Heyman, G. D., Dweck, C. S., & Cain, K. M. (1992). Young children's vulnerability to self-blame and helplessness: Relationship to beliefs about goodness. *Child Development*, 63, 401–415. https://doi.org/10.1111/j.1467-8624.1992.tb01636.x
16. Heyman, G. D., & Dweck, C. S. (1998). Children's thinking about traits: Implications for judgment of the self and others. *Child Development, 64,* 391–403. https://doi.org/10.1111/j.1467-8624.1998.tb06197.x
17. Cimpian, A., Arce, H.C., Markman, E. M., & Dweck, C. S. (2007). Subtle linguistic cures affect children's motivation. *Psychological Science, 18*(4), 314–316. https://doi.org/10.1111%2Fj.1467-9280.2007.01896.x
18. Mueller, C. M., & Dweck, C. S. (1998). Praise for intelligence can undermine children's motivation and performance. *Journal of Personality and Social Psychology, 75,* 33–52. https://doi.org/10.1037/0022-3514.75.1.33
19. Dweck, C. S. (2016). *Mindset: The new psychology of success*. New York, NY: Ballantine Books.
20. Dweck, C. S. (2017). The journey to children's mindset—and beyond. *Child Development Perspectives, 11*(2), 139–144. https://doi.org/10.1111/cdep.12225
21. Seligman, M. E. P. (2007). *The optimistic child: A proven program to safeguard children against depression and build lifelong resilience*. Boston, NY: Houghton Mifflin Company.

22. Divers, H. S., & Taylor, S. R. (2000). Exercise and sleep. *Sleep Medicine Review*, *4*, 378–402. https://doi.org/10.1053/smrv.2000.0110
23. Hamer, M. Sabia, S., Batty, G. D., Shipley, M. J., Tabák, A. G., Singh-Manoux, A. G., Singh-Manoux, A., & Kivimaki, M. (2012). Physical activity and inflammatory markers over 10 years: Follow-up in men and women from the Whitehall II cohort study. *Circulation*, *126*, 928–933. https://doi.org/10.1161/CIRCULATIONAHA.112.103879
24. Mayo Clinic. (2018, August 4). *Exercise: 7 benefits of regular physical activity*. Retrieved from www.mayoclinic.org/healthy-lifestyle/fitness/in-depth/exercise/art-20048389
25. Pate, R. R., Pratt, M., Blair, S. N., Haskell, W. L., Macera, C. A., Bouchard, C . . . . Wilmore, J. H. (1995). A recommendation from the Centers for Disease Control and Prevention and the American College of Sports Medicine. *Journal of the American Medical Association*, *23*(5), 402–407. https://doi.org/10.1001/jama.1995.03520290054029
26. Harvard Health Publishing, Harvard Medical School (2018, April). *Exercise is an all-natural treatment to fight depression: Exercise is as effective as drugs in some cases*. Retrieved from www.health.harvard.edu/mind-and-mood/exercise-is-an-all-natural-treatment-to-fight-depression
27. Anderson, E., & Shivakumar, G. (2013). Effects of exercise and physical activity on anxiety. *Frontiers of Psychiatry*, *4*(27), https://doi.org/10.3389/fpsyt.2013.00027
28. Hibbert, C. (2016). *8 Keys to mental health through exercise*. New York, NY: Norton
29. Hibbert, C. G. (2016). Mental health through exercise: How to incorporate physical activity into psychotherapeutic treatment. *The Neuropsychotherapist*, 4(5), 24–37.
30. Godman, H. (2014, April). *Regular exercise changes the brain to improve memory, thinking skills*. Harvard Health Publishing. Retrieved from www.health.harvard.edu/blog/regular-exercise-changes-brain-improve-memory-thinking-skills-201404097110
31. Szhany, K. L., Bugatti, M., & Otto, M. W. (2015). A meta-analytic review of the effects of exercise on brain-derived neurotopic factor. *Journal of Psychiatric Research*, *60*, 56–64. https://doi.org/10.1016/j.jpsychires.2014.10.003
32. Josipovic, Z. (2014). Neural correlates of nondual awareness in meditation. *Annals of The New York Academy of Science*, *1307*(1), 1–8. https://doi.org/10.1080/1047840X.2015.1064294
33. Garland, E. L., Farb, N. A., Goldin, P. R., & Fredrickson, B. L. (2015). Mindfulness broadens awareness and builds eudaimonic meaning: A

process model of mindful positive emotion regulation. *Psychological Inquiry*, *26*(4), 293–314. https://doi.org/10.1080/1047840X.2015.1064294

34. Jha, A., P., Krompinger, J., & Baime, M. J. (2007). Mindfulness training modifies subsystems of attention. *Cognitive, Affective, & Behavioral Neuroscience*, *7*(2), 109–119. https://doi.org/10.3758/CABN.7.2.109
35. Evans, S., Ling, M., Hill, B., Rinehart, N., Austin, D., & Sciberras, E. (2018). Systemic review of meditation-based interventions for children with ADHD. *European Journal of Child and Adolescent Psychiatry*, 27, 9–27. https://doi.org/10.1007/s00787-017-1008-9
36. Greenberg, M. T., & Harris, A. R. (2011). Nurturing mindfulness in children and youth: Current state of research. *Child Development Perspectives*, 6(12), 161–166. https://doi.org/10.1111/j.1750-8606.2011.00215.x
37. Waechter, R. L., Wekerle, C. (2015). Promoting resilience among maltreated youth using meditation, yoga, tai chi, and Qigong: A scoping review of the literature. *Child & Adolescents Social Work Journal*, *32*, 7–31. https://doi.org/10.1007/s10560-014-0356-2
38. Earley, M. D., Chesney, M., Frye, J., Greene, P.A., Berman, B., & Kimbrough, E. (2014). Mindfulness intervention for child abuse survivors: A 2.5 year follow-up. *Journal of Clinical Psychology*, *70*(10), 933–941. https://doi.org/10.1002/jclp.22102
39. Jazaieri, H., McGonigal, K., Lee, I., Jinpa, T., Doty, J. R., Gross, J. J., & Goldin, P. R. (2017). Altering the trajectory of affect and affect regulation: The impact of compassion training. *Mindfulness*,1(9), 283–293. https://doi.org/10.1007/s12671-017-0773-3

Index

CPSIA information can be obtained
at www.ICGtesting.com
Printed in the USA
LVHW101719020320
648715LV00008B/358